Charles Marshall

The Canadian Dominion

Charles Marshall

The Canadian Dominion

ISBN/EAN: 9783337186548

Printed in Europe, USA, Canada, Australia, Japan

Cover: Foto ©ninafisch / pixelio.de

More available books at **www.hansebooks.com**

THE

CANADIAN DOMINION

BY

CHARLES MARSHALL

LONDON
LONGMANS, GREEN, AND CO.
1871

PREFACE.

I AM not conscious that this book is written with undue partiality. I am certain that I entered Canada without prepossessions in favour of the country. During a tour of five months through the Dominion, I endeavoured to judge fairly of the present condition—social, commercial, religious, and political—of the country, and of its future prospects. I have tried to give the result of my impressions and inquiries in the simplest and most condensed manner possible.

I believe that, to estimate Canada justly, the country must be compared not only with England, but also with the United States. The contrast which Canada presents to the garden-like condition of the old country and the highly-developed state of English society, is calculated to startle and sometimes to aggrieve the sensitive observer. These impressions are modified when it is perceived that the crudity and roughness of the civilisation are not peculiar to the British provinces, but are incident to the youthfulness of the civilisation of the whole of this new continent. I had the advantage of passing into Canada from a tour through the Eastern States of the American Union, and of preparing this volume after the completion of a visit to the Western States.

THE AUTHOR.

April, 1871.

CONTENTS.

CHAPTER		PAGE
	PREFACE	v
I.	THE DOMINION	1
II.	QUEBEC	12
III.	THE 'HABITANS'	21
IV.	LUMBER	37
V.	THE FREE-GRANT LANDS	49
VI.	THE FARMING INTEREST	70
VII.	NIAGARA	85
VIII.	OIL SPRINGS AND SALT	93
IX.	LITTLE AFRICA	99
X.	THE INDIANS	105
XI.	ACROSS THE PRAIRIES	120
XII.	THE RED RIVER REVOLT	145
XIII.	THE GREAT NORTH-WEST	174

CHAPTER		PAGE
XIV.	The Air-Line to China	199
XV.	The Maritime Provinces	206
XVI.	Inter-Continental Communication	217
XVII.	Immigration	220
XVIII.	The Political Question	239
XIX.	Canadian Defence	254
XX.	The Future of Great Britain and her Colonies	270
	Appendix	275

LIST

OF

ILLUSTRATIONS.

1. THE AUTHOR IN A RED RIVER COSTUME   *Frontispiece.*
2. QUEBEC FROM POINT ST. LÉVY . . *To face page* 12
3. THE FALLS OF THE CHAUDIÈRE . . ,, 17
4. THE FALLS OF MONTMORENCI . . ,, 20
5. FORT GARRY, ON THE RED RIVER . . ,, 143
6. THE PARLIAMENT BUILDINGS, OTTAWA, FROM ABOVE THE RIDEAU CANAL . . ,, 183

THE CANADIAN DOMINION.

CHAPTER I.

THE DOMINION.

CENTURIES AGO a few wigwams on the shore of one of the magnificent rivers of the New World gave a characteristic name to the strip of land on which they stood. The Indians called it 'Kanata,' the Place of Huts.

The French applied the name to a wide piece of country; the English to a great territory. The term now includes an empire stretching from ocean to ocean. The Dominion of Canada is the Land of Homes.[1]

The settlement of the country by Europeans is scarcely two centuries old. The English occupation dates from 1760.

The first explorers of the New World supposed, from the appearance of the indigenous races, that

---

[1] See Note III., at the end of this volume.

they were the 'Indians' of that rich country of the east, which was sought by the long westward voyage. The name still clung to the red men, after the discovery that a greater India had been found.

The native races hesitated whether to unite against the intrusion of the pale-faced races from across the great sea, or to bid for their aid in their own internecine wars. Champlain, one of the earliest and most distinguished explorers of Canada, leagued with the Hurons and Algonquins, put an army of their foes, the warlike Iroquois, to flight, by suddenly appearing in the midst of a battle in glittering armour, with miraculous firearms. A god in resplendent light with uplifted thunderbolts could not have produced greater dismay before the walls of Troy. But the Indians soon learnt that their new foes were mortal. Traders from the seas supplied them with fire-arms for the slaughter of the white settlers, and with fire-water for their own swifter destruction. The diminished tribes fought on both sides in the fierce struggle for supremacy on this continent, waged by French and English. Now they have for the most part settled down to habits of peace. Under the wise and kindly policy persistently followed towards them by the English Government, they live in security on their settled reserves. By mixture of blood, and the agency of teachers and missionaries, the Indian tribes are slowly approximating to the condition of the white races. We may watch in Canada the interesting experiment of a fairly-conducted effort to elevate a lower race of people; meanwhile their presence in the country adds to the picturesqueness of life.

It is a fact of more interest, however, and of much greater importance, both social and political, that in Canada at this time a large proportion of the white population, perhaps even one quarter, under the English domination, is composed of a race foreign in blood, speaking a strange language, professing another religion, and yet living in assured content and peace.

The French are the discoverers of Canada. In 1534 Jacques Cartier appropriated its unknown extent to France, by erecting on the shore of the coast of Gaspé, a cross thirty feet high, inscribed with the arms of Francis I. Champlain established the first colonies. Colbert organised a great scheme for strengthening 'La Nouvelle France.' War-captains by sea and land, and martyrs tortured to death, make a long list of French names to emblazon 'the heroic age of Canada.' The gallantry of Montcalm, glad that his wounds should kill him before the English entered Quebec, fitly closes the period of French rule over the country.

The people learnt quickly to acquiesce in the new order. They refused all solicitation to fight against the English during the war of American Independence. In 1812 and the following years, when the American forces invaded Canada for its conquest, the French shared with the English the honour of making a successful defence of the country. At this moment French Canada is as loyal as any part of the English dominions. The French do not forget their past; they do not lose their distinctness of race; they retain fondly their language, their old customs and social order, their separate system of law, and their ancient faith. But they are prosperous and contented. They have been treated by the Imperial Government with fairness and consideration. They have responded with good-will, and have learnt to feel an attachment to the English rule, and a deep devotion to the country of their birth. The French are as thoroughly Canadian as the English.

But the country has been conquered not only from the Indians, and from the French, but with severer effort from the tyranny of Nature herself. The fertile lands of the Dominion, covered with homesteads, villages, and towns along a measureless network of railways, roads, rivers, and canals, once formed part of the limitless northern forest wilds. With infinite labour vast forests have been hewn down, and their tangled growths of interlacing roots torn up from the soil. Free way has been made for the sunlight and air, and the climate meliorated. Countless streams and rivers have been spanned with bridges. The rapid waters have everywhere been made to repay the damage of their tumultuous overflows by working the saws and hammers, the looms and mills of the settlers.

The labour of making this country habitable has been beyond all estimate; but the result is a full compensation. The older-settled districts have become a fair garden. The farmsteads are homes of comfort and ease, and often of culture and refinement. The log-hut gives place to the frame-house, and this to a substantial building of stone or brick. Meanwhile the line of invasion on the old realm of forest everywhere extends. The lumberman advances further and further north with his axe, and removes by the snow-roads of winter and the great water highways a mass of choice timber for all the markets of the world. The backwood's-man, more than reconciled to his life of excitement and variety, clears a space for his log-hut, fires the useless timber, and sows his first irregular crop.

The cleared land is worth all the pains. The Ontario wheat is one of the finest in the world. Oats, barley, maize, and other grains, yield excellent crops. Fruits and vegetables grow generously. The Canadian apple is the standard of excellence. Melons and the tomato grow equally with the potato, pea, turnip, and the rest of the vegetables known in England. The grape thrives well. Raspberries, cranberries, cherries, and other fruits grow wild. Orchards everywhere prosper.

But the great labour demanded in settling the country has produced a further result of great consequence. It has developed a fine race of people. The Canadian, whether French, English, Irish, or

Scotch, is well-proportioned and vigorous, often tall, with broad shoulders, sinewy frame, and capable of great endurance. He may not have much book-learning, but he is quick of resource, and apt at many things. He is enterprising, but unhurried. He does not move in his affairs over-fast, but very surely. He is sober-minded, persistent, and trustworthy. The races of the British isles and of Normandy have certainly not degenerated here.

The remarkable advance in material prosperity made by the country may be indicated by a comparison of statistics.

In 1851, the export returns of the four provinces of Quebec (then Lower Canada), Ontario (then Upper Canada), Nova Scotia, and New Brunswick, amounted to four millions of dollars.

In the following ten years the exports of these provinces increased more than tenfold; in 1861 the returns were $43 millions.

For the past year, 1869, the exports came to $60 millions, or twelve millions sterling.

For the same provinces the imports were:—In 1851, seven millions of dollars; in 1861, fifty-one millions; in 1869, seventy millions.

The increasing quantity of land brought under cultivation—one of the most important elements in the well-being of a new country—is shown to be eminently satisfactory by the Government returns. In 1851 the extent of land actually under culture in the Provinces of Upper and Lower Canada was seven million acres. By the year 1861 the amount had increased to eleven millions. It is estimated that the returns to be made at the next census will show a corresponding increase to the present date.

The returns of population afford significant proof of the rapid progress of the country. In 1841, the date of the union of Upper and Lower Canada, the population of the two provinces was 1,090,000. In 1852 an approximate estimate for the whole of the British North American provinces gave the population as 2,471,366. From the census returns for 1861 the numbers for all the provinces was 3,447,706. A carefully-prepared estimate of the population for the present year—1870—for all the provinces, as before, makes the numbers 4,525,000.

But statistics of the present condition of the country, and of its past progress, can scarcely suggest an adequate idea of the prosperity and importance which Canada appears destined to attain. Her various sources of wealth waiting to be developed are immeasurable and exhaustless. Tracts of prairie and woodland as large as European kingdoms wait for settlers. Lands already cleared will yield double and fourfold their present increase when the farmer shall have sufficient time to adopt improved methods of culture. Mineral wealth, vast beyond conception, of iron, coal, copper, gold, silver, lead, lies stored away in ready waiting for the appliances of science. A great variety of exquisite marbles rest in yet untroubled quarries, to make a full amends for the unproductiveness of some regions of the soil. Ornamental woods will yet give greatly increased value to the returns of the forest. Inland and ocean fisheries, great as they are, are capable of indefinite expansion.

From its northern position on the American continent, the Dominion of Canada possesses one remarkable commercial advantage, the importance of which is not yet appreciated either in the country itself or in England. It possesses the shortest and easiest route for the trans-continental traffic between England and China. The most direct practicable line from Shanghae to Liverpool passes through British Columbia, traverses the fertile Saskatchewan valley, crosses Red River, follows the Ottawa, strikes Montreal on the St. Lawrence, and then passes from Halifax across the Atlantic. This route is over one thousand miles nearer than that through United States territory. By a happy freak of Nature a pass is prepared for this Canadian Pacific railway across the Rocky Mountains at an elevation less than half that which the United States line has had to climb. Sooner or later commerce is certain to find its way along this channel between Europe and Asia.

This brief view of the Canadian Dominion may suggest the importance which it may one day attain in the British empire. By its social order, by its political institutions, and by unbroken ties of association and of interest, Canada is still firmly attached to the mother-country. Nothing but English indifference, or a persistent policy of alienation, will be likely to lead to a severance of the present connexion. Canada is proud of the English name, and of the fame of English history. In any time of national danger this true New England would eagerly lend her aid to the country from which she springs. At this moment Canada in many respects is more like the England of Elizabeth, and more intensely English, than England herself. The bonds that hold her in the empire may be weakened, no doubt, with ease; but they might be strengthened with greater ease.

Perhaps there exists at present no question affecting the future of the English race so deeply as the determination whether the Canadian Dominion will be retained in the empire, or become alienated from us with the almost certain result of being incorporated with the United States. The permanent place of the mother-country among the nations of the world will probably be determined by the way in which this question is solved.

Canada is no longer a puny stripling needing protection, incompetent for self-defence, and useless as an ally. The Dominion possesses an active militia force of over 40,000 men, with a trained reserve of 600,000. She has reared a large and hardy population of seamen. By a singular caprice of destiny almost all the great inlets and bays on the Atlantic coast suitable for fisheries are placed within her boundaries. Her marine already ranks in order of importance next to France.

The empire perhaps can ill afford to suffer the loss to its prestige and power which would follow upon the alienation of its great colony.

An impressive view of the magnitude and importance of the interests involved may, I conceive, be obtained by a comparison of the extent of the Dominion with the countries of the Old World.

In the year 1867 the provinces of Upper and Lower Canada, New Brunswick, and Nova Scotia were confederated under the title of the Dominion of Canada. This year, during my stay in the country, the territory of the Hudson Bay Company has been ceded to the Canadian Government. At the present moment the terms are already arranged for the admission of the important province of British Columbia. The Dominion territory will therefore extend from the Atlantic to the Pacific Ocean.

Now for our comparison.

The old-settled, contented, industrious, French-speaking province of Quebec contains more square miles than all France.

The English-speaking, energetic province of Ontario counts more square miles than Great Britain and Ireland.

New Brunswick has a greater territory than Holland and Belgium combined.

Nova Scotia exceeds Switzerland in size.

British Columbia surpasses in extent the whole of the North German Confederation, giving in the South German States to boot.

The newly-added Far West is vaster than all Russia in Europe, counting in, and counting twice over, Sweden, Norway, Denmark, Faroe, and Iceland.

This is the empire, with its hardy, high-spirited population, already to be counted by millions, and growing to tens and scores of millions; with its exhaustless sources of all kinds of material wealth; with its commanding position as the highway to China and all Asia; and with its assured future of greatness and power, which England may now retain in intimate association with herself to aid her prestige and influence, but which is apparently in danger of being lost to the empire by negligence or indifference.

CHAPTER II.

QUEBEC.

UNEXAMPLED for picturesqueness and magnificence of position on the American continent, and for the romance of her historic associations, Quebec sits on her impregnable heights a queen among the cities of the New World.

At her feet flows the noble St. Lawrence, the fit highway into a great empire, here narrowed to a couple of miles' breadth, though lower down the waters widen to a score of miles, and at the gulf to a hundred. From the compression of the great river at this spot the city derives its name, the word signifying, in the native Indian tongue, the Strait. On the east of the city, along a richly fertile valley, flows the beautiful St. Charles, to join its waters with those of the great river. The mingled waters divide to enclasp the fair and fertile Isle of Orleans.

The city as seen from a distance rises stately and solemn, like a grand pile of monumental buildings. Clustering houses, tall, irregular, with high-pitched roofs, crowd the long line of shore and climb the rocky heights. Great piles of stone churches, col-

QUEBEC FROM POINT ST. LÉVY.

leges, and public buildings, crowned with gleaming minarets, rise above the mass of dwellings. The clear air permits the free use of tin for the roofs and spires, and the dark stone-work is relieved with gleaming light. Above all rise the long dark lines of one of the world's famous citadels, the Gibraltar of America.

Let the spectator stand on the Flag-staff Battery within the lines won by Wolfe's gallantry, but which he could not live to enter. Below lie the steep, tortuous, narrow streets of a city as French as Havre or Calais. Yonder is an open market-place, with groups of women sitting at their stalls with kerchiefed heads. At a distant corner-house you may see a shrine to Our Lady, newly-whitewashed by the piety of the inmates. The vast stone block adjoining the cathedral is the celebrated Roman Catholic College, the Laval University, named in memory of the first bishop of Quebec. Another great pile of stone is the Parliament House for the provincial legislature. Unhappily, it must be admitted that the public buildings of Quebec look less imposing the nearer they are approached. From the citadel these two buildings look like dismal factories or workhouses. However, the parliament buildings at least have already been burnt down more than once.

Then, still below, the shores are lined with warehouses, and quays, and masses of shipping. All the surrounding waters are filled with sails; the scene is one of sunlight and life. Steamers with their filmy lines of smoke pass up and down the river, or rapidly across, or tug with much noise and short breath the heavy rafts of wood, acres wide, covered with hut villages that float down from the inland waters. At Point St. Lévy, opposite the citadel, lie stranded or lazily floating incalculable masses of this lumber, waiting for transit to the British Isles, South America, or Australia.

The abrupt or gently undulating banks of the opposite shore, of the Island of Orleans, and of the northern bank of the St. Lawrence, are fringed with rich woods, except where spaces have been cleared for villas and country houses, and for the long line of farm houses of the *habitans* of the country.

As I stood within this citadel made famous for ever in the annals of English war, the place seemed to me a fitting one for some reflections on the policy which has been lately adopted by the home Government. At the quay below lay a ship loading with old war material for England.

'A ship load of stores goes home now every week,' an officer of the garrison told me.

'And very much of it not worth carrying on to the ship,' exclaimed a Quebec gentleman, somewhat querulously. 'If your Government has determined not to use it for the defence of the country, then in the name of common sense let it be sold to the Dominion Government here!'

'Don't appeal to common sense, pray,' said another Canadian with good humour. 'Do you remember the story of the shanty guard-house brought here from Australia ?'

'The home policy is an admirable one,' said the officer; 'it is to teach the colonies self-reliance, and compel them to develop their strength.'

'Well and good,' was the reply. 'But it would be better to tell us this plainly instead of making us think we are to be thrown off altogether.'

My attention was directed to a long line of earthworks thrown up on the heights on the further shore of the St. Lawrence. Modern warfare demands another system of defence than that of stone ramparts. But I learned that the progress of the works was interrupted, and that it was not known whether the proposed line of defence was to be completed.

At the time of my visit one regiment only remained in garrison at Quebec.

I visited one day the convent of the Ursulines below the citadel. A mild-eyed nun passed me a key through the *guichet* in the wall, and left me to wander about the chapel at my will. I found a few indifferent paintings, and a tablet on the wall that arrested my attention :—

Honneur
à Montcalm !
Le destin, en lui dérobant La Victoire,
L'a récompensée par
Un Mort Glorieuse.

I wondered if, when the time comes for England to fall from her place among the nations, she will make an end worthy of her past.

In 1861 the population of the city of Quebec was 51,109 souls. The census to be taken next year will show a large increase. The building of wooden ships for the carrying trade was formerly the chief industry of the place, but has greatly decreased since the introduction of iron vessels. The annual returns that were formerly 100,000 tons, sank in 1869 to 27,000 tons. But other industries will fill up this loss. Quebec has a large operative class in its population, and many advantages for the manufacturing trades.

As an inland port Quebec must always remain a place of great importance. Though it stands two hundred miles up the St. Lawrence, the city is still full three hundred miles nearer to Liverpool than New York is. In proportions always increasing, the export produce of the west is finding its way down the St. Lawrence to Quebec for ocean transport. At the St. Charles river, which has a tidal flow of fourteen feet, Quebec possesses the means of constructing docks that may one day equal those of Liverpool.

For picturesque beauty the environs of Quebec vie with those of any city in the world. A short drive will take the visitor to the Plains of Abraham, where he will wish to see a nobler monument to Wolfe than that at present erected. Or he may proceed along the picturesque St. Foy road, and pause at another monument in memory of the men who fell on this spot at the second battle of the

Plains, when the brave De Lévis snatched a victory from the English, and almost succeeded in winning back the great citadel lost the year before.

A sunset seen from the heights above the wide valley of the St. Charles, bathing in tender light the long undulating lines of remote hills, and transfiguring with glory the great chain of the Laurentides, is a sight of beauty to rest in the memory for ever.

Crossing the St. Lawrence ferry with a light *calèche*, or with one of the handsomely appointed carriages that wait for hire in the open squares, the visitor will pass in an afternoon's drive through a wild and romantic piece of country along the St. Léry river to the highly picturesque Falls of the Chaudière. For the last half-mile you wend your way afoot across fields and through a small wood, and then find unexpectedly a scene of bewildering beauty. In a long still reach of waters, where the bending forest trees and the clear sky overhead reflect themselves, the river sleeps in dreams of profound tranquillity, then suddenly leaps a precipice jagged with projecting masses of rock, and falls white and foaming a hundred and thirty feet into the seething caldron below. The spray rises in a thin mist to cool your brow where you stand in the hot sun. Below stretch the gleaming reaches of the winding river, and around a wide range of undulating country soothes and satisfies the eye.

It may add to the traveller's interest in this river to know that it flows with gold. At one spot near its source a mining company obtained last year 838 ounces of the precious metal.

At a similar distance of an afternoon's drive from Quebec to the north, lies the picturesque Indian village of Lorette. I had the pleasure of making a visit to this place in company with the Honourable Mr. Chauveau, the Minister of Instruction for the province of Quebec. The tribe settled here is of the Huron race; but a glance at the features of the people proves that there has been a considerable intermixture of white blood. The chief of the tribe, M. Paul, a finely-made middle-aged man of much intelligence and good humour, introduced us to his family, and courteously conducted us through the settlement. All traces of the old savage life have disappeared. The people live in neat, well-made frame-houses, each with its garden or piece of cultivated land. Many of them are well-to-do farmers; others make a comfortable living by the manufacture of snow-shoes, canoes, basket-work, and Indian curiosities. The people all speak French. We attended divine service at the Roman Catholic chapel; here the prayer was intoned in the old Huron language, but not a soul in the congregation, I was assured, understood a word. Over the altar was a painting, done, I should think, by one of the Indians, of the very house of Lorette, miraculously removed from Jerusalem to Rome, from which this village has its name. The people, old and young, attended to the service with devotion.

Many of the houses we visited had an appearance of comfort, and even of elegance. The rooms were carpeted, and tastefully furnished. In some a piano would stand open, with a piece of classic music on the stand. In such a room as this the good-natured chief showed us a collection of Indian dresses and war implements; then suddenly swinging aloft his tomahawk, he shouted the war whoop, and performed one of the old dances. In conclusion, of course, the sacred pipe of peace was fitted to the war weapon, and offered to each of us. At another house we found a well-to-do Frenchman from Quebec, who introduced us with pride to his pretty Indian wife and two of the loveliest children in the world.

The Indians were nearly all dressed in the ordinary costume of modern civilisation, but a few of the women wore short skirts, with full trousers, and a graceful short cloak.

The name by which the Indians call my friend Mr. Chauveau, not without a just appreciation of his character, is 'Hodilonrawasti,' or 'Le bel esprit,' as it was explained to me. The name given to me at once was no less than 'Alonhiawasti Chialontarati,' which I shall find too long for customary use.

The village is built on the St. Charles river, and here, too, are some exceedingly pretty falls. It is not too much to say that the Lorette cascades would give fame and fortune to any spot in England or France; yet here, dwarfed by grander waters, they remain comparatively unknown.

For, after all, the great pride of Quebec is the Falls of Montmorenci. Nine miles from the city, the Montmorenci river, escaping from the tangled network of rocky pools through which it has forced its crawling way, plunges magnificently, in a snow-white mass, a sheer depth of 250 feet into a dark chasm below, where, stunned and broken, it slowly melts into the great St. Lawrence. A few stray silver lines of the river descending on either side suggest the great width of the Falls, else lost in their extreme height.

The roar of waters is deafening; you cannot speak to your friend; but perhaps you grasp his hand to stay the strange impulse that seizes you to fling yourself on the madly hurrying waters, and feel for one supreme instant the ecstasy of their frightful leap.

The white waters fall into a black gorge of utter desolation. Here the glowing iris spans the rolling clouds of foam, turning the spray to jewels. A rocky ridge from the coast-line bends round in front of the great Falls, as if expressly to afford a perfect view of their majesty.

THE FALLS OF MONTMORENCI.

CHAPTER III.

THE 'HABITANS.'

I WAS ushered one morning into the reception-room of the Laval University. One end of the handsome apartment was occupied by two paintings not badly executed, and the space for a third. In the centre appeared the Holy Virgin, robed in fair white and pink, standing on massive clouds that hung over the long line of the city and shipping of Quebec. The painting on the right was a full-length portrait by Pas-qualoui of His Holiness Pope Pius IX., in gorgeous robes. The vacant space was for Her Sacred Majesty, Victoria, Queen of the British Empire.

'The Blessed Virgin, the Holy Father, and Her Majesty, they are our three patrons,' the attendant explained to me.

I was presently conducted by many corridors up to the private apartment of the Abbé Brunet, to whom I had letters of introduction. 'Entrez, entrez!' cried the good father from within at the knock of my guide.

The door opened, and discovered the holy father,

razor in hand, half-way through the delicate operation of shaving. Wholly unembarrassed, the abbé welcomed me heartily, and proceeded to give me all kinds of information, with such breaks as the employment of the moment necessitated.

The French population of Canada, he assured me, was prosperous, contented, and eminently loyal. On the cession of the province to England, the integrity of their institutions, social order, language, and religion had been secured to the inhabitants; England had scrupulously respected these treaties, and had won the attachment and gratitude of the people. They had no causes of discontent, and prospered to the extent of their ambition. The Confederation of the Provinces had been attended with one great advantage to the French race. Formerly, while Upper and Lower Canada had been united under one Government, there had been a constant struggle for rule between the two provinces, the occasional diversity of interests and the general difference in religion often causing strife and ill-will, and leading sometimes to a political 'dead-lock.' All this was changed. The province of Quebec, like that of Ontario, had now its own local legislature, and unseemly strife for power had given place to a wholesome rivalry in advancing the general good.

I have subsequently met on all sides with confirmation of these statements.

At two o'clock I found the Rev. Mr. Laverdière, Librarian of the Laval University, in readiness for me. We took one of the quaint Quebec cars, and drove to the Custom-house landing-stage. Here we were joined by another priest, M. Roussel. We descended a perpendicular ladder to a boat waiting at the quay. In a few moments we rigged the sails, pushed her off, and were speeding before the wind on the wide St. Lawrence. The little yacht was the private property of M. Laverdière, in which he and his brother priests were accustomed to make excursions thirty-five miles down the river to an old chateau under Cape Tourment, the summer resort of the professors and students of the University.

The day was perfect. Gleaming waters with rafts and shipping, fair hill-slopes dotted with farms and villages, the magnificent pile of the mountain city, a heaven overspread with fleecy clouds and full of sunlight, made up a scene of enchantment. We passed along the channel between the Island of Orleans and the north shore. Till the chaloupe grated on the shallow bottom, we crept in closer and closer below the magnificent Montmorenci Falls. The wind grew perverse and coquettish, changing its mind every moment. It was an odd sight to watch the two tall thin priests, in their long black robes buttoned to the feet, and their tall black beaver hats, made for dignity rather than convenience, managing the boat, nevertheless, with a skill that would have done credit to practised sailors. We lifted a wooden plank in the stern seat, and produced a repast which I considered one of the most delicious I had ever eaten. It consisted of cold ham served on white bread for plates, and of excellent claret drank from a piece of delf as a loving cup. We lay in the sun, and talked, and sang. Then the wind, tired of coquetry, pretended an absurd modesty, and left us altogether. We reefed the sails and took to the oars. The tide was changing, and our progress was slow. Evening fell, and we doubted if we could reach our destined resting-place for the night. The wind laughingly took pity on us, let us put in our oars, and carried us swiftly, without pausing once to take breath, on to the picturesque French village of Chateau Richet.

On the further shore we cast anchor. Two of us stripped, and plunged into the delicious waters. Then we sped straight across to the village. M. le Curé, with smiling face, stood on the shore to welcome us. We walked through the village, touching our hats to the salutations of the pleasant-looking people, and pausing at times for talk.

A simple but most hospitable supper was prepared for us at the curé's house. Good-natured gossip about Church matters and the affairs of the village finished the day.

In the morning we went to see, and seeing to admire, the new church of stone just erected through the indefatigable exertions of our host. The walls of the interior were still bare, showing the lines of the great stones. The open timber work supporting the roof was all exposed. I am not sure that I succeeded in proving to my friends that my admiration of the effect was sincere. M. le Curé listened at first with incredulity and then with pity to the expression of my strong abhorrence of plaster. They meant to get the whole place finished off smooth and white as soon as ever they could, he assured me, and then, when they had funds enough, they might fresco it with columns and cornices of marble.

We went to inspect, too, the alterations in progress at a large stone house below the church, to fit it for an educational establishment, under the management of the Sisters of the Society of Le bon Pasteur. This was also one of the pet projects of our kind host.

'M. le Curé is a very good man, and we all love and respect him very much,' said one of the villagers to me; 'but what with the new church and the new convent, and other things, he burdens us heavily and keeps all the village poor.'

A little sparkling stream coming down from the Laurentian chain forces for itself with difficulty a way into the St. Lawrence at this spot, and makes the Falls of La Puce prettier than their name.

At eleven A.M. we resumed our course. There was more sun and wind than on the previous day, and we reached Cape Tourment quickly. With sails all set we drove the little chaloupe as far as she could go into a swamp of waving rushes on the river shore. Then, with our light baggage in the hand, with boots off, and with trousers (and robes) rolled up above the knees, we waded cheerfully through the sludge to the firm land. This was the ordinary means of disembarkation at this spot. Half an hour's walk, by pretty French farmsteads and through a scented pine wood, led us to the Chateau Bellevue—a long, square, massive mansion, built of the dark limestone of the district. We were received, literally, with open arms. At dinner we sat down to a well-served and tastefully-appointed table. In the reading-room I found a large collection of religious periodicals, mostly French; but among them 'The Tablet.' A quaint old billiard-board, evidently much used, stood in one of the great rooms.

Twenty of the professors and about as many students are accustomed to spend the summer vacation here. One party had gone away this day fishing; another to make the ascent of Mount Tourment. Two priests, coming home from some religious duty, splashed to the hat-top in mud from a swamp, were received with hearty laughter. The whole company showed an extraordinary gaiety of heart, simplicity, and kindliness.

Half a dozen of us strolled out into the noble woods surrounding the cluster of buildings. We came presently to a small shrine, erected by some pious brethren to the honour of St. Joseph. A white plaster image of the saint himself stood inside, profusely decorated with vivid artificial flowers. I was informed that the figure was taken within doors in the winter, to save it from being cracked by the frost. Further on we came to a still prettier shrine, erected to Our Lady; but unfortunately the frost, or some strange lack of care, had slightly interfered with the regularity of the Virgin's features.

The glory of the day was still undimmed when M. de Laverdière and I got into one of the small springless carts of this country, and were driven to the woods by a man sitting on a kind of undeveloped splash-board, with his legs stretched forwards on to the shafts. The roadway wandered across country and into the cool depths of the forest, over most irregular ground, filled with blocks of stone, and broken with gaps and ruts.

'As this car has no springs,' said my kind friend, 'I fear the jolting will shake you.'

I suggested that the motion might be beneficial to digestion, or to the liver, or to something or other inside us.

'But if you would like to ride easy,' he resumed, 'don't hold on to anything at all, but let your body go freely with the motion of the cart.'

I tried this plan, and found the exercise quite exhilarating.

During the ride M. de Laverdière advised me on no account to omit a visit to the church of St. Ann, which I should pass on my way home on the morrow.

It was the only place of pilgrimage in all Canada, he explained,—being the chosen spot for the performance of miraculous cures. He kindly informed me of the whole supernatural history of the place: how a little child had received the honour of a heavenly vision on the identical spot where the church now stands; how this was repeated a second and yet a third time, when the Virgin commanded the child to tell the people of the village that a church was to be built in that place; how, when the church was ready, the first beggar threw away his crutch in the midst of a great assembly of people, and so became the first of a line of cured cripples which remains unbroken to the present date. The priest proceeded to tell me of a number of extraordinary and interesting cases of cure, some of which he had heard of from actual spectators. And then he argued philosophically on the great question of miracles.

'It showed absurdity,' he said, 'and, what was worse, a tendency to infidelity, when people urge that the cures of the church occur through occult but simply natural causes. Some cases there might be of that order, but all were not.

'For instance, when a man with a shrunken limb, in which there remains no use or life, suddenly stretched it out sound and well, or when a man stone dead is brought back to life, what power can have done this short of a true miracle? Must not a cause be always sufficient for the result?'

We left the car in the heart of the woods, and proceeded along a faintly-traced pathway, till the roar of falling waters told us we were near the object of our search. A magnificent spectacle burst upon our sight. A rapid stream, breaking its way through the dark woods, and from pool to pool among masses of jagged rock, suddenly cleaves for itself a narrow chasm, over which you may spring if you have an iron nerve, and then falls, broken into a thousand fantastic forms of spray along the steep face of the rock, into a deep gorge of horrid darkness.

I do not know the volume of water; I forgot to guess the height—it may be two hundred feet. Figures are absurd in the estimate of the beauty and grandeur of a scene like this. I only know that the whole impression of the scene was one of the most intense I have ever experienced. The disposition of the mass of broken waters is the most graceful conceivable. The irresistible might of the rush of the fall, the stupendous upright masses of black rock that form the chasm; the heavy fringe of dark woods all around; the utter solitariness and gloom of the scene—all add to impress the imagination. An artist might prefer this spot to Niagara.

The precarious footway down which we climbed half-way to the bed of the gorge was fashioned in part by the labour of my companion in former days. Climbing back and beyond the Falls, we reached a sheltered pool, and bathed in the icy waters. We were careful to avoid the current. Swimming back to our dressing-place, the priest indicated the spot where one of the students had recently been drowned.

We drove back through the wood a new way. Then, with sincere expressions of regard, I left the priest, and walked on to the inn, like an auberge of Brittany, that stands by the long wooden bridge crossing the St. Ann river, on the route to Quebec.

Of course I visited St. Ann's Church in the morning. There were at least thirty crutches suspended in the church, the grateful offerings of men who needed them no more. One thing struck me painfully: the crutches were too much alike, and were not old and picturesque enough.

I walked back to Quebec by Chateau Richet and Montmorenci, visiting many of the houses and talking with the 'habitans,' the term by which the French Canadians are known.

The division of inheritance being the rule here, the separate holdings are comparatively small. The nominal extent of the holdings rarely falls below ninety or a hundred acres, but a large part of this will probably be unfit for cultivation.

The disposition of the land along the St. Lawrence is very peculiar. The divisions have been made longitudinally, leaving to each holding a frontage on the river. The present farms, therefore, are about two acres wide and fifty deep. This arrangement must increase the difficulty and labour of working; but it is attended with an odd advantage. The farmsteads are all built on the line of road that traverses the country; an unceasing succession of villas, cottages, and barns stretches from Quebec to St. Ann's, and I know not how far beyond. The people are social, and everyone thus has the advantage of near neighbours.

The houses of the 'habitans' are generally well-built, wholly or in part of stone, and afford abundant evidence of comfort and prosperity. Many of them are surrounded with verandahs or balconies of wood; and some are decorated artistically with porches and terraces, and painted to the best effect in low colours, pricked out with deeper tints at the mouldings and ornaments. Flowers often grow on the window-sills or before the door.

The scene by the winding roadway is often eminently picturesque. By the side of the pretty dwellings, or in the rear, stands the larger building of the barn. A team of good horses is being put to the strongly built market-cart. An old-fashioned plough lies rusting in a mass of tall weeds, discarded in favour of an improved implement. Screened by some large stones, there blazes in the open air a fire of wood, over which hangs a great black cauldron for washing or cooking. Sometimes you see also an oven for baking, built out by itself in the garden. Near almost every door a streamlet trickles down from the wooded heights, affording the ready means for that peculiar kind of washing with a stone or wooden beater which the Frenchwoman especially loves.

The houses inside are neat and orderly, and are comfortably and sometimes elegantly furnished. In very many a cottage sits the old grandmother, with dreamy eyes but busy hands, before the picturesque, murmuring spinning-wheel. And not unfrequently the house-wife may be seen at work at the antiquated, but still useful, hand-loom. The people showed me with pride the stuffs they wove, and boasted their superior durability over city goods.

'Would Monsieur like to see the way the machine goes?' a bright-eyed brunette asked of me, as I stood talking in one of the cottages.

'But Mademoiselle has hurt her hand, I fear.'

'Ce ne fait rien;' the girl answered, gaily, proceeding to wind round the cut hand a long piece of linen.

She allowed me to assist her in the delicate operation, and then sat at the loom, making the shuttle fly from hand to hand with astonishing quickness.

'How very fast you work!' I exclaimed.

'Ah, yes; I do not like to be slow. And, besides, I have so much work to do.'

'But, Mademoiselle, why so?'

'I have twelve brothers and sisters, and they all want coats and dresses. And, besides, I like to have a piece over now and then to sell.'

The French Canadians are, as a race, cheerful, frugal, pious, and eminently industrious. They make admirable settlers in a new country. They have overspread and reduced to cultivation a vast extent of country which would scarcely have attracted other settlers. They cling to the historic soil of the Lower Provinces, and push backward their settlements deeper and deeper into the back-woods, adding parish to parish till the saints' names from which they name them are well-nigh exhausted. Recently they have begun to occupy the upper regions of the noble Saguenay River, and have formed large settlements round the inland lake of St. John's. And still they swarm, and extend, and colonise, and help to build up a great prosperity for the future.

For, beyond all other staples, the great product of French Canada is children. An amazing quantity swarm along the traveller's route. Families of twelve, fourteen, sixteen are not uncommon. A family of children under nine in number is below the average, and is deemed insignificant.

The 'habitans' have settled both sides of the St. Lawrence down to the ocean. If the climate is severe in the winter, at least it is delightfully cool and invigorating in the hot months of the year.

Each summer their picturesque villages suffer invasion from Quebec, Montreal, Toronto, and all the cities of the Dominion. The wealth, and beauty, and fashion of Canada crowd to these delightful spots, and constitute a brief and brilliant order of existence, midway between the extremes of dull reserve and extravagant gaiety of the English and

American watering-places. To many a wearied frequenter of the well-known *bads* and springs of Europe, the wilderness watering-places of Murray Bay, Tadousac, and Cacouna, with their wild scenery, their falls and mountains, their excursions, pic-nics, and balls, their duck-shooting and plenteous fishing, would prove a welcome change after Tronville, Wiesbaden, Bagnières, or Long Branch, and well repay the long voyage to reach them.

At Murray Bay the visitor is, unwittingly, in an old settlement of Scotchmen, who have become so identified with the French among whom they settled as even to have forgotten their own language.

Charming Cacouna claims the first place for fashion and gaiety. Here we talked politics all day and danced all night—breaking up, however, at ten o'clock, for Canada keeps very proper hours. Here we were initiated into the mysteries of bowls, and saw with unfeigned admiration young girls of the fairest type of grace and beauty make successful 'spares' and 'strikes.'

No lover of the picturesque could wish to find a more wildly romantic spot than Tadousac. And, to increase his interest, here stands the little wooden church built by Champlain, two full centuries ago, the oldest church in Canada.

By Tadousac the St. Lawrence receives the deep, cold, black waters of the Saguenay. A hundred miles up this romantic river lies the great lake of St. John. The visitor to this northern continent should not fail to pass up at least as far as Ha-ha Bay, through the magnificent scenery of this river, a precipitous gorge cloven in the Laurentian Mountains. Above Ha-ha the prospect opens, and the land begins to be capable of cultivation. At the time of my visit a vessel was being laden here with lumber for Australia.

Coming back, the steamer lies, a mere nutshell, under the precipitous range of Cape Trinity, to let the traveller judge of the height of the cliffs that make this river gorge.

The scene is scarcely to be surpassed for stern magnificence. The mass of rock towers sheer above to a height of 1,500 or 1,800 feet. The broken mountain-shores, fringed and tasselled with clusters of pine, give their dark reflection to the cold, motionless waters. No sail, or canoe, or trace of life is visible. Silence and awe rest on the wonderful scene.

I have indicated but a few of the points of interest in the French province which would be sure to repay the English traveller here. The artist would find perpetual occasion for his sketch-book. The geologist must come here to study the oldest known formation of rock. The whole country seems a sporting reserve. And to all kinds of visitors the simple and gay mode of existence of the inhabitants, older in style than the French of the old country, offers a pleasant subject of study. To the Englishman, concerned with some anxious thoughts for the future of the British Empire, a personal persuasion of the loyalty of this million of his fellow-subjects of another language may be found an agreeable reassurance.

'Pray tell me, Sir George Cartier,' said a lady in an English drawing-room—'pray tell me what you mean by a French Canadian?'

'Madam,' replied the witty baronet, 'he is an Englishman who speaks French.'

CHAPTER IV.

LUMBER.

THE peculiarly characteristic industry of Canada is the lumber trade. It adds enormously to the wealth of the country, develops a vigorous race of men, and hastens the settlement of distant and still savage regions of forest. From first to last all the operations of this business are full of interest to the stranger, and possess a high fascination for the men actually employed. The lumber-man is as devoted to his vocation as the sailor to his, and leads a life as free and as adventurous.

At the fall of the year a whole army of stalwart men, in expeditionary bands of thirty to forty, move up the great rivers and their tributaries and penetrate the woods, to prepare for the winter campaign.

In some spot as romantic as it is solitary the shanty is built, for it must be erected near some stream or mountain lake for a supply of water, and the virgin forest rises sombre and magnificent around. The winter-house for the shelter of the forty men is constructed with extreme facility. A number of trees are marked by the leader, great pines from 100 to 200 feet in height. A couple of lumberers take a tree standing erect, one on either side, with well-planted feet, and the small, thick Canadian axe swinging over the head. But first, with practised eye, they look to see in which direction the great creature would prefer to fall, willing to let it have its way. Then follow the ringing strokes of the axes, with quick and measured rhythm, beating out the wild song to which the great son of the forest must die. Every stroke falls true, every stroke tells; the tree groans and cries in despair to its strange assailants, gives up its life in one long, wild shriek, and crashes resounding to the ground. These fifteen minutes are the 'mauvais quartre d'heure' in the life of the tree. The branches are lopped away, the trunk is divided into lengths of forty feet, and these are dragged by a chain and a powerful team of horses to the spot chosen for the shanty.

By a simple device of notches the logs are built on one another, in the form of a great square, to a height of six or eight feet. A massive roof, sloping to the sides, is formed of split logs, hollowed and roughly fitted one into the other. The gaps are filled in with branches and mud. A great aperture five feet square in the roof serves for chimney, ventilation, and light. A strong frame door is put in at one side, but rarely a window. The fireplace is peculiar; it is built in the centre of the shanty, ten or twelve feet square, of logs two feet thick, and is filled in with sand or dry earth. Here smoke and crackle and roar the mighty logs dragged in from a great pile outside. From one of the upright supports of the roof, and at the corner of the fireplace, swings a strong limb of timber bearing the mighty caldron for the general cooking of the company. Small delicacies are prepared by sticking some pot or kettle into the hot sand along the wide margin of the fire.

The sleeping berths or 'bunks' are arranged all round the place in two tiers of wooden shelves. On these the men sleep two and two, usually sharing the two pairs of thick Canadian blankets which each man is allowed for his use by the employer for whom he works.

The one dish eaten by the lumber-man is salt pork; his one drink is tea. It is highly creditable to the wise forethought of the masters, and no less to the good sense of the men, that no strong drinks are permitted within the limits of the lumbering operations. The men are provided with an abundance of a food particularly suited to their wants, and which they prefer to all other meats, and with tea ad libitum, strong enough, as one of them said to me, to float an axe in; and they are content to do without intoxicating liquors.

Close by the shanty is built a similar log-house as a smithy; a great deal of smith's work being wanted for the sleighs, chains, and the horses. A less elegant place is put up as the stables.

The men employed by one lumbering firm may

occupy half-a-dozen shanties in a district. At some central spot a 'depôt' is built, where the head director lives, where a general store of implements and clothing is kept on hand, and from which the supplies of pork, flour, molasses, &c., are distributed. When one region is stripped of its best timber—for only the choice trees are marked and cut—the shanties are left standing, and fresh ones are built further up the country.

Meanwhile, the most available spots of land for agricultural purposes have been noted by the lumbermen, and one of them marries a wife expressly, or brings up his family, if he has one already, from Quebec, and commences life as a back-woods settler. Double prices can always be obtained for everything in the neighbourhood of the shanties, in consequence of the distance from the regular markets.

Usually the men agree very well together, French, Irish, Scotch, and English; but it is not an uncommon thing for a foreman to prefer to employ all of one race. All through the winter months they work in the woods, from sunrise to sunset, and accomplish an extraordinary amount of work. They divide into bands of six or eight men, and each company strives to outrival the others. At night, after the evening meal, they sit in groups in the flickering light of the blazing logs, and smoke, and sing, and tell stories. In every shanty there is certain to be at least one fiddle, and the more hilarious dance, while the sedate look sympathizingly on.

On the Sunday labour stops. The men take their guns, or their springs and snares, for game. Some of the men, however, make the Sunday a day of rest, and remain in the shanty to tell yarns and mend their clothes. Once or twice in the season the Catholic priest comes round to confess the faithful, and about as often the itinerant Methodist arrives to exhort and hold a prayer meeting.

As soon as a thaw comes the lumbering parties break up. Part of them at once descend to the saw-mills, now ready for work again, and part are occupied in directing the passage of the logs to the mills. At certain bends of the rivers, and especially at the frequent rapids, the hurrying logs are apt to rest and ground. Tens of thousands of logs are sometimes obstructed thus on the passage down. To obviate this the raftsmen, in canoes, or stationed at certain points on land, armed with steel-pointed poles, move and guide the logs along. Lower down, where the waters become broad, the men are actively occupied in fastening securely together a certain number of the logs, about twenty or thirty, into what are called 'cribs.' Each of these is destined to proceed intact as far as the saw-mills, or probably to Quebec or the Hudson. But not separately. The 'cribs' are mutually attached by bonds of withies into great rafts acres wide, on which are sometimes built whole villages of huts. The lumber-man now has a lazy, luxurious life. He eats fat pork, and smokes his pipe, and lies in the hot sun, lulled to dreams by the light motion of his floating home. Very often he does not even guide the great raft; a steam-tug saves him the trouble.

Sometimes the logs are not fastened into 'cribs' at all. On rivers where the course is easy and unobstructed the logs are simply gathered within great booms, formed by attaching a number of the logs together end to end, inclosing the rest; and so the heavy mass floats lazily down or is tugged by steam.

The saw-mills are built where a great water-power can be obtained, and consequently are found in the most romantic situations — at Montmorenci, the Gatineau Falls, and the Phandière on the Ottawa, for example. The operations of a lumber-mill present an extraordinary spectacle. By a more or less complicated system of dams and flumes the danger of inundation is averted, and a sufficient water-power is ensured to work the mills through the season. The buildings, often picturesque in their variety and strange outline, press close upon the very edge of the falls. Up the stream, in some sheltered reach of water, float whole fields of loosened logs, awaiting now indifferently the fate for which they have been brought so far. One by one they are fixed to the endless chains that dip down for miles, and are dragged up a wooden slope on to the floor of the mill. There work incessantly, with a perpendicular motion, the multitudinous sets of glittering teeth of the eager saws, hungry and insatiable for ever. A stalwart workman fixes the dripping log with an iron lever, and before the preceding log is two-thirds cut dexterously turns the new one on to an endless platform that passes beneath the gleaming saws. Without the loss of an instant the fresh log follows along the platform; four, six, sometimes eight saws bite, and rend, and sunder it remorselessly, and the log has become planks.

These are examined, marked, measured, and cut up for the different markets. The best is set aside for the English trade; the rest goes to the United States, to South America, Australia, and all parts of the world. The smaller pieces are worked up for rail-fences, 'shingles,' fire-wood, and matches. The refuse, ground to chips, not to impede navigation, falls into the hurrying stream below.

Summer is over before the last raft reaches Quebec. With the first snow-fall the mills close, and the scattered army of axemen make their way back to the woods.

The valley of the Ottawa is at present the principal seat of the lumber trade. It was my fortune to be making a somewhat long stay in the neighbourhood at a time without parallel, happily, in the history of the district.

The Ottawa is but a tributary of the magnificent St. Lawrence; but it is no less than six hundred miles in length, it drains 80,000 square miles, and will one day support a population to be counted by millions. Already settlements are spreading far up the course of the river, and invading the depths of the primeval forests by the tributary streams; while villages and towns are springing up in lower districts.

Beyond question the Ottawa is one of the most picturesque rivers of the world; in other words, it is not easily navigable. It is one long succession of reaches studded with islands, narrow passes, fair lakes, impetuous rapids, and magnificent falls. The voyage on its waters, day after day, is a succession of charming surprises. At one time a wide prospect of open lakes reaches almost to the horizon; at another, you look over an endless undulating extent of hill and dale; then you are shut up in a narrow gorge without visible escape. To increase the feeling of exhilaration which variety gives, the traveller is compelled to change perpetually his mode of conveyance —from steam to stage, from boat to ferry, from car to scow. At some intervals the traveller may have to walk; for instance, where the narrow platform, thirty feet high, crossing a rocky valley, has been burnt by a fire in the woods.

At present the steamers plying on their several reaches of water go up as far as Deux Joachims, three hundred miles by water above Quebec. Beyond this place the canoe is used.

The steamers are constructed expressly for this traffic; some of them have a draught of but two feet six inches. The captain does not scruple to bring his boat gently on to the mud of the shore, where there is no wharf or landing-stage, to land or take up freight and passengers.

Where the steamboat runs you are still within the range of civilisation ; on board an excellent English dinner is served at a moderate price. The inns ashore are well kept, and will supply unexpected delicacies in drinks and meats, if you wish. The back-woods are not barbarous. In a remote inn by one of the portages I noticed among a collection of books on the landlady's table Faber's 'All for Jesus,' 'Gil Blas,' and the Waverley novels.

On special occasions the farmers and settlers will dress wonderfully. It was my happy fortune to fall in with a large pic-nic party at the limits of civilisation. The young men were dressed like Hampton Court dandies, and the girls in short flounces, coloured scarfs, tiny hats, and shoes with two-inch heels. The staying-power of their gaiety was extraordinary. After dancing all night they danced all the next day, on a poop without rails to save the giddy couples from a waltz into the river.

A prosperous little city on this river has been made the capital of the Dominion. The Canada Central Railroad passes through it. It is on the highway of the projected trans-continental route, along which the commerce of Europe and Asia is destined to pass. The place was not formerly called Bytown because it was out of the way of traffic, but in honour of Colonel By, the superintendent of the magnificent military canal uniting the Ottawa at this point with the St. Lawrence at Kingston, one of the finest engineering works in America.

On one of the many fine sites of the picturesque city of Ottawa stand the Parliament buildings—the noblest pile on this continent, with the exception of the white marble capitol at Washington. Wide streets of fine buildings are rising in all directions through the city; and pretty villas and cottages are spreading over the suburbs.

On the termination of the Reciprocity Treaty in 1864 the United States imposed a heavy duty on lumber, the principal article of Canadian export, with the view of influencing Canadian feeling in favour of entering the American union. This policy does not appear to have had the effect intended. Meanwhile the Canadian merchants have asked and obtained higher prices than before. Within the past few years the rates of lumber have increased fifty per cent., and still promise to rise.

The figures of the lumber business are not without interest and importance. On the Ottawa River 250,000,000 board measure (i.e., superficial feet) are prepared for the American market alone. A similar quantity is sent to the English market, in the following proportion: 50,000,000 superficial feet and 18,000,000 cubic feet of square timber.

From one of the principal merchants engaged in the American trade I obtained the favour of the following singular figures, the result of careful investigation and estimate:—

For the business alone of the 250,000,000 board measure above-named—

5,000 men are employed in taking out the logs;
2,000 teams used;
9,000 sleighs used;
2,500 tons of hay consumed;
3,500 barrels of pork;
4,000 barrels of flour;
23,000 lbs. of tea;
14,500 lbs. of soap consumed;
400,000 lbs. of iron chain used; and
2,000 men further employed in sawing and shipping the lumber.

But far larger figures are needed to express the amount of the whole of the Canadian lumber trade.

It is estimated at 700,000,000 feet for the American market, and an equivalent quantity for England, South America, Australia, &c. Or a grand total, in a row of ten figures, of 1,400,000,000 feet. To carry on this trade, over 30,000 men are employed, at an average of probably a dollar a day. The present prices average nine to ten dollars a thousand feet for America, and twelve dollars and over for England.

In point of fact, Canada possesses a great staple which all the world requires, and which must be obtained at any cost. The lumber will remain a vast source of national wealth to the Dominion in perpetuity.

Immense tracts of rocky territory, stretching northwards towards the Pole, and wholly unfit for agricultural productions, may continue to rival lands of wheat for use and value. As the great trees are thinned out young ones grow to take their place. As prices increase, and labour becomes more abundant, it will be found advisable to promote the growth of the large timber by thinning the overcrowded woods. And, still later, it will even become profitable to encourage artificially, by planting or other means, the superior qualities of wood in the place of less valuable kinds.

The lumber trade of Canada will remain, therefore, to increase the national wealth, and—a result of greater importance—to promote the growth of a hardy, adventurous race.

CHAPTER V.

THE FREE-GRANT LANDS.

It was my pleasant fortune to be invited by the Premier of Ontario to join him, with several members of the Government, upon a tour of inspection through the Muskoka district, a wide region of romantic lakes, and streams, and woods in the northern part of the province of Ontario. The object of the Government was to see the condition of the roads and bridges lately constructed under their order, to observe the suitability of the country for immigration, and to make themselves acquainted with the condition and wishes of the settlers. For myself, I wished to see something more of back-woods life, and to know what kind of land was given away without payment to the settler.

We proceeded from Toronto fifty-two miles by the Great Northern Railway to Belle Ewart, a picturesque little town of frame houses springing up with a rapid growth on the borders of the beautiful Lake Simcoe. This district is already settled. Along both sides of the railway farmsteads and villages occur in quick succession through the dense woods, with fields bearing a rich produce, despite the unsightly stumps which had not yet had time to rot away. This railway is to be carried on at once to Gravenhurst, the door of the free-grant district; and subsequently, without any question, it will proceed north to Lake Nipissing, to tap the line of rails that will cross the continent direct to Fort Garry and the Pacific. This line, therefore, through the free-grant Muskoka district, appears destined to be the direct channel for the north-west, and for the Asiatic trade with the province of Ontario, and with the New England States of the American Union. However, we are concerned at present with narrower prospects.

A large steamer took us, with a number of settlers and immigrants, and their multifarious wares and baggage, across Lake Simcoe. On the further side a miniature screw-steamer waited to take us over the narrow, winding, lovely lake, Couchiching. This little boat, after the excellent fashion prevailing here, and more or less all through Canada, is named, from an Indian tongue, 'Winonah' (the first-born). Other steamers we subsequently used or met were the 'Wanbuno,' the 'Chicora,' the 'Macinac.' On this Lake Couchiching—the Lake of Many Winds—we stopped at a new-born town, Orillia. The townships near by were named Rama, Mara, Vespra, and Oro. These beautiful names everywhere abound, and the country is worthy of them.

It is a pleasant indication of a natural appreciation of the graceful in this transplanted English race that sonorous and significant names are being everywhere chosen throughout the Dominion, and are even displacing old names of a vulgar sound. A certain spot on Lake Ontario—the Beautiful—could not prosper while it was styled York, or contemptuously Little York; named anew Toronto—the Meeting-Place of the Tribes—it has advanced to dignity and importance with a rapidity scarcely rivalled on the whole American continent.

There are not wanting people who say that Kingston, better named, need not have sunk to an insignificance corresponding with that of our old Saxon Kingston on the banks of the Thames. I have been told of a newly-born city which, on being called Victuallersville by a vote of the inhabitants, in grateful memory of a licensed association, perished miserably in the christening, and was abandoned by its ashamed inhabitants. From the depths of my soul I invoke a similar fate on the Pickwickvilles, Yow-Bets, Big-Jerichos, and Ulysses-Cities on this continent!

From Washago on Lake Couchiching to Gravenhurst the route passes for fourteen miles through a singularly picturesque tract of savage scenery. Precipitous broken hills, crowned with dense pine and beech, rise on every side; abrupt masses of granite block the way. The ragged road-track plunges violently down the hill-slopes to the corduroy bridge over a stream at the bottom, and toils painfully up the opposite slope. Within view we frequently pass clear lakes, as yet unnamed, reflecting the true Muskoka sky,—the name of the district being another example of the happy choice of Indian words; it means the Lake of Clear Skies. Every bend in the road opens a fresh prospect of singular beauty; but no traveller here has ever come in search of the picturesque. I believed the Minister of Crown Lands when he told me that an intending settler has been known to stop midway along this road with his family and goods, and return disheartened or resentful. But the man was wrong. Proverbially, the entrances to all lands of promise are difficult, to test the courage of the pilgrim and prepare him for his home of rest.

Midway along this road at a point named by the settler Gibraltar, from the extremely rocky character of the ground which he had chosen for his home, we found ourselves exposed to a direct fire of a battery of six mounted guns, made of the trunks of fallen trees. A defiant soldier, cut out in profile, and rather larger than life, kept ceaseless guard. These precautions were taken to overawe a Fenian invasion, should the rebels ever be absurd enough to advance so far into the heart of the country.

As our straggling cavalcade approached the spot, a brawny Highlander, in kilt and tartan, sprang from rock to rock to the battery height, and saluted our arrival with several discharges of his gun. We dismounted, and made our way to his log shanty. The place presented many appearances of comfort. The furniture was old-fashioned, but ample. Prints adorned the boarded walls. A small side room possessed a considerable library of works of piety, fiction, and history. Mr. Cuthbert had been settled for several years on this spot, had cleared a good deal of land, and, like all the other settlers through this region, was content with his rough but free life, and extremely hopeful of the future. We were presented to his wife and sister, who told us they were entirely satisfied with their new home.

'If those rascally rebels should ever come this way, gentlemen,' said our host, 'you may rely upon us here to give a good account of them.'

The Commissioner of Public Works informed him that a small brass cannon was on its way, and would be sent up to strengthen his battery with all convenient dispatch.

'I am obliged to you, sir,' said Mr. Cuthbert; 'but pray don't let it be sent up yet. All the boys about these parts are going to turn out to welcome it, and we're going to have a procession to bring it home. The boys here are much interested in my place, gentlemen.'

We said that we could not have the least doubt of that.

The Attorney-General, the Hon. Sandfield M'Donald, talked with his fellow-Scot in Gaelic, and then continued in English: 'Now, I hope you narrow but deep and very lively Muskoka river winds round the place, with a set of falls in full view, and another at a short distance. Of course, saw-mills were in busy operation. At a bend in the stream floated a quantity of saw-logs. The log huts, and wooden cottages, and frame houses two or three stories high, at different elevations on the hilly ground, with a great variety of outline, gave the most picturesque views. All around were clearings in the wood, and fields still choked with stumps. There were a number of stores, and all were bustling and prosperous. Anything conceivable, apparently, was to be obtained there, and, as I discovered, at but a trifling advance upon Toronto prices. The artisan here has a hundred acres in the bush. Free public schools are opened. Presbyterian, Methodist, and Episcopal churches are already formed. 'The Northern Advocate' has a circulation of 1,100 a week. The hotels—Victoria, the Royal, and the Dominion (signs significant)—at present sleep their superabundant guests in rows upon the floors, while their accommodation is being increased. The emigrant agent here had disposed of 60,000 acres of land within the past two months.

Muskoka is but one of a series of lakes affording a natural communication through the Free Grant district. Rousseau, beyond, is an eminently picturesque sheet of water, of irregular shape, filled with islands, large and small, with hilly, well-wooded shores; and yet perhaps Lake St. Joseph, still more north, may boast even greater beauty. This region is destined one day to be visited by summer tourists, as Lakes George and Champlain now are in New England, or our own small lakes in Old England. We bathed in each, and fished from canoes or rowboats lent us by the settlers. A considerable proportion of the land with a water frontage is already taken up. In a few years all the land will be settled, at least up to Lake Nipissing, where the Pacific route will cross.

The proportion of land capable of cultivation through the district is probably fifty per cent. In some sections it was estimated at sixty or even at seventy per cent. Scotch settlers often told us that the most stony districts were no worse than those parts of the old country from which they came; and if half the extent of a farm can be used for purposes of agriculture it is abundantly sufficient. The wooded half will supply the settler with material for his out-buildings, barns, and fences, and with the important article of fuel. In the wildest parts, too, a rank grass grows freely round the stones, on which the cattle feed well. The settlers send out their beasts into the woods in the spring, and find them in the fall in excellent condition. We frequently met with roaming cattle, marked and belled, and always plump and healthy.

Bears are now very rarely to be met. Moose and elk are occasionally stalked. Partridge, duck, and various small game are common. The lakes and streams afford an extraordinary abundance of fine trout, bass, white fish, and what is here called herring.

We constantly met parties of two to half a dozen men making their way with guns through the woods, with the view of choosing settlements. Sometimes one or two of these would be commissioned to select lots for friends at home who intended to join them. Some were Canadians, others old country folk; they camped out in rough style in the woods, or made their way at night to a settler's house or a shanty tavern.

I had the honour of suggesting a name for a spot that may possibly attain to importance. At a certain point the waters of St. Joseph approach within about two hundred yards of Lake Rousseau; a strip of sand, easy to work, forming the division. Some thirty men were at work cutting this through, and embanking the channel solidly with stone. We encamped here one night on a wooded knoll overlooking the two lakes. I took a lesson in wood-chopping, and felled, but with many a wasted stroke, two trees. It was a pleasant experience to stand back, just after the last blow, and see the tottering tree sweep down from among its fellows with a thundering crash. It was more difficult to stand on the trunk afterwards and cut it into logs by strokes directed between the outstretched feet.

Before our canvas tents blazed a magnificent fire of pine logs. Here we broiled our fish and pork and cooked our tea. A recent settler prayed our acceptance of the first potatoes grown on Lake Joseph; they turned out from our pot white, flaky balls of unequalled deliciousness. Another settler brought out from his pocket a specimen ear of Indian corn about a foot long, and excellently ripened.

We ate suppers hearty enough to have given us all nightmare in any spot less free and wild than this. Then members of Government sang patriotic songs, and some backwoodsmen, and the men on the works close by, attracted to our camp, sang songs, sentimental and comic. The stars were long out when we crawled into our tents, rolled ourselves in blankets, and fell asleep.

In the middle of the night our quiet was disturbed by a wild cry of alarm. I sprang up, and found the place at my side vacant. At the tent door loomed the spectral figure of the Attorney-General, dark against the glowing light of the camp fire, with extended arms and wild gestures. The cry of fire died on his lips. 'I thought I was in a house in flames,' he said penitently, and crept quietly back.

In the morning a great plank was procured. In open block letters I inscribed on it the name newly decided on for the place. The plank was nailed up to a pine before the assembled party. In the name of Her Majesty Queen Victoria and of the Dominion of Canada, the Reverend Mr. Herring christened the place Port Sandfield. We added our acclamations.

We visited a great number of the houses of the settlers up to Parry's Sound on the Georgian Bay. In no instance did we find anyone disheartened or faring ill. No doubt their life was hard, and laborious, and somewhat solitary; but they had all apparently come to like it. Every man knew his neighbours and received help from them, giving his own assistance in turn. We met at different points the son of a Devonshire clergyman and the nephew of a Lord Mayor of London, each contented and resolved to stay. We found also a number of Londoners who had been assisted out by Mr. Herring, and who were overjoyed at the unexpected sight of the face of an old friend. Without any exception, such settlers from the old country expressed their satisfaction at the change in their condition, and declined the thought of returning. I do not question that, on the whole, they were getting on as well as the Canadians from the old province.

Now that roads and steamboats are opening communication through the country, the course of raising a new home in the back-woods is by no means so arduous an undertaking as it may appear to our imagination at home. The first thing to be done is the selection of a piece of land. The Government agent for the district will always assist intelligently with his advice. Some old settler or hotel-keeper can always be found, for a dollar or a dollar and a half a day, to go out with a new comer, and show him the country and the most eligible plots.

The allotment decided on and secured at the agent's office, the settler must find a lodging till his own house is up. But this is no difficult matter; all the people are neighbourly, and will gladly offer what accommodation they have for a small remuneration for the short time the new comer remains houseless.

Not far from the roadway, and, if possible, near some stream or lake, the settler fixes upon the site for his dwelling. Then he strips to his shirt sleeves, and falls to work vigorously with his axe. At felling two men should work together, for the saving of labour and for company's sake. If the settler has no friend or sturdy son with him, he can hire or borrow help near by.

It is a pleasant sight to see a good axeman at work. He stands erect; with well-planted feet, with throat bare, and probably with bare arms, he lifts his axe aloft against the towering majesty of the forest-tree. The Canadian axe is small and very thick, and seems a ridiculous weapon against its great opponents. The handle is very long and bent in shape. The man swings the axe high above his head; his right hand, slipping down the long handle, guides the stroke; the weight of the falling blow, with little muscular effort, drives the axe-edge deep into the trunk. After some practice not a stroke is lost. The woods resound with the gay rhythm of the alternating blows. A great notch, a foot or two across, grows on either side of the tree. The forest giant totters. The men pause and look up; wield the axe again, then step back. The direction in which the tree must fall is always determined by some irregularity in its growth or eccentricity of its position. It is a splendid moment when it comes crashing down, shaking the earth and sending the noise of its fall through the woods. The branches are lopped off and piled for burning. The trunk is divided into logs for the house.

When enough logs are ready, a 'bee' is held, and all the neighbours round flock to assist in raising the new dwelling. The 'bee' is popular; it affords a pleasant variety and excitement to the back-woods life, it appeals to the social propensities, it allows opportunity for talk, advice, and the forming of new acquaintanceships. Besides, everyone who comes is expecting to have a bee himself, for getting in his wheat, or raising a shed, or building his second house. The bee in the backwoods is the fête, the club, the ball, the town-hall, the labour convention of the whole community.

Several members of our Muskoka party assisted for a short time at one of these gatherings. A finer score of men than those whom we found assembled it would be difficult anywhere to meet. Most of them were young, but the new settler himself and several of the others were men past the prime of life. They all worked with a will, whistling or singing, with bits of talk and an occasional joke. At a neighbour's house, lent for the occasion, there was a table well spread with pork and beans, and good bread, and strong tea, for the noonday meal. It is a general custom, well honoured in the observance, not to offer ale or strong drink on these occasions. The expense would be too great for many an immigrant; and, besides, the men meet together for hard work.

I tried to use an axe upon the new house, but rather to the amusement of the men by my awkwardness than to their assistance. The Attorney-General, however, was pronounced by them with admiration 'an old hand.' The great logs are laid on the beaten earth in a square, perhaps of forty feet by thirty. By deep notches the corners are jointed together. Some inequalities of the surface are removed. The next tier of selected logs is placed on, and so jointed as to make the ends of the side logs fit between those of the front and back. The bark outside is left on, and aids the picturesqueness of the building. The inside throughout is smoothed level. The interstices are filled in with small branches and clay. The doorways and windows are cut through after the whole wall is raised. All this can be done in a day. The sloping roof, built of hollow, divided logs, fitted one into the other, can be put on by two men afterwards.

Sometimes the log-house is built of two stories, or at least with a loft. It is solid and comfortable, wind-proof and rain-proof, and will last many years. The morticed corners are often smoothed plain, and the bark is sometimes cut away in a pattern round the windows. Some of these log dwellings suggest a model type for a gentleman's country residence.

There is one absolute essential which the new settler must procure, and with that he may move at once into his new home. He must have a stove for cooking, and for warmth through the long winter. Of course it is better if he can take with him also bed, boxes, chairs, a gun, and a few books. And, if he has a family with him, he should certainly take pork, flour, and tea to last till the next summer, or money enough to buy these. Forty or fifty pounds will carry a man with a small family pretty comfortably through his first winter and spring, the time of his chief difficulties.

But a lusty young man, with a taste for 'roughing it,' need not hesitate to commence in the bush without a cent. He can get work enough on the first day of his arrival to pay for his food. He can join a settler in clearing his plot on condition of receiving similar assistance. In the growing towns he can always earn some spare money. If put to a push, he can get a dollar or a dollar and a quarter a day at some lumbering works, and there is always one near. We found such men, who had come there penniless, and were now doing well.

The dwelling up, the man proceeds at once, with what help he can, to clear two or three or more acres. The best lumber he can sell, paying certain government dues; the rest he burns, with all the underwood. His first crop—wheat, barley, beans, potatoes—will be an extraordinary one, unless he is a man born without luck. Of grain he should get fifty bushels to the acre, notwithstanding the stumps. Of potatoes he will get a preposterous yield. Then he will lay this down in grass, and proceed to clear four acres more.

The good wife should have her cows, and pigs, and multitudinous poultry.

The settler has no need to seek a market. The lumbering shanties will buy of him at double prices everything eatable he can offer. The rising industrial centres also aid the demand.

In three or four years the log-house becomes too small for the settler's increased family and growing importance. He builds a new one of squared timbers, and uses the old place for cattle or horses.

In five years more a new change is necessary. The wilderness has become a cultivated settlement. The stumps are rotted and pulled out; save for the snake-fence his farm looks like a piece of Old England. He has built great barns, for they cost nothing but the labour. His cattle and sheep are well housed; but he is always wanting more room. Once more he sets to work building, but by this time a town has grown up near him, and he can obtain any kind of labour he desires. If his tastes are pretentious, he decides on a stone residence, with a handsome portico. But, more probably, he will build an elegant frame house, with pretty balconies and a wide verandah.

These are the steps of progress to be seen all through Canada. The man of industry and intelligence is certain to achieve an independent position for himself and his family.

He will have hardships on the way, no doubt. One well-to-do farmer told me of a time when he and his family, snowed up, were reduced to a diet of barley-meal seasoned with rat-skins. Another man, whose farmhouse is now surrounded by villas, told me humorously of his return once from market, with a big saucepan, when, through the darkness of the night, he searched about on his own farm for hours for his shanty in vain, and at length slept on the ground, with his head inside the pot for shelter. He stated that he had often passed a week on his clearing without the sight of a human creature, and at last had married a wife to save himself growing deaf and dumb. The old lady told me that on her marrying she used to drive to market in the winter on the smooth snow roads with a hogshead for her carriage.

'It was just as good driving as in a sleigh,' said she; 'but my daughter would not think so, I guess.'

'I should be afraid of tipping out, mamma,' was the answer.

'And what harm? you could get in again,' the

old lady rejoined testily. 'But the girls think themselves quite young ladies now-a-days!'

I confess I thought this myself of the blooming, blushing girl who sat by.

In some instances considerable difficulty is found in obtaining suitable instruction for the children. The settlers, however, as a rule, are well aware of the importance of education, and the first public enterprise in a new settlement is usually the building of a school-house. The educational department, alive to the importance of providing instruction in the new districts, always assists liberally in meeting the annual expenses. The use of the school-house is allowed to the various denominations for religious services on the Sunday.

At Port Carling, a small cluster of huts in Muskoka, we found a school of twenty-two children in the upper story of a general store. Many of the children were bonnetless, some had bare feet; but they were all healthy-looking, and seemed fairly intelligent. The copy-books and reading were very creditable. 'What is the meaning of that word you have just read, "stumbling?"' we asked. 'It is half-falling, sir,' replied one of the boys, after a moment's pause.

On the whole, there does not appear the least doubt that tens of thousands of our hard-working population at home would find their position greatly improved on these free-grant settlements. It was our general conviction that new comers just out from the old country did quite as well here as Canadians from the settled districts. If a man is healthy and strong and means to work, he has nothing to fear here, and everything to hope.

The regulations of the government-grant are very simple. To an unmarried man one hundred acres is the quantity given freely, but he is permitted to purchase an additional hundred acres at the nominal rate of fifty cents per acre, or two shillings English. The head of a family is allowed two hundred acres, and an additional hundred for every boy and girl over eighteen years of age. He has also the privilege of buying a limited quantity in addition, if he desire it, at the rate of fifty cents per acre. The land is absolutely given without charge; but always, and solely, on condition of fulfilling the 'settlement duties.' These are : to clear at least fifteen acres out of every hundred within five years, and to build a dwelling-house on the property.

These conditions fulfilled—and they are found wholly unburdensome—the settler receives at the end of the five years a patent establishing his right to the land. He is then at liberty to sell, but not before.

These regulations are framed with the intention of securing bonâ-fide settlers, and not land speculators, or mere fellers of timber.

The free-grant lands are practically inexhaustible. About twenty townships are now open to settlers in Muskoka; others are being surveyed.

The vast region reaching up to Lake Nipissing is being surveyed.

Nine townships in County Victoria and four townships in North Peterborough are open for settlement.

These are in Ontario. Similar districts are already open, and others are being rapidly prepared, in the lower province of Quebec.

In both provinces the government are engaged in surveying and building new roads. Railway companies are finding it to their interest to run lines of the new narrow gauge to open up the new country.

Then west of Lake Superior stretches an enormous tract of rich prairie and woodland, destined to be the home of new and powerful states.

Immigration to Canada, which for some years past has been steadily increasing, is likely soon to attain to very large dimensions.

CHAPTER VI.

THE FARMING INTEREST.

BEYOND all question agriculture is the mainstay and the making of Canada. It is estimated that eighty per cent. of the adult male population is engaged, directly or indirectly, in the cultivation of the soil. In a constantly increasing degree intelligence is being added to labour, and larger capital employed in improved methods of farming.

In the year 1841 the province of Ontario (formerly Canada West) produced 3,221,991 bushels of wheat; in 1861, 24,620,425 bushels, an increase of 664 per cent. in twenty years.

At the date of the last census, 1861, the two Canadas, with the maritime provinces, produced over forty-three million bushels of oats, five and a half million bushels of barley, thirty-six million bushels of potatoes, twenty million bushels of turnips, over two million tons of hay, fifty-two million pounds of butter, and a hundred and twenty-three million pounds of pork. These large figures may serve to suggest the great advance Canada has already made from its primitive forest condition. It is believed that the census for 1871 will show an increase of fifty per cent. on the last returns.

The accumulated wealth of the country in stock is enormous. The figures for 1861 stood as follows for the provinces now included in the Dominion:

Horses		706,979
Horned Cattle { Milch cows . .		966,875
{ Neat cattle . .		1,309,070
Sheep		2,410,536
Swine		1,207,164
Total animals . .		6,600,624

A carefully compiled estimate of values made at the date of the last census, 1861, gave the following particulars:

Value of farms . .	$546,000,000 =	£109,000,000
„ Agricultural implements . .	25,000,000 =	5,000,000
„ Horses, cattle, &c.	120,000,000 =	24,000,000

Beyond all question the return of 1871 will show a great increase on all these items.

In one important respect—the quantities of land brought under cultivation—the progress made by Canada in the ten years preceding the last census can be made easily apparent. In 1851 the quantity of acres occupied in the two provinces Upper and Lower Canada were 17,939,825; in 1861 the figures were increased to 23,730,325. In 1851 the number of acres under actual cultivation in the two Canadas were 7,300,930; in 1861 the figures had risen most satisfactorily to 10,855,854 acres.

It is safe to predict that the next returns will show at least a corresponding advance.

For the most part the land is owned in properties of moderate extent. A numerous class of working farmers, somewhat like the yeomen of Old England, is springing up to be the strength and health of the country. The following table, in which the returns of the two provinces Upper and Lower Canada are combined, may possess in this view a peculiar interest:

Properties of 10 acres and less	11,246
From 10 acres to 20	5,861
,, 20 ,, ,, 50	46,704
,, 50 ,, ,, 100	108,932
,, 100 ,, ,, 200	53,075
Over 200	11,836

The large proportion of farmers of about a hundred acres will, without doubt, still be shown in the census figures for next year. The policy adopted by the government in the disposal of the Crown lands distinctly favours the increase of farms of about that size.

There has been but little scientific farming as yet in Canada. The men have been too busy, the capital employed has been too small, the necessity for immediate returns from the soil too great. In all the newly-settled districts the most rough-and-ready style of farming will prevail for a considerable time to come. In some sections of the country injury has resulted to the land from the farmer's lack of knowledge. This appears to be notably the case in some parts of the lower province, among the French Canadians, whose disposition and habits dispose them to an existence of content and quiet rather than to enterprises demanding risk.

But an era of improvement has already come. In the older-settled districts a scientific system of farming is being adopted. Even in the conservative lower provinces several schools of agriculture have been established, and a system of rotation of crops is becoming general.

One of the most palpable signs of this improvement is found in the greatly increasing use of excellent farming implements. Factories for improved ploughs, mowers, and reapers are everywhere springing up. The farmer has too much work to do in so short a season in Canada, and has such extreme difficulty in obtaining all the assistance he could use, that labour-saving machines have become a great necessity. Canada claims to have passed both England and the United States in the value, per head of the population, of the agricultural implements employed.

The virgin soil of the country is ordinarily so rich that the settler finds no inducement to treat it with consideration. Wheat crops are frequently raised in constant succession, and with little or no diminution of return, for over a dozen years. An utterly systemless style of farming has in consequence prevailed in many districts. Farm manure is frequently thrown away, to save the trouble of carrying it to the land. When the soil at length becomes too impoverished to yield a paying return, farmers of the old-fashioned type sell out at low prices and move to new ground. A farmer knowing his business buys the place, and quickly makes it pay better than before.

The draining of the land in the old-established districts is now proceeding in all directions. Several draining-ploughs, or ditch-excavators, have been invented, and are coming into use, for running the lines for the draining-pipes. These implements are, I understand, expressly of Canadian invention and manufacture.

Throughout Canada farmers' societies have now been formed for the discussion of agricultural matters and the dissemination of intelligence. A number of agricultural journals are also in general circulation. But perhaps the most effective, as it certainly is the most popular, means of improving the farming of the country, is to be found in the agricultural fairs that have lately become general through the Dominion. Almost every township, in Ontario at least, has its annual show of farming implements and produce; each district has its show in addition, sometimes an annual one; and, besides these, the great Provincial Agricultural Exhibitions are held annually, moving the place of exhibition each year.

A District Agricultural Fair was held in London, Ontario, during my stay there. London the Little the energetic town is called, to distinguish it from another London, by the people who have heard of both.

The fair was held for three days towards the end of September. Nearly ten thousand persons passed within the grounds during the last day. The scene presented a fair picture of prosperity, content, and advancement. The stalwart, burly, jovial farmers would have compared favourably with any similar gathering in the old country. Their wives, plainly dressed, absorbed in examining improved butter-churns and wringing machines, looked cheerful and well-to-do, but sometimes rather too sun-dried. The daughters, plump and rosy-cheeked, daintily trimmed from feather to shoe-buckle, casting demure glances from the calves and sheep among the crowd, in search of acquaintances, seemed the very models of young housewives to make a new farm complete— as many of the tall young farmers, in cut-away coats and astonishing caps, evidently concluded. There appeared little danger, I thought, of the farming lands being less well-managed by the new generation.

The fine display of produce surprised me. Wheat, barley, oats, and other cereals were well represented. Maize, or corn, as it is uniformly called on this continent, though less grown than in the United States, showed excellent samples. The roots and vegetables were surprisingly fine. A field pumpkin which I measured was four feet ten inches in circumference; a squash eight feet three inches, weighing one hundred and fifty pounds. The potatoes were the finest I have ever seen, but were too large to be ornamental on a dinner-table. There were a great number of varieties; the meshamoc, ruby seedling, and early rose being perhaps the best. Citrons, melons, marrows, and tomatoes were also exceptionally large and fine.

Many of the fruit specimens would infallibly have taken prizes at an English show. Upwards of a hundred varieties of apples were exhibited. For cooking, there were the Cayuga, Red-streak, or Twenty-ounce pippin, an imposing fruit, measuring sometimes over fifteen inches; the Alexander, of a glorious crimson; the Red Astrachan or Snow-apple, so named popularly from the whiteness of the pulp; the Gravenstein, Baldwin, and many others. For dessert, there were the Fameuse, the Streaked St. Lawrence, the Spitzenburg, the Seek-no-farther, of gold and red.

Even in California, the orchard of the Union, the superiority of Canadian apples was, to my surprise, confessed. Vast quantities are exported to England, and sold simply as American, their nationality being lost.

In pears we had the musky-flavoured Bartlett; the red and russet Beurré Clairgeaux, of ideal shape; the Flemish Beauty, with a fine melting flesh; the small, fragrant Seckel, the standard of excellence.

Plums were good; the peaches indifferent. Open-air grapes showed to great advantage. I will name a few varieties: the Delaware, a prolific vine, with a honeyed claret-coloured grape; the Concord, with a compact, shouldered cluster of dark fruit; the delicious Hertford Prolific; the sweet Creveling, the strangely-tinted Diana, the Clinton, Catawba, Isabella, and others especially fit for wine.

There was a good collection of foliage plants and of flowers. Canada has advanced far beyond the stage in which a people is solely occupied in providing for the necessities of life.

At this single district exhibition the following entries in live stock were made:

Horned cattle	330
Sheep	360
Horses	640
Pigs	200
Total	1,530

There were excellent Durhams, Devons, and Ayrshire cattle; Cotswold and Leicester sheep; Essex, Suffolk, and other well-known breeds of pigs; and many excellent draught and road horses. I had already seen at various farm establishments that much attention was given to stock-raising; but I was not prepared for the evidence of such a wide-spread interest in this branch of the farmer's occupation and such a general excellence of result as I found here.

I was still more surprised at the great variety and excellence of the agricultural implements exhibited. Beautifully made ploughs were priced at fifteen dollars and upwards. A splendid piece of machinery, a thresher and separator, with ten-horse power engines, cost 340 dollars, or about 70*l.* Others less elaborate were offered at lower prices. A newly-invented Canadian drain-tile ditching machine was at work, digging cleanly out a ditch of five or six feet in depth, and was priced at 130 dollars (26*l.*).

But the most interesting pieces of construction were perhaps the hand-raker with mower, and combined self-raker and mowing-machines, ranging from 130 dollars to 160 dollars. They were calculated to perform with ease the work of several men. And, however high the cost, it must be soon saved in a country like this, where labour is highly paid, and difficult to obtain at the needed moment.

There were, besides cultivators of different kinds, fanning-mills, straw-cutters, grain-crackers, root-cutters, &c.; and a number of improved gates, pumps, log-raisers, stump-extractors, &c.

The fair of which I have been speaking was not the result of unusual efforts. It was but one of many district exhibitions held annually, and was to be followed in ten days by the great Provincial Agricultural Fair, appointed to be held in Toronto, in the same division of the country.

At an extremely small town, Chatham, in the south-west of Ontario, I visited, a few days later, another annual exhibition, marked by all the characteristics of the Little London one, but on a smaller scale, commensurate with the diminished importance of the place. All the specimens shown of grain, roots, and vegetables were excellent, and the variety and number of improved agricultural implements noticeably large.

Increased attention is being shown throughout the Dominion to the raising of stock. Both in Quebec and Ontario there are now large stock-farms which yield heavy returns to their proprietors, and are useful in assisting to improve the breed of cattle, horses, and sheep through the country. Choice animals are imported from England, and stock raised from them is sold freely at high prices. The Canadian has the old English love of fine animals about his farm—a fondness that is not diminished by the fact that superior meat, wool, or capacity of labour more than repays the additional outlay.

It is difficult to speak with precision of the returns of grain commonly yielded to the farmer in this country; the amount varying much, according to the climate, the soil, and the cultivation. I have seen some fields that yielded forty bushels to the acre; others, not far distant, giving perhaps but fifteen. In one of the southern counties of Ontario I remarked one morning a particularly poor-looking crop of Indian corn; on the same day, in the same county, I walked through a field of, I suppose, forty acres of this splendid plant, growing to a height of eighteen to twenty feet, and yielding thirty-seven tons to the acre as a food for cattle. It was then being cut down green. I plucked an ear nearly ripe eighteen inches long, and out of curiosity counted the large grains of the ear. They numbered 600; an enormous increase on the sown grain.

An approximate average, however, of the returns of the soil can be offered. I will quote, as a trustworthy authority, a pamphlet issued in 1869 by the authority of the Government of Ontario:

'The average yield of wheat in some townships exceeds twenty-two bushels to the acre, and where an approach to good farming prevails the yield rises to thirty and often forty bushels to the acre. On new land, fifty bushels is not very uncommon; and it must not be forgotten that Canadian wheat, grown near the city of Toronto, won a first prize at the Paris Exhibition. It may truly be said that the soil of what may be termed the agricultural portion of Canada, which comprises four-fifths of the inhabited portion, and a vast area still in the hands of the government, and now open to settlement, is unexceptionable; and when deterioration takes place it is the fault of the farmer, and not of the soil.'

An impression, I think, has generally prevailed with us that, as an agricultural country, Canada compares to great disadvantage with the United States. I should not judge this, however, from personal observation and enquiry in the two countries. On both sides of the boundary line the land is cultivated with, apparently, an equal lack of the neatness and care that distinguish the farming of the long-settled countries of the Old World. And on either side of the line the soil seems to give an equally abundant return to the slight labour bestowed on it. The Canadian farm looks as prosperous as the American; the house and farm-buildings and the home comforts of the Ontario farmer compare well with those of the farmer of New York State or Ohio.

I have no kind of wish to snatch an advantage for Canada at the expense of the great Republic on her borders. It is perhaps only fair, however, to the younger and smaller people, to allow them to state their own case with the best chance of attracting attention to their position. They claim to be no whit behind their neighbours in agricultural prosperity; and dare even to assert, giving openly the figures in proof, that lately their rate of advance has been greater than that of the States. I will quote again from the authorised pamphlet mentioned above, prepared under the management of the Hon. John Carling, the Commissioner of Agriculture for Ontario, and, as I was assured by him, completed with the greatest care, to insure fairness and accuracy:

'During the interval between the last census and the preceding one the decennial increase of population in Canada exceeded that in the United States by nearly $5\frac{1}{2}$ per cent.; Canada adding 40·87 per cent. to her population in ten years, while the United States added only 35·58 per cent. to theirs. She brought her wild lands into cultivation at a rate, in nine years, exceeding the rate of increase of cultivated lands in the United States, in ten years, by nearly 6 per cent.; Canada, in 1860, having added 50 acres of cultivated land to every 100 acres under cultivation in 1851, while the United States, in 1860, had only added 44 acres to every 100 acres under cultivation in 1850. The value per cultivated acre of the farming lands of Canada in 1860 exceeded the value per cultivated acre of the farming lands of the United States; the average value per cultivated acre in Canada being $20.87, and in the United States $17.32. In Canada a larger capital was invested in agricultural implements, in proportion to the amount of land cultivated, than in the United States; the average value of agricultural implements used on a farm having 100 cultivated acres being in Canada $182, and in the United States $150. In proportion to population, Canada in 1860 raised twice as much wheat as the United States; Canada in that year raising 11·02 bushels for each inhabitant, while the United States raised only 5·50 bushels for each inhabitant. Bulking together eight leading staples of agriculture—wheat, corn, rye, barley, oats, buckwheat, peas and beans, and potatoes—Canada, between 1851 and 1860, increased her proportion of these articles from 57,000,000 to 123,000,000 bushels, an increase of 113 per cent.; while the United States in ten years, from 1850 to 1860, increased their productions of the same articles only 45 per cent. In 1860 Canada raised of those articles 49·12 bushels for each inhabitant, against a production in the United States of 43·42 bushels for each inhabitant. Excluding Indian corn from the list, Canada raised of the remaining articles 48·07 bushels for each inhabitant, almost three times the rate of production in the United States, which was 16·74 bushels for each inhabitant. As regards live stock and their products, Canada in 1860, in proportion to her population, owned more horses and more cows, made more butter, kept more sheep, and had a greater yield of wool, than the United States.'

The figures for Canada in this statement are obtained from the returns of the conjoined provinces of Ontario and Quebec; the former having, however, a greater prosperity than the latter, which is to a large extent occupied by a conservative French population. The rate of advance, therefore, of the Anglo-Saxon province of Ontario has been still more remarkable than the above comparison indicates. The Ontarians may be forgiven for asking our attention to this. I will quote Mr. Carling's pamphlet again :

'Of fall wheat New York sowed within some 28,000 acres of the breadth sown in Ontario, but we reaped over 2,000,000 bushels more than they did. The average quantity of oats raised by us in 1861 was fully more than 31 bushels per acre, but New York only averaged 17 bushels per acre. New York reaped 19,052,853 bushels of oats from 1,109,565 acres sown; whilst our Western farmers, from

678,337 acres, took off no less than 21,220,874 bushels. This fact of itself speaks volumes for the fertility of Canadian soil. The small quantity of turnips raised in New York appears singular, our returns being 18,206,950 bushels as against 1,282,388. Taking the returns all in all, they indicate that our farmers have nothing to envy in the Empire State, and that, either as regards excellent soil or good farming, we can compare favourably with our neighbours.'

CHAPTER VII.

NIAGARA.

THE Dominion may claim the dignity of possessing the most magnificent spectacle of falling waters in the world. Of the multitudes who have heard of the fame of Niagara, few perhaps are accustomed to associate the name with that of Canada.

The Falls of Niagara are shared between the New Dominion and the United States. The boundary-line passes through their troubled waters; but from the position of the Falls, broken into by a rocky island dense with woods, the chief panoramic view of the whole mass is to be obtained on the Canada side. The inferior division of the great flood, the American Falls, though within the United States, makes its tremendous plunge in full face of the Canada shore. Then, separated by an abrupt wall of rock, the exposed base of Goat Island, the main body of the river rolls headlong down, forming the world-renowned Horse-shoe Falls which divide Canada from the States. Below the feet of the observer the great river, broken into whirlpools of foam and spray, rushes hurriedly away along the deep chasm which the Falls have fashioned for it during countless ages. Rolling masses of vaporous spray rise up to the heaven; sunrise and sunset transform them to clouds of the most delicate hues; the moonlight lends them a mysterious beauty. The Indian says it is the incense of the world rising to the Great Spirit. The grandeur of the scene is heightened by the wild roar of the Falls, loud as ocean, but with no moment's lull. It is the voice of the waters sounding for ever one unvarying note in the psalm of creation, and the effect on the mortal spirit may well be too exalting. The moment of the vast plunge of the waters, though the supreme instant in the course of the river, is not its only burst of rapture. For a mile above the Falls the river leaps, foaming, thunderous, tossed to billows, lashed to whirlpools, down a long series of falls and rapids. For two or three miles below, the fierce current, hedged to one-half the width which it has wrought for itself at the present Falls, leaps madly forward in long rolling waves that scarcely touch the shore, but dash against each other in the centre of the current. Niagara fills the senses to intoxication with scenes of awe and magnificence. The art of nature here exhausts itself.

Night after night during my stay I visited the scene by moonlight. One night I wandered alone, down a precipitous footway on the Canadian side, to the spot where formerly Table Rock stood. Its shattered masses lay below me, scarcely visible through the circling clouds of foam. Above me bent forwards the overhanging mass of the hollowed rock, threatening an overwhelming ruin. In front the great flood of waters rolled headlong down, losing itself in a chaos of surge and foam. The ledge on which I stood continued forwards beneath the descending flood. Wet through with spray, with hands against the rock, and with carefully placed feet, I passed slowly behind the falling waters. The moonlight streamed in through a break in the flood, and I paused to look up. It was a spectacle never to be forgotten. From a cavern of black waters, turned here and there into cataracts of brilliants, I looked out into a strange world as fair but as intangible as seen in dreams. The blue heaven, the round moon and stars, were faint in mist. The outline of the Falls, brightened where the moonbeams fell, and the dark masses of the woods on the opposite shore, rose like a thin vision through the ascending wreaths of spray. Before me the way still led on beneath the body of the Falls; I followed. A frightful chasm yawned at my feet, up which clouds of spray came drifting against my face. Below I dimly traced the peaks of jagged rocks. Before me the black wall of the cliff struck out into the falling flood, barring further progress. My eyes threatened to grow dizzy; I closed them for an instant. The earth seemed to tremble where I stood. And, hardest of all to endure, the air was rent with the most hideous and appalling noises. It seemed as though myriads of fiends, or formless creatures of the waters, yelled curses at me from the bewildering floods, or shrieked warnings to the intruder. I returned with hurried steps.

Neither descriptions nor calculations can do more than suggest the vast volume and fury of the waters of these Falls. Professor Lyell has estimated that 1,500,000,000 cubic feet pass every minute; Dr. Dwight, of Yale College, that above 100,000,000 tons pass every hour. These figures, if they impress the mind, do as well as any other. The height of the American Falls is said to be 164 feet; of the Horse-shoe Falls, 158 feet; the depth of the water as it makes the plunge 20 feet. Good Father Hennepin, the first white man, as far as we know, who saw the Falls, may give us a better idea of them by a certain misstatement of his for which he has, no doubt with perfect complacency, suffered the ridicule of formal observers for two centuries. He thought the Falls were 600 feet high. And they still seem so, whatever they may count.

It is one of the delightful peculiarities of the Niagara Falls that you may walk with perfect safety along the brink of the waters, either on the mainland or on the islands that rise from the flood just before it leaps the abyss. You can stoop and cool your hand in the clear water at the very instant it falls from sight. You may stand on the smooth limestone over which the waters roll when a west wind blows, and look straight down into the falling flood at your side. You may touch with your cane the rock over which the flood is passing, then, letting go, see it instantly disappear. It will come up to the surface of the river at the whirlpool probably, three miles down the river.

The beautiful stream permits itself to be toyed with. Its smiling accessibility is most alluring, but is most dangerous. Every rock and ledge has its story of the fatal attraction of the waters.

One of the finest points of view is from the little Luna islet, joined by a flying bridge to the island that divides the river. The lunar rainbow is seen to a great advantage here; and when the sun shines you get a most brilliant arc painted on the rolling clouds of spray. Just here a little girl perished, and a young man in trying to save her. The rocks below have many tragic memories. Half-a-dozen spots on the Canadian side, visible from where you stand here, have been the scenes of sudden death. You see yourself that you have but to take one step. A horrible impression seizes you that more tragedies occur at the Falls than are ever known. The river hides many a mystery in its cavernous depths.

A strange story came to my recollection the first time I stood on the spot.

An excursion party were visiting the Falls; among them an engaged couple, the man singularly handsome, the girl a born coquette. She flirted; he remonstrated. At sunset he was found seated in one of the delicious rocky dells looking on to the

Falls at Luna Island. His friends intreated him in vain to return with them. His bride-elect sobbed on his shoulder, and prayed him to come away. My informant, a girl-playmate of his from childhood, pleaded with him. No; he chose to stop there, he said. The waters fascinated him; he could not go yet; he would follow presently. An old friend hid in some trees to watch him unperceived. His shattered body was found the next day caught in some rocks at the base of the fall.

'And the woman? Did she recover from her grief and self-reproach?' I asked. 'Or has her life been spoilt?'

'She was married within three months,' said my informant slowly.

One of the best views of the flood is obtained at the extremity of Iris or Goat Island, the wooded mass of rock that divides the Falls. A plank bridge crosses from rock to rock over the foaming cataract to a stone tower built at the verge of the great Horse-shoe Falls. You get here a terrible impression of the fury and might of the waters. You do not doubt that Father Hennepin spoke the truth in declaring that 200 years ago there was a third cascade falling from the Canada side. You see that the Falls are changing their form now; the horse-shoe shape is being broken in the centre by the stress of the flood. The Falls eat away the solid wall of the rock at the rate of a foot a year. You pause and speculate. The line of the Falls perhaps passed opposite where you stand when the New World was discovered. It is possible that the great floods were united in one single fall at the time of the birth of Christianity. What vast changes has the stream of time wrought while this river has been carving out its divided course! The eye glances on further. Where the fallen river bends round yonder point, and passes from sight, may possibly be the spot at which the Falls stood at the furthest date to which man can trace back his history. Before then—what? Did fauns and sylphs haunt these scenes? Or did the great river work on its slow way in utter solitariness through these earlier millenniums? It is not difficult to believe that the river is glad that young nations are now gathered on its shores to see its splendour. For, with a magnificent vanity, it has spread its charms to the best effect, and offers a grander spectacle than during its earlier course.

You turn and look up the course of the river. Many and many a long age must pass before the waters shall have cut their way inch by inch to the back of the island, and the Falls again be united. What will happen to the world through that vast reach of time? Will not this new continent, great as several Europes, produce a cluster of nations whose fame and power shall vie with that of the peoples of the Old World? Will the English language of to-day be understood by the nations of those times, or be dead, like the tongues of the great peoples of old? Will the Anglo-Saxon retain its supremacy, and renew here the splendour of its achievements, or become modified and changed by the infusion of new elements? There was a time when the tread of a hoof or the fall of a stone might have deflected the course of the river; who shall lift it from its bed now? The destinies of the people of this continent will be determined for ever by the influences at work to-day.

CHAPTER VIII.

OIL SPRINGS AND SALT.

ONE of the strangest-looking towns in the world is Petrolea, Ontario.

A branch line from the Grand Trunk reaches the place from Wyoming Station. The train that takes you has probably one passenger car and a long line of empty oil tanks of thirty-five barrels capacity each.

Approaching Petrolea, the train crawls among a heap of vast vats and tanks, and pauses at the first sight of the clustered group of oil-works. This spot is Pithole, the newest of the petrolea districts. I got out from the car here, in company with the editor of the 'Petrolea News.' For a mile on the rough the wooden scaffoldings of the oil-works are scattered irregularly through the open forest; the older division, above Pithole, is Petrolea.

Wherever oil has been 'struck,' hasty structures of wood have been at once put up for working the well. No clearing is made; no road. The great forest trees wave their green branches against the 'derricks,' the wooden open-work constructions for sinking the wells. You tread on the brushwood and fern to pass to the furnace or other works. You may count over thirty of these lean, wooden pyramids rising amid the forest as you stand at Pithole. Columns of smoke curl upwards still further in the distance. All around you the grace and freshness of nature are befouled past all imagination.

At spots convenient for the pumps, the soil, consisting of a heavy blue clay, is dug out to make great tanks, sometimes large enough to hold two or three thousand barrels. The underground position is some security against fire. Besides the mounds thus formed, the scene is diversified with vast iron tanks, holding from five to ten thousand barrels each, erected before the simpler plan of the clay tank was thought of. Instead of streams of water, the ground is intersected with rivulets of a black, filthy, pestiferous fluid that runs as refuse from the works.

The wells are about four hundred and ninety feet deep, of artesian tubing, cased for about seventy-five or a hundred feet down to the rock. The crude oil is pumped directly into a reservoir, for safe keeping. Thence it is conducted by pipes to a still, to steam off the water which comes up with it. It is then run into the underground tanks, and is ready to be pumped on to the cars for transport.

An ingenious process has been adopted for heating the furnaces. The clotted oily refuse from the tank above drips slowly down within the mouth of the furnace, is there met and scattered by a jet of steam, and converted into a blaze of gas.

Along the scattered line of oil-works a number of wooden huts have been built for the men employed. At one spot the irregularly placed oil-works and wooden hovels are grouped closely together. The intervals are filled up with provision and clothing stores, drinking and billiard saloons, printing and banking offices, and one or two churches. This is Petrolea. All around stretch wide wastes of uncultivated ground and the uncut forest. The place is too wild and singular to be called ugly, and it gives a vivid idea of the eagerness of commercial enterprise in a new country.

The atmosphere reeks with the rank odour of the mineral oil. But, through an accommodating whim of nature, the older residents come to like this—at least they say so, and should know best. A lawyer of the town, for example, assured me that he had lost his health and spirits while away from the oil for a couple of years. No sooner, however, did he return to the richly-lubricated air of Petrolea, than a process of 'recuperation,' as he termed it, rapidly set in, and he became healthy and happy once more.

The discovery of oil here was made, it is said, from observing that Indians were accustomed to resort to a certain spring, at the advice of their medicine men, and to dip their blankets in the oozy waters, for the cure of scrofulous diseases.

The present production of the district is estimated at 5,000 barrels per week. The crude oil was sold at $1.60 a barrel at the time of my visit, September 1870. The principal export market was Germany.

The distilling of the mineral oil is mainly done in the suburbs of London the Little. The crude oil is heated to steam, condensed, and turned into agitating tanks, where it is moved violently by air; it is then treated with sulphuric acid, washed with caustic soda, and deodorised in the same agitators with letharge and sulphur; it is finally bleached in tanks holding about five hundred barrels. In the last stage I observed that iridescent hues of the most delicate tints played on the surface of the oil, and was told that this was the recognised indication of the purity of the fluid. The oil had now become colourless and odourless—but not tasteless.

The manufactory I visited turned out 120,000 gallons of refined oil a week, using up 200,000 gallons of the crude oil.

A great deal of intelligent ingenuity has been expended in extracting the most value from this oil of the earth. After the refined oils have been made, benzine and benzole are obtained from the stills; paraffine is made; a lubricating oil for machinery is extracted from the refuse; the thick tar from the oil is employed in Nicolson pavement; and the hard coke remaining finally at the bottom of the stills serves as an admirable fuel.

The sulphuric acid used in the oil processes is

obtainable at works close by. At one manufactory crude brimstone imported from Italy is used; at another copper pyrites from Lennox Villa, near Quebec. This ore, stacked in heaps, burns of itself. The sulphuric acid is obtained by a newly-patented 'continuous process' with glass retorts, which appears to answer excellently well. The refuse ore contains five per cent. of copper.

The Ontarian London seems to cherish an ambition of becoming a city of manufactories. Works for starch making and other factories are in active operation there, besides those already mentioned.

When petroleum fortunes were first being made in the United States and in Canada an oil fever set in over the continent. A promising shale was found on the shores of Lake Huron. A company with $4,000 capital was started forthwith to find coal oil. The town of Goderich, Ontario, near which the discovery was made, offered $500, and the county $1,000, to induce the company to descend 1,000 feet. At length water was reached, but brine came up instead of oil. The company were disappointed and resentful. But the brine came up thick and pure, yielding a fine white salt. Fortune had favoured the venture beyond all hopes.

Goderich has already become the seat of a considerable industry. At the date of my visit a thousand barrels of salt a day were being produced; while the demand is increasing, I was told, far beyond the rate of supply. A number of companies are already at work, and others are forming.

The process is simple. The brine is pumped into wooden vats, and runs from them into long iron pans, about 100 feet by 10, with a depth of 3 inches. The pans are heated from below by steam; the water evaporates; the pure salt remains. When cool it is shovelled aside to fall into the packing rooms. There it is put up into 280-lb. barrels. One well will supply 100 barrels a day. The salt deposit is believed to be very far spread, stretching at least sixty miles from Kincardine, above Goderich, to Seaforth South.

There appears to be no reason why the number of salt works here should not be multiplied ten times, to the advantage of the capitalist and of the country.

CHAPTER IX.

LITTLE AFRICA.

In the south-west corner of the province of Ontario there still exist, in considerable proportions, the remains of a negro settlement which once promised to attain to some importance. The coloured colony dates back to the time when the Fugitive Slave Law was enacted in the States, and the negro who had escaped from a southern master found himself without legal protection in the North. One means of safety alone remained for him; to flee again, still further north, to British soil. The first spot he came to was this angle of the Canadian province, 'The Beautiful,' dipping down into the clear waters of Lake Erie. The fugitive here found a home, the most southerly portion of Canada; its climate was more tolerable to the sun-darkened negro than other portions of the Dominion. The new settlers were soon to be counted by hundreds and by thousands. In a large proportion they consisted of the best elements of the negro race; of families that brought away the proceeds of their industry, to prevent the forfeiture of their property with their persons. They overspread the district—a wide range of marshy land, then little settled—and commenced, with as much energy as their indolent nature permitted, the difficult task of improving and cultivating the soil. The settlement continued to increase in numbers until the outbreak of the late war in the States. The Fugitive Slave Law was repealed in the North; many of the negroes made their escape immediately from the severe Canadian winter. On the conclusion of the war others went South, to the black man's fitting zone of temperature, to live as free men in the scenes which had witnessed their degradation and misery.

At the date of my visit, September 1870, the numbers of the coloured population were regarded as stationary. The natural increase by births made up for the losses by removal. The black race was estimated at one-third the numbers of the white in Chatham, the principal place in the district, and in Brixton and Dresden, towns of very small proportions. The negroes were not unkindly spoken of; they were generally regarded as good citizens, quiet and orderly, easily managed, and moderately industrious. In the towns their occupations seemed to be mainly the keeping of barbers' shops and apple stores, shoe mending, and washing and ironing. Of course we must add domestic service and the ministry of religion. Most of the coloured people here, as in the States, are Methodists, though not a few are

Baptists. Prayer meetings, and other gatherings where the social and religious instincts may be gratified at once, are highly popular with them. Their piety is sincere, but sometimes lacks reverence. 'I hear de Lord a-comin' t'rough de shingles!' a cracked-visaged, bright-eyed, little, lean old man cried out in a prayer meeting at Chatham (the 'shingles' form the wooden roofing); 'Come 'long, Lord! Here's a darkie—dat's me—'ll pay for all dem shingles what gets broke up dar!'

The nigger quarter of Chatham is popularly known as Little Africa. The houses, generally of wood, are very small and poor-looking; but the manifest inferiority of the black man in position and in capacity does not distress him greatly. The negro is singularly light-hearted, and forgets, in a burst of easily-provoked laughter, any transient impression of his low place in the world.

Little Africa swarms with half-naked, grinning imps. I visited one of their schools; the children seemed merry enough, and certainly not too much in awe of their two worthy teachers. The partiality of the negro race for brilliant colours was manifested singularly in the dress of one of the few well-to-do children; she shone in more colours than appear in the rainbow. From irregularity in attendance, and other causes, most of the scholars were very backward in their learning; but—as if for the sake of an odd contrast—a dozen boys and girls were being taught trigonometry. Two or three great giggling girls, with unmended frocks, were deep in the second book of Euclid.

While I stood talking in a cottage in Little Africa with the good-natured landlady—a marvellously fat washerwoman, with a ridiculously small head—there came in a neighbour, a wrinkle-faced old lady, and we had a discussion on education. The fat washerwoman wished that the coloured and white children should be taught together, and talked profusely, but disconnectedly, in advocacy of the plan. Her friend, jet black except where grey, made strenuous opposition.

'Why,' said she, 'can't you jest rec'lect as it used to be so once? and what did we do then? Why, we coloured people sent a petition to the Queen of England to get separate schools. And the Queen replied that she didn't know no difference of colour 'mong her subjects, which is to say that she thought all jest alike. However, we did get our schools separate someways, and now you want it back agin!'

The fat lady argued that if the two races went to school together they would learn to like each other, and would intermarry.

But this was a reason for fresh objections on the part of the old lady.

The washerwoman averred that the division was unchristian.

'By gar, I'd have the black and white separate, even in heaven,' returned the old lady, with strong emphasis. 'It ain't good for neither of 'em to get mixed.'

Without any doubt there are to be found men of superior intelligence among the coloured race. A gunsmith of this place with whom I had a long conversation, a man of pure negro blood, seemed to have good natural parts, and to be particularly well informed. He quoted Livingstone and Darwin appositely in illustration of his conclusions. His table was heavily piled with newspapers and reviews. As a gunsmith he is said to have no equal in America. He showed me a pair of silver-mounted Derringer pistols for which he had received a prize from California, and a double-barrelled shot-gun, of exquisite finish, which contained properly, he said, the work of sixteen kinds of hands, but which he had made entirely himself.

The negro farms throughout the settlement are but poor. The holdings are commonly small, from thirty to fifty acres. The insignificant farm-dwellings, with ragged patches of out-buildings, appeared even more mean and comfortless than the town lanes. Specimens of their crops in the Chatham Agricultural Fair showed to little advantage.

The true destiny of the negro race is certainly not farming in a northern soil.

However, the settlement must not be regarded as a failure. A great number of the most influential members have gone South, but still the community holds on its way and thrives. It affords one among a thousand proofs that the negro race can be trained to order and industry, and to the pursuit of the civilising arts of life. Under more favourable conditions, in a climate more congenial, and with a longer space of time for his development, the negro will probably attain a position both of usefulness and respect.

CHAPTER X.

THE INDIANS.

THE statement may be made with some confidence that the Indian tribes of British North America are not fated to immediate extinction. Whether they will ultimately survive a close contact with the ever-growing white people, it were more hard to say. Observers scarcely disposed to an over-sanguine view of the case have sometimes been disposed to judge of this question very favourably. For instance, in a Report to the United States Congress for the current year, 1870, it is said: 'It is now an established fact that the Indians of Canada have passed through the most critical era of transition from barbarism to civilisation; and the assimilation of their habits to those of the white race is so far from threatening their gradual extinction that it is producing results directly opposite.' And it is absolutely a fact, if the provincial statistics are to be depended upon, that the Indians of the old Canadas have been increasing slightly in numbers during the past twenty-five years. The causes are not difficult to discover. They have been saved from the constant internecine wars which thinned their numbers perpetually in the days of their pure barbarism; and in Canada they have had to suffer no wars with the whites since the settlement of our provinces. On the contrary, we have followed towards them an undeviating policy of conciliation and protection, which appears to have won the admiration of some of our friends in America. 'The Government has assumed a friendly and painstaking guardianship over them,' says the report above quoted. We have carefully respected our treaty engagements with them, and have paid them for the lands we have required of them, or have granted them new reservations. We have supplied them with missionaries and schools, and the elements of instruction in agriculture and in various trades. Of more consequence still in estimating the causes staying their extinction, we have provided for them medical aid, and have taken especial pains to save them from the ravages of small-pox, a disease which formerly would destroy whole tribes.

The various Christianising and civilising agencies have not been without effect. Large reservations of land for farming purposes and for fishing and hunting are faithfully left to the use of various Indian tribes in Ontario, Quebec, and maritime provinces; and in each will be found small attempts at farming and the commencement of the arts of life. Some of the Indians have become carpenters, coopers, tailors, masons, blacksmiths, and have exhibited creditable skill. The Indian of pure blood, however, makes a far better fisher, trapper, or voyageur, canoe-builder, or guide.

The Indians of the Canadian provinces are slowly becoming civilised, and, probably, are not decreasing in numbers; but they are losing their savage blood. In all the older settlements they are parting with their distinctive character and peculiarities. The native costume is a thing of the past; they wear a motley dress half English, or else the complete European costume. They learn the English or the French language, and in many instances forget their own. The Indian blood becomes largely mixed with white. It appears likely, therefore, that they will escape extermination simply by ceasing to be Indians.

By common consent the most favourable example of Indian civilisation is to be found at the pretty village of La Jeune Lorette, eight miles from Quebec. A small branch of the Hurons retreated here for safety after disastrous wars with other Indian tribes near the great lake from which they take their name. Here are prosperous farms, well-built cottages, handsome houses owned by the richer men, schools, and a Catholic church. But in colour and in type of feature the people have become significantly like the whites among whom they live. The Huron language has fallen into disuse; young and old alike speak French. Of these Lorette

Hurons, Professor Wilson, of Toronto University, writes:—

'They seem likely to survive until, as a settlement of French-speaking Canadians on the banks of the St. Charles, they will have to prove their Indian descent by the baptismal register or the genealogical record of the tribe, after all external traces have disappeared.'

A less advanced Indian community is that of the Iroquois at Caughnawauga, near Montreal. They farm indifferently ill; a few of them work at trades; all of them hunt and fish with skill. I remember that during my stay in Ottawa, a gentleman, commissioned by the Government to make an exploration of the north of Lake Superior, determined to engage some Caughnawauga Indians as boatmen and voyageurs on the expedition. The uses of even the pure Indian will not be readily exhausted. Civilisation finds some unexpected occupations for him. The Indian makes a superb runner, leaper, jockey, and expert at 'La Crosse.' At Montreal I witnessed a series of exciting contests in the favourite Canadian game between a picked company of the city players and a dozen of the Caughnawauga Indians. The game is a pretty and exciting one, though inferior in science and order to our cricket. At either end of a large field double stakes are set up, the 'homes' of the respective parties of players. The ball is started midway, and is propelled solely by a kind of open-work cane bat, with which the ball can be caught and flung with great dexterity. In the games which I witnessed the whites, though players of reputation, stood apparently no chance. The noted Keraronwe, or some other Indian, would run straight away, with the ball on the 'La Crosse' bat, at will. If intercepted, he would leap aside, and fling the ball with a dexterous jerk to some other Indian in the field. Put through the white wickets, the game was won by the red man. In this contest at least Fortune appeared on the side of the fleet, agile son of the woods.

One of the most encouraging Indian agricultural communities is said to be that of a tribe of the Six Nations, on a reservation near Brantford, Ontario. If we remember the wandering, houseless, indolent, normal condition of the Indian, and his especial dislike of plodding, monotonous occupations, like those of the farmer, the results attained in this settlement may seem surprising. But again, when the Indian's farming is compared with that of the poorest white's, a conviction is forced on the mind of the hopelessness of this attempt at training him. He must have white blood, and cease in part to be Indian, before he can submit to follow the white man's patient culture of the soil.

There are many necessary occupations which would be far more congenial to him. The Indian is peculiarly adapted for the care of horses, cattle, and sheep. He has a natural love of animals, and inherits a large amount of sympathy with them and understanding of them. The Indian is volatile and versatile. That occupation suits him the best in which he finds a constant change of interest, the varied employment of his highly-trained bodily senses, and the opportunity for long spells of laziness. The care of wandering herds and flocks appears to be the ideal occupation of a civilised but pure Indian; and no inconsiderable number could thus be provided for. As Canada becomes more populous, as increasing attention is paid to stock-breeding, and as new districts are opened for settlement, it will probably be found advantageous to employ the Indian generally for this business. The breeding of goats in the mountain plains in some parts of the Dominion will probably become a profitable industry, and would increase the demand for herdsmen.

The various religious missions, Catholic and Protestant, have without doubt exercised a large influence on the native tribes. The older church, with its many condescensions to an ignorant race, its imposing ceremonialism, resembling but surpassing the Indian rites, and with its many pretensions to miracle, excelling those of the mystic or medicine man, appears to have great advantages in gaining over the superstitious Indian tribes. On the other hand, the reformed churches have directed special attention to the education of the children and the training of the Indians to trades. Both churches are generally regarded with respect and gratitude. It is a little hard, however, upon the uncultivated

Indian, to be besieged, as he sometimes is, by champions of the old and reformed faiths, and compelled to decide, on pain of his everlasting perdition, between the claims of churches supported by the learned arguments accumulated in long centuries. It is said that, in his excusable indecision, the Indian sometimes finds a welcome suggestion of the right choice in the practical form of the gift of a particoloured blanket.

Outside the small town of Sarnia, on Lake Huron, I found an interesting settlement of the Ojibways, among whom the English missionaries have laboured with, apparently, considerable success.

There are about five hundred Indians on this reservation. They have been instructed in various trades, and some of them make fair masons, carpenters, and tailors. Great pains have been taken to attach them to the cultivation of the soil, with results which the missionaries regard as encouraging. Some of them farm indifferently well as much as thirty or forty acres. Their log-houses are small, squalid, unfurnished, comfortless; but are nevertheless considered by the whites a great improvement upon the ever moving wigwam. The Indians and squaws are usually dressed in unpicturesque garments which have been discarded by the whites. Their inborn delight in colours, however, still manifests itself occasionally with fantastic effect. A bright handkerchief is twisted in the black hair, a gay scarf disposed gracefully over the head, a quantity of trinkets are attached to ears, neck, and wrists, and gleam against the dark skin. The men are tall, muscular, and well-proportioned. Many of the full-blooded Ojibways, both men and women, have intelligent and handsome countenances. It is apparent enough, however, that here, as in the other semi-civilised reservations, there has been a considerable mixture of white blood. Many of these Indians speak English.

There are two chapels, each with its school-house, on this reserve; the one Methodist, the other Episcopal. At first a sharp rivalry existed between the two missions, but now they work quietly, taking no heed one of the other.

I attended a Sunday afternoon service at the Episcopal Church. The building was small, but neat, and prettily decorated. The light from the altar window was softened by a chequer-work pattern, apparently of coloured paper. The crimson altar-cloth was inscribed in the Indian tongue, Jehovah Shahwanemeschenaum. The congregation, numbering five-and-twenty souls, was very silent and attentive. Some of the old men had really grand-looking faces, set off with long white hair; several of the half-blooded young squaws, tastefully attired in holiday dress, had pretensions to great beauty.

The form of service was extremely simple. Some prayers, and passages of Scripture were read; hymns were sung; and two short addresses were delivered, by English and Ojibway clergymen. Here is one of the hymns ('Come, let us join our cheerful songs,' &c.):

> Nuh qua uh muh wah dah nig suh
> Ish pe ning a yah jig;
> Kuh ke nuh moo je ge ze wug,
> Koo tah me gwe noo wug.

The principal address, or sermon, was spoken in English by the founder of the mission, the son of a well-known London clergyman. It was touching to witness the earnestness of the young minister in an effort apparently so hopeless. He entreated his hearers to be content with no merely formal faith, but to assure themselves of the possession of vital Christianity. One of the arguments he urged upon these semi-savages had a strange sound. The end of the age was apparently approaching. The greatest event since the Incarnation had just happened. The Man of Sin, the son of perdition, had been exalted above all that is called God, and had taken his seat in the temple of God, showing himself that he is God. Those of his hearers who had studied prophecy would perceive that all the Scriptures were being fulfilled, and that only a last opportunity remained for repentance and salvation.

The assistant minister, a pure Ojibway, one of the few Indians consecrated to the Anglican priesthood, spoke afterwards in a rich, soft, musical tongue, not without a deep touch of melancholy in the tones. In conversation afterwards he appeared to be a man of intelligence and earnest piety.

A fair and not untruthful statement of the present condition of the semi-civilised Indian tribes is submitted in an Ottawa Blue Book Report for 1868. Mr. W. Spragge, who prepared the report, says: 'There is reason to believe that there is general evidence of progress among the Indians of the province of Ontario and Quebec, and improvement in their habits of life. A portion of this is undoubtedly due to the personal influence of the clergy who minister among them, exercised as it is for the repression of intemperance and vice, and for the promotion of industry and good order. An evidence of this will be found in the population returns, showing that in twenty-two settlements there is an increase in numbers, and in two only of those from which returns have been received is there a decrease. The sanitary condition of the settlements is beyond doubt much better than it was some years since. One cause of this is that the contagious diseases, such as small-pox, which at times swept off whole families, have of late been guarded against; and, at periods sufficiently near to each other, it is our practice to require professional men to make so general a vaccination as to leave little room for apprehension of a repetition of such visitations. Another cause is the improved mode of living in comfortable habitations, better diet, and better clothing, all of which assist in diminishing the number of cases of pulmonary diseases to which the Indians when in a semi-civilised state become liable.'

The total Indian population of Ontario and Quebec, Lakes Huron and Superior, Nova Scotia and New Brunswick, was estimated to be 20,612 in 1868.

The numbers have probably increased slightly since then.

It is on various accounts desirable that the well-meant efforts for their civilisation should be continued. Their chance of surviving the process, as pure Indians, is slight; but their final extinction, if they do not undergo the change, is certain. The effects produced on the Indian by our modern civilisation and Christianity cannot fail to be an interesting study, and, if carefully observed and reported, may lead to some useful results in social science. These missions, too, have a beneficial reflex action on the whites, in preserving our traditions of a generous care for the weak and ignorant; and eventually the half-bred Indian race that will survive may prove of great service in the community in a variety of out-door occupations requiring manual dexterity.

Still one may perhaps be forgiven a regret that the picturesqueness of the Indian life will be gone. The ancient 'Kanata,' the cluster of wigwams, of boughs or skins, rich in stains of sun and storm, with light smoke curling upwards in the woods, modern Canada will soon know no more. The Indian brave, fierce with tattoo and war paint, dressed in skins of the chase, ornamented with fringes of scalp-locks, and with the feathers of birds of prey, whose arrangement and stripes of colour tell the whole story of his achievements, will bury both weapons of war and the pipe of peace, and stalk off the scene of living history, followed by his obedient squaw with her painted papoose strapped on the shoulders.

But this event is still distant. We have as yet considered only the semi-civilised Indians of the older Canadas. There remain numerous tribes in the Far West in a condition of almost primitive simplicity and unmitigated barbarism. It will be long before the white man will require their vast hunting-grounds. The opportunity still exists for studying the natural mode of life of the red man, his singular and poetic superstitions, and the social and political institutions which he inherits by long tradition, and considers a true civilisation.

Their numbers can be estimated with but a faint chance of approximate correctness. There are, perhaps, 120,000 on this side the Rocky Mountains; and possibly 30,000 more on the Western Slopes reaching to the Pacific. One-tenth of them possibly are semi-christianised; the rest are pagans.

They pursue, with their old ardour, fishing and the chase, and engage frequently in those internecine wars which are apparently the chief means of giving interest to existence, and which afford the men their principal opportunity for acquiring distinction and influence. These wars do not appear to be nearly as destructive to the red men as contact with the white race. The diseases introduced with our modern civilisation, and the fire of our 'burning water,' fearfully reduce the numbers of any tribes in whose countries the white men settle in amity. As we have already seen in the Canadas, this process appears to be stayed when the Indians have become accustomed to our methods of life, and when the white blood has been mingled with theirs.

It is greatly to the credit of the Imperial and Canadian Governments that since the conquest of the country no wars have been waged with the Indian tribes. Treaties have been made for the cession of the tracts of country claimed by the various tribes, and these engagements have been scrupulously respected. Large sums of money are still paid annually, in accordance with the terms of these treaties. To a certain extent these moneys are applied by commissioners to the establishment of schools, &c., on the Indian reservations. The rest is spent readily by the people for food, clothing, and trinkets.

This policy of peace and protection towards the Indians has proved a wise one. It has cost far less than the aggressive policy of the United States towards the tribes within their boundaries. England is regarded with respect and affection by these rude savages. 'King George's men,' as our soldiers are called, are spoken of with admiration, and are believed to be invincible. Medals and buttons, strips of ribbon and bits of accoutrements, relics of the wars when the red men had the honour of fighting for 'King George,' are preserved as precious heirlooms, and worn upon great feasts.

A very satisfactory proof of the attachment of the Indians to the British rule was afforded during the current year in circumstances that rendered their good-will of the greatest consequence to us. All the cost we have incurred in making presents to them, and in purchasing their lands, was more than compensated in this one occurrence.

When the English and Canadian forces started across the Continent for the Red River, attempts were made by the half-breed rebels of the settlement to induce the Indians to offer resistance. It was an opportunity for the kind of warfare which the braves especially like, and for which they are admirably suited—a war of ambushes and surprises, in a country of rocks and woods familiar to these sons of the forest, and entirely unknown to the white troops. There was rich booty, of food, arms, and uniforms, to be secured. At some of the portages, where the flat-bottomed boats had to be carried along narrow defiles, a few score of these Indians could have inflicted heavy losses on the troops without exposing themselves to a shot in return. The half-breeds were allied by blood with many of the tribes, and yet failed to obtain their concurrence in the scheme. The Indians had learnt that the advancing troops were 'King George's men,' and refused to molest them. Yet more; the Red Lake Indians, a body of about five hundred, living to the east of

Fort Garry, sent messages to the Red River rebels that they intended to resist the passage through their country of any half-breeds proceeding against the troops.

Red River stories are always open to suspicion; but this one was told me on the best authority on the spot, and is commonly believed in the country.

There is one special reason just now why the traditional policy of a kindly treatment of the Indians should be followed.

In all probability the Canada Pacific Railway will soon be constructed. It will pass through 1,500 miles of Indian country. Some management will be needed to reconcile the Indians to the undertaking, for the railroad and the line of settlements along its route will tend to ruin the great remaining buffalo grounds, and, in doing this, will threaten the continued prosperity of these wild children of nature.

For the sake of our own interests, if not from pity for a race destined apparently to extinction, we should deal with these Indian tribes kindly, and let them pass from the world unstained by the shedding of English blood.

CHAPTER XI.

ACROSS THE PRAIRIES.

ON the last day of September, 1870, I left Ontario to make my way through United States territory to the new Canadian province of Manitoba.

I should have preferred the route taken by the Red River Expeditionary Force, in order to judge for myself of the suitability of the country for a line of settlements on British soil; but the last party, proceeding with the Lieutenant-Governor, Mr. Archibald, had already passed through, and the season had become too advanced for a single traveller with but one or two attendants to make the journey without extreme difficulty.

A day on the cars took me from Detroit to Chicago, across the wooded state of Michigan. We passed no town of importance; but the country appeared to be generally occupied and cultivated. This is but a run of 284 miles, a trifling distance here. Lines of great cars, worn with much use, impressed the imagination by their inscriptions with the true extent of American travel. They were labelled—

Great Central Through Route.

New York	Omaha
Boston	Salt Lake
Detroit	Sacramento
Chicago	San Francisco

I remained in Chicago three days; but there is really little in the city to detain a visitor. It is built on the flat prairie at the south of Lake Michigan. The streets, of course, are at right angles. Several of them are very wide, and in these there are some large stores ornamented profusely in stucco; and there are several fine new comfortable churches. But the majority of the houses are petty wooden frame structures, and all the streets present an unfinished and slovenly appearance. It is easy enough to understand here how three or four story houses can be moved about without extreme damage; they are merely big square boxes, with sashes and doors let in. I met such frame houses constantly blocking up the traffic of the larger streets, with wooden rollers placed and replaced under the flooring timbers, as they were being slowly drawn along by horses, towards the outskirts of the city, to make room for more pretentious structures in the older quarters.

But the inhabitants are with reason very proud of their city. It has been built up in an incredibly short time, and has increased in population and in wealth beyond all precedent. The situation is a commanding one, as an entrepôt for the through traffic of the continent, and for the supply of the Western States; and the inhabitants have displayed an extraordinary energy in availing themselves of the natural advantages of the position, by opening up railway and steamboat communication to determine the lines of commerce to their city. 'Every other merchant in Chicago has failed twice,' Mr. Wendell Phillips said to me in Boston, in illustration of that restless energy of his countrymen which he termed go-a-headitiveness, and the excess of which he deprecated. 'Or, at any rate, every merchant you see on our streets has failed once,' said a Chicago merchant to me smilingly, in mitigation of the former judgment.

No visitor is expected to leave the city without seeing its peculiar sights. These are the corn elevators, that lift the grain from the rail-cars to boats; the bridges that swing on a pivot to allow barges and schooners to go up the creeks; and a roadway that runs under a shallow river. Besides these, you may see a pig-killing establishment, and, five miles away, a vast range of out-buildings for Texan and other cattle.

This is Chicago, the Queen City of the West. But its great title to distinction remains to be told. Its pride and glory are expressed in a single fact—it has attained a population of 300,000 souls within the duration of a single lifetime.

It seems a pity that so ill an odour should attach to the name of this great city. Chicago signifies, in the Indian, ' The Place of Skunks.'

A thousand miles of prairie now lay between me and Fort Garry. But the railway already traversed half this distance, and will be continued over the remaining half, probably before the end of 1872.

The rich lands of Wisconsin and Minnesota still wait for the tens of thousands of immigrants needed for their cultivation. Northwards from the picturesque station on the Mississippi Prairie du Chien, the railway proceeds through a scarcely broken wilderness. The small, irregular, hastily-built, but rapidly-progressing St. Paul's is the present limit of civilisation. At this point the traveller bids an unregretful farewell to the prosaic, ungainly, hideous new clusters of houses which must at present pass for cities on this new continent, waiting blankly the ministry of time to give them picturesqueness and dignity.

At St. Paul's the small party had already arrived with whom I was to make the journey to the Red River settlement; the wife and daughter of the Lieut.-Governor, in charge of an old friend of the family, Mr. Loo Gouge. Sir John A. Macdonald had done me the honour to ask me to render any help that might be in my power on this journey. We were fortunate enough to obtain here the services of Mr. Robert Tait, of Red River, who was just returning from St. Paul's, and who kindly undertook to make all the necessary arrangements for our passage across the prairies.

We could still avail ourselves of a small piece of railway. Rails laid on the open prairie took us on seventy-five miles to St. Cloud, the last station on the lately commenced St. Paul and Pacific Railroad.

There were in all over thirty passengers on the cars, immigrants and others, wishing to proceed north through Minnesota; but the two lumbering stages that stood in readiness for our further progress would not by any ingenuity of packing hold nearly that number. A dozen rough men, with their non-descript masses of baggage, were left behind to wait the extemporising of 'extra' stages, or the return of the 'regulars' in three days.

The weather-beaten, sun-dried driver, with a mass of dark hair, rough as a buffalo mane, flowing beneath his battered sombrero, got his six horses well in hand, and dashed off on a devious coach-track across the prairies at about one o'clock in the day. When we came to a swamp in the interminable flats, half-a-dozen roadways would break off, and our driver would choose the one he hoped would have the fewest 'quags' and holes. We drove on, with varying speed, for twelve hours. Five times we changed horses, and three times our driver. We passed clearings pretty frequently during this first day; but the houses of settlers, often Swedes, were miserably small and poor-looking, and the rich ground was cultivated apparently with but the most barbarous ideas of farming.

At the roadside shanty inns where we stopped to water or change horses, our motley crowd of fellow-passengers usually turned out to stretch their legs and 'liquor-up.' They made a most picturesque group. There were tall, rough, tawny-haired miners from Fraser River and Montana; thin, hollow-jawed Yankee traders, with hair shaven from the cheeks, but hanging long from the chin, aiding that impression of long-headedness which our American cousins delight to produce. Then we had some fine specimens of the French half-breed population of Red River, men of large frame, with swarthy complexion, long coal-black hair, and great black eyes. In our coach we had a big straw-haired Swedish woman, who could not speak one word of English, French, or German, and who was labelled to be taken through about one hundred miles, with her four bundles of fat-faced children, and other baggage. On the other stage, that sometimes followed, sometimes passed ours, were several fur-traders and a government official, proceeding on a visit to the United States forts scattered through the Indian territories.

It is pleasant to be able to say that throughout the journey our fellow-passengers and all the people we met showed the greatest consideration for the comfort of the two lady-passengers; and, with a large amount of rough frankness, behaved with the utmost good humour amongst themselves. A certain amount of very vigorous language we were compelled to hear; but there never was occasion for an instant's fear of rudeness or incivility.

At dusk we stopped at a long rambling frame house for a supper of pork, eggs, bread, excellent potatoes, and strong tea. Our driver from this place had not been over the ground for six years, and heavy clouds perpetually veiled the moon; our roadway amid the deep ruts had to be guessed at. Besides this, the coach was top-heavy, and reeled at each sudden curve in the most ominous manner. Despite the night cold, we had thought it better that our party should occupy outside seats to escape the peril of asphyxia and paralysis in the interior; but as we were now in danger of being swung into space on the lurching of the coach, we doubted the wisdom of our decision.

Still that night's ride was a grand one. It was our first experience of the open prairie. The moon broke through the clouds and lit up endless tracts of country, sombre-hued with the autumn grasses. Here and there a scrap of scrub-oak served to indicate the receding distances, and impress the imagination with the wide extent of the wilderness.

At two o'clock in the morning the stages pulled up at a small cluster of log-houses called Saukcentre. At the 'Hotel' we obtained, with some difficulty, one private room. We men rolled on to a line of rough beds, or on to the floor, in a long garret, as much or as little undressed as we pleased.

At half-past five the next morning we were called for breakfast—of course of pork, eggs, potatoes, and tea. At six rang the drivers' cry of 'All aboard,' and we swung off into interminable space again. But the heavy, tall stages were fortunately exchanged here for light, low, canvas-covered wagons; the baggage following behind. Towards midday we passed through a wide straggling wood of scrub-oak, poplar, and birch, where the ground was so broken, and the ruts so preposterous, that our former conveyance would assuredly have met with disaster.

We stopped for dinner beyond the wood at a dozen or so of log-houses, called Alexandra Villa; and rested at night at the city of Pomme-de-Terre, which consists of a single farm-house with its out-buildings in a palisaded inclosure, dating from the time of the Sioux massacres here seven years ago.

'For a city, I consider this here Pomme-de-Terre very small potatoes indeed,' observed one of our fellow-passengers reflectively, as he broke up a mass of stick-tobacco in his hands for a plug.

We arrived here at the seasonable hour of 8.30 P.M., having again driven our sixty miles in the day.

We started the next morning about six, and in eleven hours reached Fort Abercrombie, the terminus of the stage-route. Our distance this day was probably fifty-five miles.

Beyond all question, the country we passed through is eminently suitable for settlement. The farmers with whom we talked along the route spoke in the highest terms of the productive qualities of the soil. The remark of one rough-visaged, keen-eyed, old Yankee may well stand as the expression of the general testimony.

'This prairie land,' said he, solemnly, 'is jest about the best there is *lying out of doors* in the hull creation.'

At Pomme-de-Terre the last signs of settlement ceased. During our third day we saw no traces of cultivation whatsoever, nor indeed once again, till we arrived, in five days more, at the Red River settlement, with the sole exception of the few farmsteads gathered round the United States Forts Abercrombie and Pembina. The land waits for the settlers whom it is ready to support and enrich to superfluity.

By the third day our travelling companions were reduced to less than half their original numbers, and we could stow ourselves in the wagon with comparative comfort. One of our remaining acquaintances had seen all the course of the Red River troubles; another had been employed as a government scout in the time of the Sioux massacres. Notwithstanding our many discomforts, our three days' staging was enjoyed, I suspect, by all of us. We sang songs or hymns, discussed politics, or told anecdotes all the way through. Nothing could exceed the good humour with which the ladies submitted to the rough break in their ordinary life which this journey involved. We were afraid they would find the new experience too barbarous; but they quickly perceived that the rough manners of the men hid a true courtesy of disposition, and henceforth they felt at ease. In fact, the strangeness of the scene and the people, the singular contrast presented to ordinary life, afforded us all a constant fund of entertainment.

One of the stories told us by a travelling companion, who had himself witnessed the circumstances, may be found interesting as illustrative of the Indian life.

A Sioux warrior had been found guilty of stealing a horse, and was condemned to pay its value in certain instalments. He brought the last sum to one of the Hudson Bay Company's forts, and tendered it to the man, a Métis or half-breed, who had been mainly concerned in bringing him to justice. The transaction was completed, the quittance given, and the Indian withdrew. In a few moments the Sioux reentered the office, advanced on his noiseless moccasins within a pace of the writing-table, and levelled his musket full at the half-breed's head. At the instant of the descent of the trigger the half-breed raised the hand with which he was writing, and touched lightly the muzzle of the gun; the shot passed over his head, but the hair was singed off in a broad mass. The smoke cleared away, and the Indian saw with superstitious amazement that his enemy still lived. The other looked up at him for an instant full in the eyes, and quietly resumed his writing. The Indian rushed away for his life without one word. Our informant saw this through the open door and rushed in with some others, offering to follow the fugitive and bring him to justice. 'No,' said the Métis; 'go back and finish dinner; leave this affair to me.'

In the evening a few whites accompanied the Métis to the Sioux encampment, outside the fort, to see how the matter would end. At a certain distance, within sight, he bade them wait. The Métis advanced straight to the Indian tents.

The ordinary employments of the encampment were going on—cooking, talking, smoking. No preparations had been made for battle. By one of the tents sat crouched the murderous Sioux, with no weapon in his hand, but the Indian tom-tom, to which he was singing his own death hymn. He mournfully complained that the hour had come when he must say good-bye to wife and child, to the sunlight, to his gun and the chase. He sent messages beforehand to his friends in the spirit-land to meet him on his arrival, and to expect him that night. He told them he would bring all the news of their tribe. He swung his body backwards and forwards as he chanted monotonously the strange song; the sweat poured from his brow; he never once looked up.

The Métis stood quietly over him and spurned him with his foot.

The crouching Indian sang on, unheeding the insult, and awaiting his fate.

His musket, discharged within a foot of his enemy's head, had failed to kill. Some spirit had intervened. The Indian felt himself powerless, and acquiesced in his doom.

The Sioux around looked up now and then, but with no pretence of interfering in the affair. It was a private quarrel, with which they had no concern.

Still the Métis waited; still the murderer sang on his death song.

Then the half-breed bent his head and spat down on his crouched foe before the tribe, and turned leisurely away.

It was a crueller revenge, said our friend, than if he had levelled his pistol and shot him dead.

It was not until this third day of our journey that we saw the spectacle of a fire on the prairie. Afterwards we saw fires, near or remote, almost daily up to Fort Garry. But the first fire we encountered will live the longest in our recollection. Even in the midday the heavens were made red with the flames. For hours we approached the scene of the conflagration, wondering, and in part fearing, whether we should have to pass through it.

At length we reached the black and smouldering country; the fires were passing before us, and away to the right, before a slight wind. Another hour, and we came to the fire in its full glory. A vast line of leaping flames, rendered vivid in the dark rolling masses of smoke, extended before and behind us for a distance of many miles. In some spots the flames, beating back against the wind, came right up to the edge of the track along which we drove. The horses showed no fear. It was singular to notice that all along the line the slightly-beaten track made by the passing of the stages proved enough to stay the progress of the flames. The country on one side was charred and black; on the other an endless wilderness of brown and russet grasses gleamed wave-like before the wind. In the fires where the grasses were thick the flames leapt up perhaps twelve feet; but ordinarily the fire ran much nearer the ground. Our drivers were entirely content at the sight. The burnt land would prevent an accumulation of snow along their track during the winter. Snow-drifts, they explained, cannot lodge except where the grass is thick to hold them.

It was five o'clock when we reached the farmhouse outside Fort Abercrombie where we intended to pass the night, and where Mr. Tait's wagons awaited us for our further journey. With the falling darkness the magnificence of the fires increased, until the whole horizon became a spectacle of awful beauty. In the west the sun set in calm splendour, changing the moveless clouds to the fair image of a world with seas of gold and peaks of translucent glory, with dreamy regions of endless repose. But all the east was reddened with rolling masses of lurid smoke, from which broke forth white leaping flames and circling columns red as blood,—a fearful picture of wrath, desolation, and magnificence; but on the one side lay the majestic repose of heaven, on the other the mad fury of a hell. Only on the ocean could we have seen such a sunset; but not even a battle-field could have given so vast a spectacle of rolling clouds and blazing fires.

Early on the morrow we inspected Fort Abercrombie, and received much courtesy from the United States officers. At noon Monday, October 10, 1870, our small party started over the uninhabited plains. We had struck the Red River, here a turbid stream of perhaps one hundred yards in width, and were to follow it north direct to Fort Garry, a distance of some two hundred and fifty miles.

But the Red River itself, especially through this part of its course, crawls through a flat country with most persistent windings, trebling the distance, as if reluctant to leave a congenial land. Our course lay from bend to bend of the river almost due north.

Our procession was one of picturesque simplicity. First, a light spring wagon, with a canvas awning for protection against the hot noonday sun and the keen morning winds. In this sat the ladies, carefully heaped with shawls, buffalo-robes, and rugs, all needed during our starlight journeyings. Next came a baggage wagon, drawn by two long-eared zebra-marked mules, of excellent patience and strength. At the end of our five days' journey of fifty miles a day these creatures still seemed in good condition, though we could afford them little but the prairie grass all the way. They carried, with other luggage, our tent gear and provisions. Then a second wagon, of two horses, piled with many boxes, which we took only as far as Frog Point, about seventy miles from Fort Abercrombie. Paul, a fine, young, strong Indian, a pure Saulteaux, with black eyes and long black hair, a somewhat sallow but intelligent countenance, dressed in the rough wide garments worn by the whites of these parts, proved of great service to us in our campings, and in finding the horses each morning. He always drove the mules. Mr. Tait, Mr. Loo, and myself drove the other wagons, one of us, however, by turns riding a spare horse with a Mexican saddle and a blanket.

At six o'clock the first evening we struck a bend of the Red River, chose a good spot for wood, water, and fodder, and made our encampment. The horses and mules were unloosened and allowed to roam at their own free will; Paul cut tent poles, and, with crooked tops and notched pegs, in half an hour our tent was well fixed. We strewed it inside with thick grass, and placed on this buffalo robes and white blankets. Various carpet bags were taken in from the wagon, and of course wash-basin and towels. Mrs. Archibald was kind enough to say that she found this sleeping chamber extemporised in the desert as comfortable as it was picturesque. Meanwhile a great camp-fire was built, one of the pleasantest of the day's duties. The fire easily takes in the keen air, and the logs burn clear away. My lumbering experience now proved of service, and I explained carefully the proper method of cutting a log. I was less successful in reducing science to practice. Both Mr. Tait and Paul could use the axe better than could the lecturer.

For the sake of neatness, and to prevent a prairie fire spreading from our camp, we burnt the grass for a distance of several feet round the fire. Within the circle we spread on the ground our cloth for supper; our tin plates and tea-mugs glittered in the warm light like silver. A great saucepan was put into the red flames. Seated on a buffalo robe Miss Archibald graciously plucked a prairie hen, the result of a shot from the side of our wagon while the horses stood still. Another bird, trussed by Paul, and fantastically skewered across a mass of cinders, gave to the air a most delicious evening fragrance. Magnificent slices of ham frizzled in our stew pan; great potatoes, masses of flaky flour, steamed off their skins. Seats from the wagon were drawn up, but naturally we fell into recumbent attitudes, after the fashion of a civilisation older than chairs. It was a veritable gipsy pic-nic.

We were content and without care. The freedom and ease and independence of our prairie journey came in delightful contrast with the cramped and ordered staging; and we were proving how practicable the new mode was.

The scene around us, too, was strange. The flickering fire-light touched everything with romance. The sombre trees rose up around us weird, though protectingly. Behind stretched away the endless, silent, melancholy wilderness. No human soul was near, save perhaps some traveller like ourselves. We were scores of miles from even a log-house; hundreds from the last trace of civilisation in a shanty town.

The ladies retired. We men sat still awhile, to fill or finish a pipe. Then we put down buffalo robes on the ground, removed coat and boots, and rolled ourselves in blankets, with our feet to the fire. Good-nights were said, and a fearful stillness followed. I could easily distinguish the breathing of each of my companions. One by one all slept. It was too strange for me to sleep, feeling for the first time the great night close over me, the great earth spread close around me. The hours passed in waking dreams. Great stars glittered cold above. The moon rose high, and filled the dark scene with mysterious beauty, and with a stillness more intense than before. At one o'clock I woke and re-made the fire. At four, in the chill dawn, our camp broke up, and we resumed our desolate way. We endeavoured to arrange the wagon so that Mrs. and Miss Archibald might still find some snatches of sleep, if the roughness of the prairie road would allow it, or at least be sheltered from the bitter night wind. At six the sun rose in splendour, with a vast horizon, on which to make a scenic display. By ten we reached Georgetown, at present a cluster of five wood-huts, but the place which the United States Northern Pacific Railroad is to reach in the course of 1871, on its way from Duluth on Lake Superior to the western coast. There were no signs of preparation for the railway at the time of our visit; but the energy of American enterprise may well be counted on to carry this work through by the time arranged. At six o'clock in the evening we encamped at the junction of the Goose River with the Red River, a distance of about forty-seven miles from our morning starting point.

The next morning we again started at four; prepared our breakfast at Frog Point, a shanty station of the Hudson Bay Company, where we left the luggage of our second wagon, to be sent on by a steamer, the 'International,' on her last trip for the season down the river. At sundown we camped at Grand Forks, by a wild patch of scrub poplar, at the junction of the Red Lake River with our own stream.

At two in the morning, while Loo was feeding the fire, a mounted horseman approached our encampment from out of the darkness. We watched his coming with some uneasiness, unable to conjecture a reason for the appearance of a solitary rider on these desolate plains at such an hour. Stories of Indian atrocities came to our minds, with keener recollections of warnings which we had received of the scattered Red River rebels. Loo had his revolver in readiness; I looked to my gun.

Our precautions were unnecessary. We soon recognised a friend of the morning, an employé of the Hudson Bay Company at Frog Point. His story was characteristic. He had missed the two horses we had left with him, with our second wagon. From the 'bull-punchers' of an ox train crossing the prairies he had learnt that the horses had been seen with a certain party of travellers going north. 'They have chosen a good chance for a bullet,' he said, with significant emphasis. We took note of his detailed description of the party supposed to have 'conveyed' the horses; but saw nothing of them. Our acquaintance sat and smoked by the fire; then smoked and took breakfast with us; and finally rode away puffing dense clouds to his melancholy musings.

The next day, Thursday, we had our longest stretch of travel to do, having to cross two salt streams before we could encamp for the night. We started, therefore, at 3 A.M. At 8.30 we prepared our breakfast, and of course gave the horses a long rest, having already come some twenty-five miles. At 6 P.M., having travelled twenty-seven miles further, we encamped at a bend in the Red River just past the Long Trévasse.

This afternoon I had a small prairie adventure to myself. I threw a blanket over the saddle of our spare horse, and went with my gun to seek game. My intention was to keep our wagons in sight, but in an hour's time they were far in the distance. I imagined that, with a little coaxing, my horse would stand fire; and, at any rate, I was willing to run the risk of the creature's starting in some alarm. I was not, however, prepared for what happened. A second hour elapsed before I found a chance for a second shot. I sprang off, held the horse with a long cord, and raised my gun. But my over-curious horse turned his head to see what I was doing, and instantly started away in frantic alarm. Perforce I followed. The scarlet blanket fell from the saddle. I could not drop the gun, for a sudden whirl of the brute had entangled the cord with it. We went plunging over the prairie, until presently the unreasonable creature struck at me with his heels. At all hazards of the discharge of the piece, I threw it down, and seized the horse's head. I have never seen such a look of fear and agony as shone in that brute's eyes.

It was an odd position for a man unaccustomed to the idea of crawling a score of miles with fractured ribs. We were now far beyond sight or help. If the horse had succeeded in breaking away, I might have followed him in vain for hours.

I talked to the poor beast in an unreasonable manner, suited possibly to his demented condition. By degrees I coaxed him to quietness. I led him back in search of the blanket; its colour aided me. When I mounted the horse, pretending that he had no further cause of alarm, I showed him my hands, empty of the gun, and assured him in plain words that I had no intention of firing again in the solitary company of a horse who showed so vehement a dislike of the sport.

Then I traced my way back to a clump of bushes which I had marked near the spot where the gun fell, and, dismounting, and patting the brute, I succeeded in drawing the weapon, unobserved, by his side. Once again mounted, I struck my heels into the horse's flanks, and had the finest gallop of my life.

Evening was hastening on, but we had a splendid sunset. The travelled track, which I soon struck, was unmistakably distinct. The camp fire was lit and the tent pitched when I got in. The smoke had guided me to the spot by the woodside.

The next morning we started at 3.30. There were several reasons for the urgency with which we made our journey. Mrs. Archibald felt anxious to reach the Red River settlement with the least possible delay. Besides, the brilliant weather with which we were favoured was likely to fail us at any day on the route. More than once a slight storm-shower fell. Sometimes we could see along the horizon half-a-dozen vast vaporous clouds discharging their rain in trailing lines of blackness. A night encampment in storm would have occasioned us real inconvenience. In the advanced season hail and snow were by no means improbable.

We prepared breakfast eighteen miles on, at Big Point. At noon we passed the American outpost Fort Pembina. We took dinner in the Hudson Bay Company's fort, in the small room in which Mr. McDougal had received the peremptory notice of the Red River Provisional Government that he would not be permitted to proceed forward to the seat of his Governorship. Since that time the United States surveyors have discovered that the boundary line of the British possessions lies somewhat further north than had been presumed. In half an hour we passed the new post just set up, and reverently saluted British soil. In the evening we encamped on Little Lake, seventeen miles on, in the new province of Manitoba.

The most magnificent spectacle we had ever beheld in the heavens was displayed for us this evening, as if in celebration of our arrival on our national soil. At a quarter past six a vivid belt of rosy light grew out of the still darkness in the north-east, and spanned the heavens from the horizon to the zenith. All the sky around was cloudless, but filled with a faint mist of vapour, obscuring all but the brightest stars. To the east and to the south new belts of light appeared, flame-coloured, saffron, opal, sapphire, and orange. One-half the celestial vault was ablaze with colour; the other side still black with darkness. Then the splendour of mingled colours poured slowly down on the western slopes of heaven, until the whole earth was enshrined in a gorgeous canopy of light. Broken sheets of flame, varying streams of liquid colours of the most delicate hues, descended from the zenith to the edge of the world, save at one spot due north, where the stars still shone in utter darkness. Our little camp was hushed to stillness. No word was spoken until one of us repeated the words of a sacred scene for which the spectacle alone seemed worthy :—' Then shall appear the sign of the Son of Man in heaven : and then shall all the tribes of the earth mourn : and they shall see the Son of Man coming in the clouds of heaven with power and great glory.'

The next day, Saturday, October 5, completed our journey. We started at 4 A.M., and in eighteen miles reached the first house on British soil, the hut of a kindly French half-breed, five miles from the boundary line. Here we found waiting us, with a large travelling carriage, the private secretary of the Lieut.-Governor. Twelve miles further on we partook of a civilised luncheon, sitting without reluctance on chairs round a table. At four o'clock we were met by the Hon. Mr. Archibald himself.

This part of our way led through a belt of scrub poplar, with an occasional clearing and a settler's log-house.

At dusk we descried the long lines of the now celebrated Fort Garry, built at the confluence of the Assineboine with the Red River, with the straggling town of Winnipeg, a cluster of wooden houses, scattered over the plains close by. Our pleasant journey was done.

There are no difficulties on the route even now that need prevent the immediate entrance of Canadian and English immigrants. From the experience of our party I can confidently assert that the journey may well be made a continuous pleasure excursion. No intending settler need hesitate to bring out his wife and children. The freedom and novelty of camp life for a few weeks in good weather would fully compensate for a few slight inconveniences.

Let no traveller, however, of delicate organisation willingly undertake this journey in a period of winter storms, as I perforce did, in the middle of November, on my return. The travelling would have been more agreeable in the settled, intense cold, a month later, when two feet of snow would have covered the prairies, and the jolting wagon have been exchanged for the gliding sleigh.

The farmer proceeding now to the Red River country should certainly take through his own horses and wagons, his farming implements, and household goods. If he need extra draught after leaving the railroad, let him buy more horses and carts, or oxen and the charettes of the country. Everything he takes to Red River will be worth twenty-five to fifty per cent. in advance on its cost upon arrival; and if he travels with his own teams, the expense of transit will be nothing.

With each year, however, the facilities of communication will increase.

By the close of 1871 an American railroad will probably strike the Red River, meeting a line of steamers running to Fort Garry. One or two years later, the iron rails will be laid all the way.

Long before this, however, a new route will be opened through British territory, saving several hundred miles to the immigrant from Canada. First the stage and steamer, and finally continuous railroad, will render communication easy by this route also.

The interior country will be developed rapidly to a condition of great prosperity; but the romance of travel will be gone.

CHAPTER XII.

THE RED RIVER REVOLT.

EVERYTHING connected with Red River is exceptional. The country is unlike any other in the world; its settlement differed widely from that of any colony ever established; its mingled races of people form a community unrivalled in eccentricities. The variety of divergent interests here—social, commercial, political, and religious—presents one of the most intricate puzzles ever offered for the ingenious treatment of politicians. The settlement has attained a world-wide fame ludicrously disproportioned to its positive achievements. Its wars have been more innocent than school-boy sports; its heroes young men of absurd insignificance, its revolutions the by-play of the oddest chances. It has been the appropriate theatre of the most ridiculous mistakes ever made in the blundering art of politics. Statesmen even of acknowledged ability have, in dealing with Red River, lost all regard for expediency, policy, or common sense. Its recent troubles, the direst tempest in a wash-pot ever known, have attracted the attention and consideration of the American continent and of Europe. Its minute parish squabbles have become questions of imperial magnitude. When the history of Red River shall some day be written gravely, it will be read as an extravagant burlesque.

The settlement has existed for half a century in the centre of a vast continent, remote from all external influence. A circle drawn round it with a radius of a thousand miles would scarcely touch civilisation anywhere in its sweep. Northwards lie great lakes and streams without a solitary sail, vast plains and woods without a settler, the inland ocean of Hudson Bay, and the frozen wilderness that reaches to the Pole. To the south stretch boundless uninhabited prairies to the British frontier, and endless prairies still through United States territories downwards for hundreds of miles. Eastwards reaches a vast country of dense woods, reeking swamps, tortuous streams broken with rapids, irregular lakes, and wilderness of rock, far beyond Lake Superior, in a line that twelve hundred miles would not measure.

To the west stretches the magnificently fertile, but utterly desolate, Valley of the Saskatchewan, with verdant slopes and navigable rivers, up to the base of the Rocky Mountains; and then a vast wilderness of rock, woodland, and prairie, on to the Pacific. The next settlement in this direction counts fifteen hundred miles from Winnipeg.

The only routes of travel through the country are the trails opened by the Honourable Hudson Bay

Company for the conduct of their business in furs. In the summer months the trader and the occasional traveller find their way to the settlement in the Indian bark-canoe, or in light flat-bottomed boats, which may be carried over the portages in order to pass the rapids; or light wagons and ox-carts bring them over the prairie. In the winter the sleigh is used, with horses, or preferably with a long train of dogs. Fort Garry is the principal station of the Hudson Bay Company, and the seat of the former government, and has therefore become the terminus of their wandering lines of travel.

This strangely-isolated colony owes its origin to the ancient feud that subsisted between the Hudson Bay Company and its French rival the North-West Company before their amalgamation. With the view of opposing the influence of the French company, Lord Selkirk brought out in 1813, by way of Hudson Bay and York-Factory, 300 Scotch families, mostly from the Orkneys. All kinds of Macs flourish to this day equally among the white settlers and the half-breeds. The North-West Company refused to submit tamely to this intrusion. War was declared. A conflict took place, known in the history of the Territory as the Battle of Red River, in which no fewer than twenty-two lives were lost, including that of the Hudson Bay Governor. This is the most bloody encounter known through all the wars which have signalised the history of this settlement.

This battle is supposed popularly to have taken place in the year, day, and hour of the Battle of Waterloo, which name has consequently found a place, through the power of association, in the memory of the people. I shall not be ungenerous enough to attempt to disturb so innocent and natural an illusion.

The troops of the Hudson Bay Company subsequently gained some compensating victories in the capture of various rival forts; and finally an amalgamation of the two companies was effected, as a result of which the efforts of the allied belligerents were turned to the trapping of moose and mink, and to trading with the Indian tribes with flour and blankets for the winter furs. Peace reigned in the settlement; prosperity followed.

Lord Selkirk had brought his Scotch settlers to Red River partly on account of the amazing fertility of the soil, and partly because the position was a very central one for conducting the operations of the fur company. In a long line of farms with river frontage the Scotch have mainly settled on the left or west bank of the Red River, northwards from Fort Garry to the Lower or Stone Fort, a distance of fifteen miles. The French and French half-breeds have settled on the right bank and up the Rivière Rouge. The English residents, generally old servants of the Company, and the English half-breeds, have scattered themselves along the Assineboine for a distance of sixty miles to The Portage.

Speaking in general terms, no care has been expended on the cultivation of the soil. In a slovenly manner, with miserable implements, its surface has been scratched over and grain sown, with a total heedlessness of any order of rotation of crops. In some instances wheat has been put into the same ground year after year since the commencement of the settlement; yet such is the richness of the land that the farmer tells you he knows of no falling off in the quantity or quality of the crop.

The peculiarity of the Red River farmer is to pitch all his manure into the river; it is his way of getting rid of a nuisance. To save himself this trouble, however, he adopts sometimes another expedient. He piles his cattle dung round his roughly-built log-barn and stables till the light is shut out and the wood has rotted to tottering; then he makes a sudden escape from the accumulated filth by raising new frame buildings, or possibly by removing to some fresh tract of land. He can present, however, one single excuse for his neglect of valuable manure—the whole soil consists of a rich compost.

The less said about the dwelling-houses of the old settlers the better. There is a complete dearth of large timber throughout the district, and the cost of transport on the rivers has hitherto been very heavy. The extensive woods on the river banks are composed of small trees growing much too densely to allow of the formation of large timber.

In obtaining fuel and wood for fences it has never been the fashion here to thin these woods, so as to let the larger trees grow to a fit size for building purposes; but instead of this successive strips are cleared wholly away—and this in pure despite of the fact that the chief disadvantage of the country is its scarcity of timber. Of course, no one has ever yet been guilty of the prudence of planting trees. When this is done on a large scale, the climate will be ameliorated, greater dampness secured, and the crops of the farmer rendered as secure from early frosts as in the older Canadas.

But though timber for building is scarce, limestone abounds within easy access. Two or three of the many churches of the settlement are built of this, and it is used in the foundations of some of the wooden houses; but no quarry is regularly worked. Excellent brick-clay occurs constantly through the country; but not a single kiln is in operation. A small attempt at brick-making was made some year or two ago, and the bricks sold readily at 3*l.* a thousand. Four stout English brick-labourers here, with 10*l.* a piece in their pocket, might make a competency in a few years, and a large fortune, if they had wit and enterprise.

A fair idea may now be formed of the character of the Red River settlers for business activity and intelligence. I am delighted to allow that a number of examples are to be found of another order of men; but they are exceptional. It is also certain that a number of excellent virtues may be discovered in men who may disdain to devote themselves to the material improvement of the country. The Red River settlers claim to be singularly moral, sober, religious, and patriotic. I for one shall not venture to question the propriety of the claim.

But the mode in which the great qualities of the inhabitants of Red River have displayed themselves has occasionally been somewhat singular. We should not be speaking of Red River if this were not so. Some years ago, a clergyman, found guilty of a very grave offence before the highest court of justice in the land, was sentenced to six months' imprisonment; but the gaol at Fort Garry was broken open by his sympathising friends, and the reverend gentleman set at liberty. One of the leaders in this brilliant exploit was secured, by order of the authorities, and imprisoned, with the view of asserting the injured majesty of the law. But this imprisonment could no more be tolerated in Red River than the other. The friends of the gentleman collected, broke open the prison again, and set the captive free.

From this time the Hudson Bay Company became increasingly anxious to hand over the government of the country into stronger hands. At a later date a professional gentleman, whose name afterwards became a rallying cry for one of the parties in the late disturbance, had the misfortune to be sentenced to imprisonment for debt. Once again the prison was broken, and the gentleman quietly resumed his position in the town of Winnipeg, under Fort Garry, without molestation.

Of the one town of the settlement a word should be said. It is named Winnipeg, though forty miles from the lake of that name, and still more distant from the river; but this strikes no one in the place as incongruous. It is composed of fourscore wooden buildings, the stores, dwelling-houses, and barns all counted; and no one will lightly venture the calumny that any of these show the least pretentiousness of style, or betray any undue regard to outward appearance. The uniformity of an American town is happily avoided. The houses might very well have been shaken carelessly out of a magician's bag, who had done with them for old boxes.

It remains only to state the estimated numbers of the population. The figures are—

2,000 Pure Whites, English-speaking Protestants.
5,000 English Half-breeds, Protestants.
5,000 French Half-breeds, Catholics.

Within the settlement are scattered also a few scores of semi-civilised Indians, whose bits of farms do not compare to such disadvantage with those of the whites as one might beforehand have expected. These families all migrate during the summer for the chase, as do many among the half-breed population. All around the settlement, especially north and west, roam wandering tribes of Saulteaux, Sioux, Swampies, Crees, Chippewyans, and Blackfeet. These are mostly Pagans, and may number throughout the whole North-West 150,000 souls.

The scene is now sufficiently prepared before the reader for an account of the heroic events which have given Red River its fame with the Canadian and English public.

The outside world knows the main course of the history. Under the guidance of English statesmanship, a transfer was arranged, to be completed at the close of 1869, of the North-West Territories of the Hudson Bay Company to the Dominion of Canada. A gentleman, Mr. McDougall, was selected by the Canadian administration to occupy the position of the first Lieutenant-Governor of Manitoba, the name by which a new province, including the old Red River Settlement, was to be known. At the close of 1869 he proceeded by the easiest route— that through the United States—to be in the place of his government at the time when, by the Queen's Proclamation, it should become a portion of the Dominion of Canada. On November 2, 1869, Mr. McDougall's progress was arrested at the British boundary line, by a small force of French half-breeds, and he was ignominiously driven back to United States soil, in obedience to a brief requisition which may be given here as commencing the documentary history of the insurrection :—

A Monsieur W. McDougall.

Monsieur,—Le Comité national des Métis de la Rivière Rouge intime à Monsieur W. McDougall l'ordre de ne pas entrer sur le territoire du nord-ouest sans une permission spéciale de ce Comité.

Par ordre du Président, John Bruce,
Louis Riel, Secrétaire.

Daté à St.-Norbert, Rivière Rouge.
Ce 21° jour d'octobre 1869.

The English-speaking population of Red River appear to have been taken completely by suprise by the energetic action of their French neighbours; but they declined to make any effective efforts for the re-establishment of order. Mr. McDougall waited vainly at Pembina for his friends within the settlement, and notably for one Colonel Dennis, whom he constituted his representative, to prepare by a counter display of arms for his entry within the country. The authority of the Hudson Bay Company, disrespected in the former days of peace, now fell utterly into contempt. Mr. McTavish, the governor of the Hudson Bay Company, issued a proclamation calling on the people to lay down their arms, to which no one gave the slightest heed. Mr. McDougall issued proclamations, though he was not yet constituted the governor, nor held any legal status of authority. Louis Riel issued proclamations on his side, which had the one merit of getting respected. Five or ten score rebels—a disorderly, ill-armed rabble of French half-breeds—walked into

Fort Garry, took possession of the cannon, small arms, and ammunition, and henceforth held the inconstant, divided, ill-armed mob of the English-speaking population at a great disadvantage. At any time before the taking of the Fort a dozen determined men might have overawed the incipient rebellion. At any time after the capture two score of English soldiers could have retaken the Fort by a night assault, and probably without effusion of blood.

But this could only have been done at one risk of great magnitude. It might have led to a conflict of races through the bitter winter—a miserable calamity in an isolated province like this, cut off by distance from all interference and succour. The Indians, appealed to, as it were, on both sides, might have made an effectual clearance of the whole white population. At the very least, a deep sense of injury and of hatred would probably have been established between the rival races here which years or centuries might have failed to remove. As the event has proved, the sensible men of each party are disposed to bury the ridiculous errors of the past in a speedy oblivion.

To appreciate at all the inner history of the Red River revolt it is necessary to observe the exceptional variety and intricacy of the interests that were involved. Never was there such a mixture of elements in such a little pot before! No wonder it came to spasmodic ebullition, and boiled over in wide-spread confusion.

First must be named the difference of race, dividing the little community with natural rivalries. Next the difference of religion, separating the people into two antagonistic parties. Then must be considered the separate interests of the powerful Hudson Bay Trading Company, with its own policy to pursue and its great profits to make—an association surrounded, of course, with enemies, as every monopoly is sure to be. With all this, however, it must be remembered that the isolated condition which the people here all shared tended strongly to unite all interests against the outside world of foreigners. But to assist the complication we must take into account the divergent interest of a number of energetic American residents, and their sympathisers within and without the settlement, who covertly or openly avowed a policy of annexation to the United States. Add still the influence of a restless but imbecile Fenian party, whose aim was to establish an Independent Republic, from which they might make wars upon Canada and Great Britain. The imbroglio is not yet complete. It is no secret that the Government at Ottawa were themselves divided as to the policy to be adopted in Manitoba. The Quebec party were naturally for increasing their own influence, perpetuating the Catholic religion, and strengthening the French interests in the new country. The Ontario party were equally determined to prevent the growth of a second Quebec in the Dominion, and set themselves in unreasoning haste to secure Protestant and English ascendency.

Here are the ingredients of our olla podrida: Rivalries of race and of creed; Orangeism, Ultramontanism, Red-republicanism, Monopolies, Fenianism, Spread-Eagling and Annexation; and, not least active, Ishmaelism, the natural sentiment of the country. Each party had representatives in the disturbances, while some of the prominent actors, however, represented especially themselves. It would require infinite patience and the rarest powers of discrimination to determine which party acted with the most, and which with the least, indiscretion. Now, of course, each one seeks charitably to distribute the burden of blame among his choice enemies. The present government shows admirable sense in devoting its energies to the pacification and development of the country, and in avoiding inquiry into past affairs. The only tribunal fit to deal with these is one of Omniscience. No practical good could be gained by distributing equal doles of censure all round.

The initial and chief blunder in the Red River affairs was, without doubt, committed by the statesmen of Canada and England. The Territories, with their populations, were made over to a new government without consulting the people in the slightest degree. And this omission occurred notwithstanding the obtrusive fact that in recent annexations of territory—of Nice, of Venetia, of Rome, for instance—a vote of the peoples was considered a political necessity. Their destiny may have been pre-ordained and the *plébiscite* a managed formality; but nevertheless it was permitted in deference to an international sense of justice, and as a show, if an empty one, of regard for the wishes of the people. In the present case, if, as it has since been urged in extenuation of the mistake, the Governments were possessed with the conviction that the population of Red River were eager for the projected change, the more reason surely existed for allowing them an exercise of the privilege of professedly disposing of their destiny. But no commissioners were appointed to inquire into the wishes of the people; no votes were taken; no representatives called for to express the popular feeling. It is a singular fact that no official communication of the transfer of the Territory was ever sent to Red River. No official notice was sent even to the resident governor of the Hudson Bay Company; nor was there any formal announcement made to the settlement that a Lieut.-Governor was to assume authority over it, or that Mr. McDougall was on his way to his seat of government. The people learnt the fate prepared for them through the newspapers. The Ishmaelism of the whole community felt itself outraged. 'We are sold as a flock of sheep,' was everywhere said. The first popular expression of displeasure was made by a party which, although it afterwards considered itself expressly loyal, publicly avowed its persuasion that, since the people of Red River had been sold for 300,000*l.*, they ought to adopt measures for securing the division of the purchase-money among themselves.

A second blunder was made by the Canadian Government in a generous eagerness to improve their new possessions. A Mr. Snow was sent in the fall of 1869 to prepare a road between the Lake of the Woods and Fort Garry before the transfer of the Territory had been made. The Hudson Bay Company and the Red River people, at one in indignation at this interference with their prescriptive rights, made urgent remonstrance against the premature action of the Government. A worse mistake followed. A number of surveyors appeared in the settlement, running lines through the claims of the inhabitants and marking off fresh plots. With or without reason, the people imagined that their property would be appropriated at the caprice of a crowd of new-comers. Ishmaelism revolted.

But perhaps the most extraordinary mistake committed throughout these transactions was the issuing of a bogus proclamation by Mr. McDougall. While in retreat at Pembina, before the transfer of the Territory by Her Majesty, without any official notice of his actual status as Lieut.-Governor, and of course without having taken the oaths of office, Mr. McDougall judged it well to issue a Proclamation in the Queen's name announcing himself as the

Lieut.-Governor of the North-West Territory, and requiring 'our Loving Subjects of our Territory, and all others whom these Presents may concern,' to govern themselves accordingly. It is understood that on the night of the first of December, the appointed day of the transfer, Mr. McDougall stole down to the boundary line and signed this manifesto on British territory. But far more than this was needed to make the thing legal. The occurrence of the disturbances had rendered a delay in the transfer imperative, in the opinion at least of the Government which Mr. McDougall served.

Another extraordinary document of these days was this gentleman's Commission issued to Lieut.-Colonel Dennis, authorising him to commence civil war in the disturbed district. After a long recital of particulars, it proceeds in the following manner :—

'Know you that, reposing trust and confidence in your courage, loyalty, fidelity, discretion, and ability, and under and in virtue of the authority in me vested, I have nominated and appointed, and by these presents do nominate and appoint, you, the said John Stoughton Dennis, to be my Lieutenant and a Conservator of the Peace in and for the North-West Territories, and do hereby authorise and empower you as such to raise, organise, arm, equip, and provision a sufficient force within the said Territories, and with the said force to attack, arrest, disarm, or disperse the said armed men so unlawfully assembled and disturbing the public peace; and for that purpose, and with the force aforesaid, to assault, fire upon, pull down, or break into any fort, house, stronghold, or other place in which the same armed men may be found; and I hereby authorise you, as such Lieutenant and Conservator of the Peace, to hire, purchase, impress, and take all necessary clothing, arms, ammunition, and supplies, and all cattle, horses, waggons, sleighs, or other vehicles, which may be required for the use of the force to be raised as aforesaid '—and so on to double this length.

But injustice would be done to the other actors in the comedy if it were supposed that the blunders made were all on the side of the Canadian Government and its representatives. The Hudson Bay Company's officials received notice in advance of the intended attack on Fort Garry by the insurgents, and yet took no precautions for securing the place. This fault has perhaps been expiated by the loss of 50,000*l.* worth (so the figures have been estimated) of provisions and stores appropriated by Mr. Riel and his party during their half-year's occupancy of the Fort. The Canadian or loyal party, through disunited counsels and the want of a leader, failed to do anything but make themselves ridiculous. Their impotent displays of force served to encourage rather than to check the rebels. Some forty of this party, well armed, assembled in the house of Dr. Schultz in Winnipeg, while the main body gathered, and talked, and disputed at the Lower or Stone

Fort, twenty miles off, under Colonel Dennis. Three separate orders were sent from Mr. McDougall's Lieutenant and Conservator of the Peace, requiring this detached force to fall back and join the main body. The orders were ignored. Out came the rebel Conservator of the Peace and the military generals from Fort Garry, with a small field-piece, which they trundled in front of Dr. Schultz's house, and waited there for a couple of days, demanding submission. On the third day the garrison yielded. Quarter was given. The forty men were disarmed and marched into Fort Garry as prisoners. This affair is known as the Siege of Winnipeg. Not one fired shot mars the glory of the victory.

Colonel Dennis issued more proclamations, and suddenly disappeared from the country. Mr. McDougall wrote some more papers, and then returned to Canada. Mr. McTavish, the Governor of the Hudson Bay Company, grew more sick and ill at the indignity of his position as a prisoner in his own house, and at the miserable issue of events which he could no longer control, and eventually obtained permission to leave the country and die.

The rebel party reigned. A lull took place in the tea-pot tempest. The less obnoxious of the prisoners were set at liberty. The most obnoxious of them, Dr. Schultz, effected his escape in a singularly daring and ingenious manner. The self-elected Provisional Government occupied itself over Fort

Garry wine with discussions on the fate to be chosen for their country. The first president, Mr. John Bruce, was early supplanted. I found him in the parish of St. Boniface, near the Fort, usefully engaged in his proper avocation as a journeyman carpenter. He speaks only French, but told me that his grandfather was Scotch. His persistent idea, he assured me, had been the establishment of the province as a Crown Colony. But the fame of Mr. Bruce has failed before that of the triumvirate, Riel, O'Donoghue, and Lépine. Louis Riel was born in the province; had shown some ability at school; and had been sent by Bishop Taché to the Montreal Roman Catholic College for the completion of his education. The young man, however, eventually declined to enter the priesthood, and wandered into the States for a fortune or a living. Shortly before the Red River outbreak he was 'clerking' in a store in some small State town. But he was back in Red River in good time. This young man is 'the Little Napoleon' of Red River fame. It is not known, however, to what circumstance he owes the flattering title.

The Honourable W. B. O'Donoghue, Secretary of the Treasury, was an escaped lay brother from one of the Roman Catholic Red River schools. It is understood that he chiefly represented the Fenian party in the insurrection.

The Honourable Mr. Lépine was only the Adjutant-General. It was believed, however, that he would have been made Commander-in-chief, or at least a Lord Marshal, after the murder of Thomas Scott. Popular expectation was disappointed. Even at Red River courage and generosity would go unrewarded.

The Provisional Committee found time for some pieces of business. To imitate other great States, a Convention of Representatives was called at Winnipeg. It consisted of forty members. For the sake of present quiet the English-speaking districts sent delegates with the rest. By this assembly Riel was recognised as President of the Provisional Government, and a Chief Justice, a Secretary of State, and various other high functionaries were elected. After fifteen days of talk the Convention broke up in February 1870, having produced a long Bill of Rights.

And now occurred one of the greatest events of this history. The columns of the rebel newspaper, the 'New Nation,' containing the thrilling story, are headed in startling type, 'The Revolution! Battle of Winnipeg!'

But, as the excitement of the conflict has now passed away, I shall content myself with a condensed and unimpassioned narrative.

During the sitting of the Convention the Canadian or loyal party had a second time assembled in arms—on this occasion at Kildonan, the Scotch settlement *par excellence*, about six miles north of Fort Garry. Their purpose appeared to be the overawing of the Riel party, the storming of Fort Garry, the overturning of the Provisional Government, and the establishment of a new one of their own. But they could only agree positively on one thing—the peremptory demand of the release of the remainder of the prisoners captured in the Siege of Winnipeg. Awed by the Kildonan demonstration, the Little Napoleon agreed to the demand, and let the two dozen remaining prisoners free. The whole country trembled to hear what desperate thing would next be done. Nothing the first day. The suspense grew fearful. Nothing the second day. Men breathed. Nothing the third day. The women laughed in scorn. The Kildonan army, of perhaps five hundred men, broke up and dispersed. The leaders could not agree that a sufficient cause existed for embroiling the settlement in strife, with murder, and pillage, and fire. And possibly they were right.

The Little Napoleon and his court of generals plucked up heart. From the wall of the Fort a soldier descried a small party of men making their way across the prairie in the snow. They were proceeding from the direction of Kildonan, and were apparently on their way to Portage la Prairie. The conviction flashed upon some man of genius in the Fort that this was the detachment from Portage la Prairie that went up several days before to swell the number of the loyal army. The wild clarion of the bugle sounded; every available horseman was urged forward. Adjutant-General Lépine and the redoubtable O'Donoghue headed the tumultuous charge. The horsemen stood in a ring round the entrapped party. The loyalists were called upon to surrender; they obeyed. Forty-eight fresh prisoners were conducted into the Fort.

This was the great Battle of Winnipeg, fought on Thursday morning, February 1870. Once more a complete victory had been gained without the expenditure of one ounce of powder.

Some remarks of a writer in the 'New Nation' may find a place here, for, rebel as he probably was, the fellow had a stroke of wit in him:—

'Between 500 and 600 of the English people sprang to arms to liberate the prisoners, and about 24, all that remained, were set at liberty by the President. Thirty-six hours subsequently a whole detachment, *en route* home to the Portage, was gobbled up by the French. Here, then, is a summary: English prisoners released, 24; made prisoners, 48. If we were not a peculiar people this result would astonish us. But in this country we have learnt to be astonished at nothing. The war of proclamations inaugurated by Dennis & Co. has been followed up by a series of campaigns—the principal feature of which is that nobody was hurt (*sic*).'

A fortnight after this capture the Riel Government perpetrated their one damning fault in the cold-blooded murder of one of these prisoners, a young man named Thomas Scott. He gave offence to the petty usurpers of a little power by a dangerous firmness of character and a remarkable plainness of speech. To quote a representation made in the behalf of the rebels, 'He was very violent and abusive in his language and actions, annoying and insulting the guards, and even threatening the President.'

For these offences the young man was sentenced to death by a court-martial held March 3, 1870. Until ten o'clock the next day was given him for preparation for his end. Mr. Donald Smith, a Commissioner recently sent out by the Ottawa Government, and held in semi-captivity in his own house in the Hudson Bay Company's Buildings, made the most strenuous efforts to show the rebel leaders the character of the deed they were committing, and to obtain at least a delay of the sentence. Clergymen and priests also entreated in vain. 'During all this time nothing could convince the prisoner that his sentence would be carried out.' On the fatal morning, the Rev. George Young, the minister chosen by the prisoner to attend him, earnestly urged delay, on the ground that the condemned man 'was not prepared to die.' An extraordinary piece of generosity was now shown on the part of the rebel government. In deference to this statement the execution was postponed from 10 A.M. to noon. The prisoner was then led out into the court-yard within Fort Garry, and shot down like a dog.

The miserable playing at government of the rebels has a certain fit culmination in the cold-blooded murder of a powerless prisoner with an aping of the forms of military law.

All previous mistakes by other parties were diminished to insignificance before this malignant and imbecile blunder.

But for awhile peace reigned—a very still quiet—for the people were seized generally with an invincible fear. That one murderous volley, the only shots fired in the rebellion, woke in every home echoes of indignation and dread. Riel's cause and that of his party received its death that morning in the Fort.

It is not difficult to conjecture the underlying reasons for this so-called 'military execution.' The rebel Government wished to strike awe through the settlement, and prevent any further attempts against their usurped authority. It was their purpose, further, to commit their party irrevocably to a policy of opposition by some deed not to be lightly passed over by the Canadian Government. A temporary success attended their plan.

Five days after the execution of Thomas Scott Dr. Taché, the Roman Catholic Bishop of St. Boniface, arrived in the settlement. News of the disturbances in his diocese had been sent to him at Rome, where he was assisting at the Œcumenical Council; and a special telegram from the Ottawa Government urged his immediate return. With extreme anxiety the prelate set out, crossed half the world, and came back to his people—unfortunately, too late to prevent their crowning blunder and crime. It is morally certain that if Bishop Taché had been present Scott would have been saved. Among the French of the settlement the Bishop's influence is supreme. On his arrival he set himself to moderate parties, and to prepare for the friendly reception of the Imperial and Volunteer Expeditionary Force. It is probably owing especially to this one man's influence that the playing at war did not eventually become a grave reality, and that our North-West Territory has been saved from wide-spread calamity.

Having said this, I must in candour add my conviction that, but for the influence of the Roman Catholic Church, the Red River difficulty would never have occurred at all, or, at least, would not have attained serious dimensions. The most mischievous element in the first excitement of public feeling in the settlement was a wide-spread alarm that the interests of the Romish Church were to be sacrificed, and that the Catholic religion was to be forced into the holes and corners of the provinces by the horde of English adventurers that would come in with the new order of things. The priests themselves were afraid of this, and increased the alarm of their flocks. It is, unfortunately, certain that several of the Catholic priests openly abetted the acts of the insurgents; and I have reason to know that at one moment, at least, the Catholic clergy hesitated in their loyalty to the English rule, and questioned if annexation to the United States might not be a better fate than the treatment they were likely to receive from the Canadian Government.

A month after Scott's murder, Mr. Riel issued a proclamation to the population of the North-West which is one of the choice literary curiosities in Red River history. I will quote some of the characteristic sentences :—

Elevated by the Grace of Providence and the suffrages of my fellow citizens to the highest position in the Government of my country, I proclaim that peace reigns in our midst this day.

Happy country to have escaped many misfortunes that were preparing for her!

O, my fellow countrymen, without distinction of language or without distinction of creed—keep my words in your heart! If ever the time should unhappily come when another division should take place amongst us, such as foreigners heretofore sought to create, that will be the signal for all the disasters which we have had the happiness to avoid.

LOUIS RIEL.

GOVERNMENT HOUSE, FORT GARRY, *April* 9, 1870.

The spring of 1870 came hastily on. Red River heard the news, at first with incredulity, of the starting of the expeditionary force. It was proposed by the rebels to equip and discipline an army in opposition. They debated on the advisability of raising the wild Indians on the line of march against the coming troops. Fenian aid was talked of, and indeed was to have been tendered, if Canada had first been conquered. It was agreeable to Fenian imbecility to neglect a practicable opportunity for striking a blow at England on this remote expedition of our troops, where, at some of the portages, a hundred men might have occasioned a great, or even a fatal, disaster. And of course it was the fitting thing in Red River to depend on these Fenians, and on the action of the United States, and on the intervention of the gods, and on big talk, to stop the English force. Up to the end the rebels did nothing; the empty wind-bag of the revolution had not one last breath left in it.

On August 24, 1870, at ten o'clock in the morning, the first detachment of English troops entered Fort Garry. At nine o'clock Mr. Riel and the honourable gentlemen of his government left by the back door. Up to the last moment resistance appears to have been intended, or at least dreamt of. The rifles flung down by the rebel soldiers on their retreat were found ready loaded. But, agreeably to the peculiar genius of the Red River warfare, not one shot was fired. Little Napoleon and his army ignominiously disappeared. The farce ended befittingly; the Red River Revolt was done.

Despite the ludicrous aspect of this burlesque of a revolution, it is only too certain that at one time it threatened to involve the empire in serious difficulty. A certain party of American political agitators were in active correspondence with sympathisers within the settlement. An incursion of filibusters to aid Riel, and then to take the conduct of affairs, was by no means a distant probability. It is happily beyond question that the Government of the United States would have considered seriously any representations England might have chosen to make; but it is by no means clear that the Washington Government could have taken any effective part in aiding us to a recovery of the province if a rabble of miners from Montana and Colorado had already entered the Red River Territory and established an independent government.

Fortunately, such an untoward event did not happen, and will not now. At the time of my visit, in October 1870, order was completely re-established. The careful selection of the first Lieutenant-Governor of Manitoba has proved a happy one. From all parties the Honourable Mr. Archibald has won favourable opinions by the impartiality, and kindliness, and ability of his administration. Already the resentments and jealousies of the population are giving way to milder moods. A vigorous stream of emigration will shortly flow in, and give the new blood, the enterprise, and the healthy ambition which the settlement alone needs to make it one of the most prosperous countries on the face of the earth.

An Anglo-Saxon race has to spread across this continent. The loss of the Red River would have prevented effectually the confederation of the North American Colonies and the consolidation of British power in the New World. Let Red River and the magnificent Saskatchewan be filled up. Our island is too small both for the population and the energy of our race. We can establish a new and vaster England here, with advantage to ourselves and to the world. The importance of the possession of this country to Canada is beyond calculation. For the first time she has vast plains, large enough to be carved into great states, to which she can invite immigration upon a scale of national magnitude. Let Canada endeavour to colonise from the Atlantic to the Pacific with Anglo-Saxon blood, for the sake of a great destiny for her children; race still remains the determining element in deciding the fortunes of nations. Of course, no sort of unfairness must be shown to the present French population; and none will be. On this vast continent they will find use and place wide enough, however large the influx of the English race may be.

The scope of her territory now dignifies Canada. It is no mean thing to be a citizen of a Dominion which in extent is a new Europe. Let Canada cherish here the sense of honour, the high courage, and the hatred of corruption which we think made Old England strong, and her fame will be worthy of her descent.

CHAPTER XIII.

THE GREAT NORTH-WEST.

It has now passed beyond all question that a vast country of extraordinary fertility occupies the central portions of British American North-West territory. Until recently few travellers had explored these remote and inaccessible regions. No sufficient inducement was supposed to exist for the pains. The great fur-trading Company, claiming the whole region, jealously kept hidden their knowledge of the country. The traditional policy of the Company has always been opposed to any scheme of public immigration. The dominant Church here, foreseeing that its influence would be jeopardised by a large Protestant settlement, has also naturally favoured a Conservative policy. No suspicion of dishonesty or want of right intention is implied in this. Self-interest influences men unceasingly in biassing and blinding the judgment.

Nor has much good time been lost through the long neglect of this country. Canada was not prepared to occupy it; England would not have felt disposed to do so. The United States, with all their amazing eagerness to promote immigration, have not spread onwards the line of settlements within hundreds of miles of this part of the continent. The open discovery of the magnificent resources of the Red River and of the Saskatchewan come at a most fitting moment. It affords a safe and wide field for the display of a new-born ambition natural to the age of the new-born Dominion. It gives scope for petty provincial politics to expand into a generous statesmanship. It suddenly presents the idea of empire and national pride before the spirit of the Ontarians and Quebecois and the peoples of the maritime provinces at the earliest moment in which they were prepared to forget their local jealousies. And once more the existence of this wide Red River country, and of the fertile belt of the North-West, renders practicable the opening of a direct route from the Pacific to the Atlantic for the extension of the Japan and China trade at the earliest moment in which such an undertaking was likely to be carried through by English and Canadian enterprise. And yet again it may be added that the better time has only just come, if indeed it be come yet, when England has awakened to the fact that, for preserving her own position among the nations of the world, it is essential for her to adopt a policy of strengthening her great family of colonies, and of binding them to her more closely, by generous sentiment and by material advantages. England may now probably be disposed to assist a great scheme of emigration to these wide western wilds, in order to build up here a power favourable to her own honour and interest.

To assist distinctness of apprehension, the old Hudson Bay and North-West Territories may be divided into three great sections:—First, the barren, frost-bound, polar north. Second, eastward of Red River a wide region of lakes, swamps, disjointed streams, dense woods, and wildernesses of rock full of ore, extending beyond Lake Superior. Through a section of this difficult country the Expeditionary Force made its way in the summer of 1870. Third, the fertile region of plains extending west of Red River for 1,000 miles to the base of the Rocky Mountains; the country destined to be the granary of the Dominion.

The country contained in this last division is of vast extent. From its eastern boundary, the Lake of the Woods, to the sources of the Saskatchewan in the west, it stretches 880 miles. Its breadth, reckoned from the British boundary line, latitude 49° to 60° north, is 760 miles. It includes an area of 480,000 square miles—an extent of country equal to that of Great Britain, France, and Prussia united. The greater proportion of the land appears to be well fitted for cultivation; many great districts possess a richness of soil unparalleled.

This region of flowing plains, that may be called the basin of Lake Winnipeg, was once probably a vast inland sheet of water. Its elevation above the level of the sea is inconsiderable, rarely rising to 1,000 feet. The soil is a fine alluvial deposit, or frequently a black vegetable compost. Roots, vegetables, melons, and certain fruits, grow with an extraordinary luxuriance. Good crops of barley, oats, and rye, are raised even by the poorest skill where any attempts at farming have been made. Wheat will yield fifty bushels to the acre, but requires more care than the people know how to give.

All the rivers from the British boundary line flow northwards. The whole country tilts that way. Lakes Athabasca and Winnipeg, at the north and north-east of this division, are estimated at but 600 feet above the sea. The effect of this depression of level on the climate is very great, and wholly favourable. The isothermal lines strike directly upwards from the Lake of the Woods as far as Peace River and Athabasca Lake. The rigour of a northern winter is mitigated. The increased heat of summer rapidly ripens all grain. It is possible that the warm current of the Pacific, striking upon the Columbian Coast, may aid in modifying the climate of the north-west of America, as the Gulf Stream is popularly supposed to temper that of England. At any rate, the resemblance holds that in the north-west of America, as in the north-west of Europe, the climate is naturally less severe than in the eastern extremities of these continents in the same degrees of latitude. In Red River, and in other districts, only 18 inches of snow fall. Horses and cattle keep in good condition through the winter without shelter. No snow-drifts occur to impede railway communication.

'We have in a very great part of this central prairie country an open or summer season of seven months, the mean temperature of which is fully as warm as Toronto for the same period, with a winter season of five very cold months, but clear and dry—as cold as the northern parts of Minnesota—a winter fully colder than that of Quebec, but without its obstructively deep snow, or the drawback it presents in the difficulty of feeding cattle through it.'[1]

The natural system of water communication existing throughout this country will prove of immense service in facilitating its settlement, and in developing its resources. Close together in the Rocky Mountains, about two hundred miles from the United States boundary line, two streams have their rise, flowing east. One bends somewhat to the north, the other much to the south. At five hundred miles from the starting point they meet, each having run about eight hundred miles. One is the north, the other the south or main branch of the great Saskatchewan. The river is a thousand feet wide at the junction of its branches, and flows on east two hundred and eighty miles further, and falls into Lake Winnipeg. A natural highway, west and east,

---

[1] Mr. Russell's Pamphlet on the North-West.

is provided through the country. The occurrence of several rapids will necessitate the construction of canals and locks, to avoid trans-shipment. There is no doubt that for grain and heavy produce water communication will be used even after the construction of railways. Vast beds of coal lie exposed on the banks of the Saskatchewan, two hundred and fifty miles from its mouth, in readiness for steamers. Woods abound; marshes wait to be drained; and vast reaches of fertile prairie attend the coming of the husbandman.

The great sheet of water into which the Saskatchewan flows, Lake Winnipeg, will prove of immense value in the water communication of this country. It lies north and south with a length of two hundred and eighty miles, and a breadth varying between six and sixty. Its area is said to be over eight thousand square miles. It empties itself northwards, by navigable rivers, into the Hudson Bay. Heavy freight that will not pay for transmission will probably leave by this route for England, as return cargoes. It is the route hitherto chiefly used for the great import and export business of the Hudson Bay Company. Its chief disadvantage is that it can be used with certainty for only five months in the year, as the early formation of ice impedes navigation.

At a southern bend of this lake the waters of the Winnipeg river flow in, after a course of five hundred miles from the east. The volume of this river is more than double that of the Rhine. In its turn this river communicates with the Lake of the Woods, Rainy river (whose banks are singularly fertile and beautiful), Rainy Lake, the river Seine, and the lovely but greatly obstructed Lac des Mille Lacs, within forty miles of Lake Superior. Various locks on the way, and a tram-road or railway over this forty miles, will complete the direct communication between the Rocky Mountains and the settled provinces of Canada. From Lake Superior, canals and great lakes, and the magnificent St. Lawrence, present an open route to the Atlantic and the Old World. The inland ports of Toronto, Montreal, and Quebec, have a great interest in the opening up of these western territories. The future will see a water highway, crowded with commerce, from the Gulf of St. Lawrence to the foot of the Rocky Mountains, a distance of three thousand miles across the continent.

Two large streams, the *Assiniboine* and the *Red River*, uniting at Port Garry, flow into Winnipeg from the south. Each of them runs a course of about five hundred miles, through a soil of extreme fertility, which one day will produce an enormous supply of grain for the European markets. The north-west corn lands of the United States will probably avail themselves of this line of transit. The difficulties of creating this trade, however great, are certain to give way before the unusual advantages which nature has beforehand arranged for it.

Lake Winnipeg is but one of several sheets of water lying together and connected by open waters. Winnipeg signifies in the Indian the Dirty, or rather Turbid Waters. The lake and river owe this name to the rich mud which tinctures their waters. The Red River has its name from its similar appearance. West of Winnipeg lies its diminutive lake Winepegoos. South-west lies the fine lake of Manitoba, which gives its name to the new province. The Indian has chosen the title from the thunder-storms that disturb its waters. It signifies 'The God who speaks.'

There is little doubt that the Red River country will be the first to receive a large incursion of settlers. The fame of its history, and the number of its already known advantages, will secure it the first preference. It has the making of a great country; but it needs the making.

I will state a few facts about the country which I gathered myself during a three weeks' stay there. The soil is a rich, black, vegetable compost, a foot deep on the Red River prairies, and two or three feet, and sometimes more, at the portage on the Assiniboine, and in many other localities. The subsoil is generally a light clay. Boulders of limestone and granite occur constantly along the banks of the rivers, and in the dry gullies of the prairies formed by storms and by the melting of the snow in spring. Lime-stone crops out in masses in various places on the prairie.

In the wretchedest hovels of the half-breed inhabitants I have seen ripened Indian corn stored away against the rafters for family use. A dilapidated old half-Indian settler showed me some particularly fine potatoes. His year's crop of three hundred bushels had been produced from eleven bushels sown. Some of his potatoes weighed four pounds each. He put in this year twenty pounds of wheat and took out two hundred and seven. But for the culture of grain better appliances are needed than the old settlers know anything about. Twenty returns of wheat, however, I am assured, are not uncommon, of sixty-five bushels to the acre.

An old Scotch settler gave me the following figures:—For his last crop he sowed 72 bushels of wheat, and raised 1,470 bushels on $2\frac{1}{4}$ acres. Barley and oats yield five or six bushels more to the acre. Of potatoes he planted 20 bushels and took out 450. About his land he said, 'It would be none the worse for being drained.'

An Ontario farmer, a recent settler, gave me some particulars of his first season's crop. His farm has a depth of fourteen feet of loam. From a field which had been planted with wheat for twenty years in succession, he raised without manure a crop of wheat of fifty bushels to the acre. Barley gave as much; oats more. 'It is the finest country in the whole world for root crops,' he said; 'I had turnips from fifteen to nineteen pounds.' His potatoes yielded enormous returns; many of them weighed from two to three

pounds. He grew excited at the thought of his vegetables. His peas, beans, cauliflowers, celery, carrots, citrons, and melons, grew with a lavish luxuriance that amazed him. 'You could not crowd a cabbage into a flour-barrel,' he said. 'The sugar-beet here will make fortunes for many manufacturers,' he went on, 'and for the culture of flax the country is without rival.' His wheat was marvellous, 'every grain as big as a little pea.'

Before me lie the Minutes of Evidence respecting the character of this country, taken before a Select Committee of the Senate at Ottawa in the year in which I write, 1870. I could fill pages with statements similar to the following :—

'I have seen a crop come off the same land for twenty-five years,' says one of the settlers examined. 'I have known farmers who have thrashed their wheat and got thirty-five bushels to one, during the last year, and that was not a good season for ripening. I have seen one grain of wheat make fifty-five heads. About sixty-five or sixty-six pounds is the average weight. Hemp grows taller than myself.'

'I had an estimate made up last year,' says another, 'and my opinion was that of all the cereals we had not less than twenty returns for every bushel sown in the whole country. The yield per acre is difficult to get, as the people do not pay any regard to that measurement. I would say thirty and thirty-five bushels to the acre would not be too large.'

'Last year about forty bushels to the acre in

some parts,' is stated as the yield of wheat by a gentleman examined. 'The average, probably, however, was not much over thirty. The wheat weighs generally over 60 lbs. to the bushel. Its weight can be so generally depended upon that the local regulation makes the bushel measured not weighed. Oats are about 32 lbs. to the bushel. Barley turns out equally well.'

These wide prairie lands present advantages beyond all countries in the world, probably, for three purposes: steam farming, stock-raising, and railway making.

Fields of grain may be raised here a mile, or ten, or a hundred miles square, without a hill or river, or even a stone, to obstruct the furrow of the plough. Steam for breaking the ground, for harrowing, for reaping, could and should be used. The grain crops, especially wheat, now suffer occasionally from the shortness of the season. The farmer can rarely put in the plough before the first of April; teams of oxen, or of horses, cannot do the requisite labour fast enough. Summer comes suddenly. The seed cannot be got in soon enough after the passing of the snow. Every day saved is of consequence. Once ripe, the crop cannot be cleared with sufficient haste. Early frosts are to be feared. A fall of snow will sometimes occur early in July; and the immediate return of fine weather, and a superb Indian summer, will not restore the frozen wheat. The latest improvements in agriculture for hastening field operations will here have their full value, not only in saving labour, scant to get, but in rendering the crops secure.

For stock-breeding this country, and perhaps still more the Saskatchewan, offers extraordinary advantages. It is the natural home of the buffalo. Herds of these great creatures, numerous beyond estimate, covering scores of miles square as they graze, find rich sustenance on these plains. The natural grasses are good, but will in time probably be replaced by grasses better still. Horses and cattle find pasture all through the year; and indeed remain in good condition, exposed on the prairie, through the rigour of winter. At present it is the common practice to save the trouble of providing shelter; but certainly the more experienced farmer will not allow his stock to suffer the keen prairie winds, and he will lose nothing by his carefulness.

For railways all that is needed is to throw up a couple of trenches, to carry off rain and melted snow, and put the rails flat on the tract thus made. There are no engineering difficulties. There are not even snow drifts to provide against, as in older Canada; the snow lies only from eighteen inches to three feet deep on the prairies. From Fort Garry right up to the summit of the Rocky Mountain pass, a distance of a thousand miles, the line can be laid down with as much speed as the rails and ties can be brought along the route. Branch lines will be constructed with all imaginable ease to develope the resources of the inland country as soon as sufficient occasion exists for them.

But there are various objections to this new country which must in candour be named. They are these: the periodical plague of grasshoppers, or locusts, as they are termed here; a persistent nuisance of mosquitoes; the mole-hill mountains made by the little gophir, which hinder the plough in some places; the presence of ague-breeding swamps; the inundations of the rivers which take place on the melting of the snows; occasional droughts; the extreme scarcity of timber; the want of communication with the outer world, and lack of a market; the indolence of the native population; the excessive length and severity of the winter. The list is a long one; for I have put down all the objections I could myself find, or could hear anything of.

These objections are of weight, at least as against the country as a place of residence for people disposed to tolerate little change from the ordered mode of life of old-established communities. They are of less account to a rough practical farmer, or to an energetic man resolved to find fortune in the New World. And they are all fated to disappear, or become greatly lessened, under the influence of a large immigration to the country.

The plague of grasshoppers is already diminishing, and is really little thought of in the settlement. They have visited Red River three times within the past fourteen years, and always in fewer numbers.

On the last occasion little damage was done. The creature, about an inch and a half long, appears in the autumn and cuts down the stalks of grain not sufficiently ripe to resist it. When the crops are well advanced little harm ensues. But commonly the grasshopper deposits its eggs before leaving the country, and from these the principal mischief comes. In the early spring the young grasshoppers swarm over the land, destroying everything green in their course. But latterly the autumn swarms have been inconsiderable, and few eggs have been left. The prairie swamps to the south in which they have their origin are drying up, or being drained. As cultivation advances this once formidable plague will disappear.

Much the same must be said of the mosquito pest. Without question this tiny fly has been hitherto a cause of grievous misery throughout the land. I have been told with a grave face, by men of unquestioned veracity, that at mid-day the clouds of mosquitoes on the plains would sometimes hide the leaders in a team of four horses from the sight of the driver. Cattle could only be recognised by the shape; all alike becoming black with an impenetrable crust of mosquitoes. The line of the route over the Red River plains would be marked by the carcases of oxen stung to death by this insignificant foe. However, this September I failed to find even a single specimen as a curiosity; and on all hands I heard that the fly, with an admirable sense of propriety, forbears to obtrude within the older settlements.

In some districts, at present, fever and ague prevail. This will surprise no one who has seen the mean log-houses of the people, built flat on the soil, and frequently in a depressed hollow by the river side. There is no draining as yet in the country. All this will be altered by a little enterprise.

In 1826 the land for thirteen miles west of Red River was flooded on the breaking up of the winter ice. This was an unusually heavy inundation, and had the happy effect of widening the bed of the river. One or two slight inundations have occurred since, doing little damage. The river banks are said to be double the width they were formerly.

Timber is so valuable, as well as so necessary for ornament in any country, that woods and parks are certain to be planted as settlement increases. Private enterprise will suffice for this, but probably the government will see fit to encourage the process. Several of the prairie States in the Union have found it expedient to grant a royalty to the settler on every acre planted with trees. The policy is a wise one; both the State and the individual become the richer. A great variety of timber will grow in the Red River district; poplar, birch, the sugar-bearing and exquisitely-leaved maple, all the white woods; and, with perhaps less facility, the hard woods, oak, elm, and the rest. Fruit trees will probably be difficult of cultivation until portions of the land are protected by large timber from the searching winds of the prairie.

With the opening up of the country markets will be found for everything that can be raised. At present the demand in the settlement for all kinds of produce, and for all descriptions of manufactured articles, greatly exceeds the supply. But an outside trade by rail or water must grow up to large dimensions with the progress of the country.

The chief difficulty remains to be mentioned— that of the climate. It is severe beyond all question, but not beyond exaggeration. 'Settle in that accursed Red River country? No, sir!' said an American to me. 'No country is gwine to fit me that has got a nine months' winter, with the three months' balance very late in the fall!'

Up to the time I remained in the country, the middle of November 1870, the weather was splendidly fine, with warm sun in the day, and mornings and nights cold but exhilarating. Half an inch only of snow had fallen, and that disappeared. The air was of an intoxicating brightness. I believe the country must be one of the healthiest in the world.

The rivers are ice-bound, and the prairies white with snow, usually in the beginning of December. The cold then lasts steadily on till the middle or end of March. No rain falls, and no thaw occurs to spoil the sleigh-roads. Sometimes the thermometer falls for days or weeks to 20° or 30° below zero, touching occasionally at 40°. At times, but infrequently, the mercury freezes. But at these low temperatures the people feel the cold very little. Men will go out without overcoats. By a happy peculiarity of the climate the wind never blows when the glass is very low, and in the absolutely tranquil bright keen air I was assured that it was impossible to tell within 20° what the temperature is.

Put briefly, the winter, trying though it may be to an Englishman accustomed to our singularly temperate insular climate, presents no unfamiliar features to a Canadian. It is generally held to be somewhat more severe than the winter of Ontario, but less extreme than that of Quebec. It is endurable at once, and makes itself liked by the settler. It helps to breed a vigorous hardy race, and so to form a strong nation.

I have been writing with an especial regard to the country of Red River; but much that I have said of its condition and peculiarities applies equally to the Great Saskatchewan plains intervening between Red River and the Rocky Mountains.

This wide region is usually termed the valley of the Saskatchewan, from the fact that it drains into that river, though its actual conformation is one of rolling prairie and broad woodland.

It is the 'Fertile Belt' of various travellers, so called because it lies between the frigid north and the great arid American desert which dips above the boundary line, and limits the Saskatchewan region along the south.

Of this country Captain Palliser, in a Blue-book Report as far back as 1857, speaks in the following terms :—

'Almost anywhere along the Saskatchewan a sufficiency of good soil is everywhere to be found fit for all purposes, both for pasture and tillage, extending towards the thick-wooded hills, and also to be found in the region of the lakes, between Forts Pitt and Edmonton. In almost every direction around Edmonton the land is fine, excepting only the hilly country at the highest levels, such as the Beacon Hills; even there there is nothing like sterility, only the surface is too much broken to be occupied while more level country can be obtained.

'In the upper part of the Saskatchewan country coal of fine quality occurs abundantly, and may hereafter be very useful. It is quite fit to be employed in the smelting of iron from the ore of that metal which occurs in large quantities in the same strata.'

Similar testimony might be collected from all writers on the country. I will content myself, however, with but one more quotation, from a Report prepared for the New York Chamber of Commerce several years ago, when the possibility of the absorption of our North American colonies by the United States seemed less remote than now.

'There is in the heart of North America a distinct

subdivision, of which Lake Winnipeg may be regarded as the centre. This subdivision, like the valley of the Mississippi, is distinguished for the fertility of its soil, and for the extent and gentle slope of its great plains, watered by rivers of great length, and admirably adapted for steam navigation. It has a climate not exceeding in severity that of many portions of Canada and the Eastern States. It will in all respects compare favourably with some of the most densely-peopled portions of the continent of Europe. In other words, it is admirably adapted to become the seat of a numerous, hardy, and prosperous community. It has an area equal to eight or ten first-class American States. Its great river, the Saskatchewan, carries a navigable water-line to the very base of the Rocky Mountains. It is not at all improbable that the valley of this river may yet offer the best route for a railroad to the Pacific. The navigable waters of this great subdivision interlock with those of the Mississippi.'

This is the country happily opened to the enterprise and capital of England and of the Dominion at a critical moment in the history of our nation. We need space in which to develope our cooped-up race, and grow to the vast numbers which make up a modern empire. There is room enough here.

I have said enough of the great fertile West, the chief of the three divisions of the British North-West Territories. It remains to speak briefly of the extreme north, and of the broken country east of

Red River, reaching to the Canadian province of Ontario.

The line of absolute sterility and of perpetual ice, however, lies far to the north of the country we have been considering. Advancing settlement and cultivation will push the line still further towards the pole, as in the old countries of Europe. North of the Saskatchewan valley immense districts remain which are at least as well fitted for civilised populations as Scotland, Sweden, or Northern Russia.

For example, there are the valleys of Peau River and the Athabasca, consisting of fertile prairie and woodland, with a climate not more severe than that of Canada. The two rivers just named, flowing northwards, unite near the beautiful Lake Athabasca to form one of the great rivers of the world, the M'Kenzie, that makes its way to the Arctic Sea. Immense districts along this river, too, are capable of cultivation, and possess a moderate climate.

Lake Athabasca, Bishop Taché says, is 'a beautiful expanse of deep limpid water, measuring over two hundred miles in length, at an elevation of about 600 feet above the sea level.' The Peace River he describes as a noble river, with few rapids; its valleys as rich and beautiful.

'Mineral riches,' says Bishop Taché, 'including sulphur, iron, bitumen, and plumbago, abound all over the district. I think there are also petroleum springs there. Peace River has plaster quarries and

o

carboniferous deposits supposed to be of great value. Gold dust concealed in large quantities of sand is washed from the Rocky Mountains by its rapid stream.'

Athabasca and Peace rivers flow east from their source to their junction about a thousand miles; then, forming the wide M'Kenzie, they journey still another thousand miles directly north to the ocean. It is difficult to realise fairly the extent of country on this northern continent waiting to be developed.

'The M'Kenzie,' Mr. Alex. J. Russell writes, 'offers a great navigable communication for large vessels, with coals on its banks, connecting the vast interior region south of it, suitable for cultivation, with the rich fisheries of the Arctic Sea.

'The whale fisheries it leads to, inside of Behring's Straits, are the richest known, and are fished extensively by American whale fishers, who have to sail sixteen thousand miles to get there. When our great central prairie country is occupied by millions of people, they will have but one-tenth of the distance to reach these fisheries by the M'Kenzie, to obtain the products of the sea; it will no doubt then be a highway of some importance.'

It appears probable that districts of the barren north, which must remain for ever unsuitable for cultivation, will yet prove valuable for stone and marbles, and for their mineral wealth.

And the utterly desolate, melancholy, frozen northern frontier is not without its service. It affords a flank that can never be turned. The northern line of defence nature guards for ever, and from that north breathes down the strength and vigour necessary to enable a race to defend its other boundaries.

The remaining portion of the North-West Territory, the country between Ontario and Red River, possesses a character wholly distinct from the divisions we have been considering. It is a wild region of rock and river, morass and forest, hitherto almost impassable. But for this natural barrier, the fertile plains of the West would long since have attracted the immigration of the Old World. The barrier is now, however, effectually broken through. Formerly only the Hudson's Bay Company's trails led through this rocky wilderness. No settler ever passed through. But this year, 1870, the Imperial and Dominion Expeditionary Force, a thousand strong, made its way with stores and guns from Lake Superior to Red River, and the route selected is now being slowly made ready for ordinary traffic, and for the passage of immigrants.

The trail followed was that known as the old Canoe Route, passing from Thunder Bay on Lake Superior, by the Kaministiquia River, the connected lakes Shebandowan, Kashaboiwe, Lac des Mille Lacs, Windigoostigan, and a number of other small strips of water with incongruously long names, and Rainy Lake and River, to the Lake of the Woods; a distance of about three hundred and fifty miles. From the Lake of the Woods a roadway of ninety miles is in process of completion, across prairie land and swamp, direct into the heart of the Red River Settlement.

This is the route that will probably be used for several years to come by travellers from Canada. Though the country is generally unfit for settlement, many small patches, and occasional tracts of good land, are found along the line. This is notably the case along the Rainy River, the boundary of the United States and the Dominion. 'This tract is of the very richest alluvial soil,' Mr. Dawson said in his Report, submitted in 1869 to the Ottawa Parliament; 'in the whole distance there is not apparently an acre unsusceptible of cultivation.'

But this entire range of country will be found of the utmost economic importance, from its hidden mineral treasures and its illimitable supply of timber.

'For a great part of the way,' Mr. Dawson's Report says, 'the line which it is proposed to take will pass over schists of the Lower Silurian period, such as yield silver at Lake Superior and gold in Nova Scotia.' Indications of a variety of the useful metals also have been found, though the country as yet has been very imperfectly explored.

The value of the great woods covering this region can scarcely be overestimated. A vast lumbering country is here provided, as if expressly, for the supply of the treeless prairie lands beyond. The abounding water communications will float the logs wherever they are wanted. 'On the streams flowing towards Rainy Lake,' Mr. Dawson says, 'there is an abundance of timber, such as red and white pine, of a large size and good quality. This section would compare not unfavourably with some of the timber regions on the Upper Ottawa.'

As the great prairie lands settle up, the demand for timber will grow immeasurably; but the supply from the hill country will also be practically inexhaustible.

The route here indicated, however, through the tangled country of rock and lake and stream near the United States borders, will not finally be the highway to the Red River country and the fertile West. A line of railroad is imperative, and is practicable. Fortunately, the direct Canadian route to the Red River coincides with the shortest line from Canton to Liverpool. A railroad from Ottawa to Fort Garry would form a link in the Dominion Pacific Railroad. It will pass probably much to the north of the water-route of which we have been speaking. By recent explorations a practicable railroad route has been found, passing thirty or forty miles north of Lake Superior, a little to the south of Lakes Nipigon and Seul, and north of the Lake of the Woods. This appears to be a far more promising range of country for settlers than that more to the south.

The north shore of Lake Superior is a broken mass of rock, hopeless for cultivation, wholly unfit for the construction of a railroad, but full of mineral wealth. A considerable distance to the north, however, the aspect of the country changes to comparatively level woods and plains.

Lake Nipigon is still another of the great inland sheets of water, adding to the beauty, and healthfulness, and value of the northern part of this continent. It is estimated by Dr. Bell, in his Report for the present year, 1870, at seventy-five miles north and south, with a breadth of about fifty. This, 'the most beautiful of all lakes,' as Dr. Bell calls it, is in the same latitude as Fort Garry, with a similar climate. The Report states that the land between Nipigon and Sturgeon lakes is admirably fitted for cultivation, consisting principally of black loam.

The country of the Lake of the Woods is known to be fit for settlement, and practicable for the railway.

Let the direct Canadian line be constructed without unnecessary delay, and the immediate prosperity of the North-West will be assured.

CHAPTER XIV.

THE AIR-LINE TO CHINA.

A LINE of railway from ocean to ocean across British territory is, perhaps, the most important undertaking waiting to be accomplished for the development and strengthening of the empire. It is needed to make the Confederation of the British North American Provinces true in fact, and not in name only. It is essential to the opening of the rich countries of the North-West to English and Canadian enterprise. It cannot fail to be of important service as the direct communication between Asia and Europe.

With this railway, and a stream of immigration following it, and overflowing the northern continent along its course, the Dominion will grow in strength and influence, and will hold its place as a distinct power in the New World. If this immigration should take place mainly from Great Britain and the British American colonies, as very certainly it would, the power that would grow up here would be another and larger England, willing to remain in political union with the mother country, and certain to remain attached to us in the closest bonds of sympathy and of alliance and good-will. In preparation for the threatening future, with our European alliances proving untrustworthy, we should surely direct our policy to the strengthening of the peoples of our own flesh and blood, formed to be our natural allies. The means that may secure this are of imperial and vital consequence.

For this Canadian line of railway, Nature herself has apparently gone out of her way to accumulate a variety of favourable conditions. At the Atlantic terminus of the rail vast beds of coal lie exposed, on the very coast, in readiness for the steamers that will ply between Halifax and Liverpool; this being the only example of coal so situated along the whole Atlantic seaboard. Similarly, at the Pacific terminus, great coal mines wait at Vancouver's Island for the traffic to China and Japan; this again being the only coal on the Pacific seaboard. But this is not all. Along the very line which the railroad must traverse, coalfields of measureless extent lie along the Saskatchewan, obtruding often to the surface to save the trouble of mining.

'Along the eastern base of the Rocky Mountains,' Mr. Alex. J. Russell writes, 'there extends a broad belt of geological formation, throughout the entire length (nearly a thousand miles), containing an inexhaustible amount of lignite coal; it has been seen in many places in beds from two to eight feet thick, and in some parts over a breadth of nearly two hundred miles.'

But nature has been kinder still. By a happy eccentricity in the formation of the Rocky Mountains, a wide, and easy, and remarkably low pass has been scooped out, almost immediately in the direct air-line to China. The greatest elevation, 3,760 feet above the sea, is less than half the height of the passes which the United States Pacific line has had to cross.* The ascent to this pass—the Yellow-head, or Leather-head Pass—is, from the east, simply a gradual upward sloping of the vast prairie plains. The descent into British Columbia is perfectly practicable for railroads.

'There are,' says Lord Milton, 'no engineering difficulties of any importance. From the Red River settlement to Edmonton, a distance of about 400 miles, the surface is slightly undulating, the lower ground universally swampy, and everywhere covered with thick forest. There is little doubt that a better trail than the one at present used might be found for this portion of the way, by keeping to the higher ground. From Jasper House to Tête Jaune Cache— the pass through the main ridge of the Rocky Mountains, about 100 or 120 miles in length—a wide break in the chain, running nearly east and west, offers a natural highway, unobstructed except by timber. The rivers, with the exception of the Athabasca and

* Evans' Pass in the United States Pacific line is 8,242 feet; the Rattlesnake, 7,560; Bridger's, 7,534.

the Frazer, are small and fordable, even at their highest. The ascent to the height of land is very gradual, and indeed hardly perceptible; and the level only 3,760 feet above the sea; the descent on the western side, although more rapid, is neither steep nor difficult. From the Cache the road might be carried in almost a straight line to Richfield in Cariboo, lying nearly due west ... and a road has already been made from the mouth of Quesnelle, on the Frazer, to Richfield, through a similar country. This would therefore complete the line of communication through Cariboo to Victoria.'*

The line is a northern one, but still it is only in the latitude of Amiens and Prague. The difficulties which it presents are fewer than those already overcome by the United States Pacific Railroad. As a result of the tempering influence of the warm waters of the Pacific, and of the descent in northing of the great inland plains, the winter reigns here with no undue severity. Through parts of the rocky ascent from British Columbia, snow sheds will doubtless have to be constructed, as along the American Pacific Railroad. On the thousand miles of the Saskatchewan plains, however, the snow lies but two or three feet deep, and does not collect in drifts. The traffic, even in the depth of winter, will probably be more easy than on the lines in constant use in Ontario and Quebec, and on the nearly completed Intercolonial Railway to Halifax.

* Milton and Cheadle.

The country traversed by the line is all valuable. There are no tracts of country like the five hundred miles of arid and saline plains from Laramie to Salt Lake valley, over which American enterprise has successfully carried the first Pacific railway. From Halifax to Ottawa a line is already almost completed through a fertile and partly-settled country. North of Lake Superior and south of Lake Seul, the railway will help to develope a region of inexhaustible mineral wealth. It will pass on westward through a magnificent lumbering country— then through the midst of the future granary of the Dominion and the wide grazing lands of the Saskatchewan. Then, crossing by Tête Jaune Pass, the line will run once more through a wide mineral country rich with the gold of Frazer River and Cariboo. If only for the means of exchange between these different portions of the northern continent, the line of rails will become a commercial necessity.

But the Imperial policy is also concerned in the establishment of this line of communication. British Columbia declines to enter the Confederation, it is understood, without a guarantee that this Pacific railroad, which would unite her with the other provinces, shall be constructed within a limited series of years. The exceptional importance of the case, and the unusual circumstances attending it, may possibly justify the English Government in affording this enterprise its all-powerful assistance.

To the New Dominion this enterprise means real dominion, influence, and increased national prosperity. Sacrifices should be made, and some risks incurred by the Government, to avoid any tedious delay in the execution of this project.

The separate provinces—at least Ontario in the east, Manitoba in the centre, and British Columbia on the Pacific—have interests so great in the line, that by grants in aid, or by other available means, they should seek to secure its early construction.

But if Parliaments and Provincial Assemblies are too busily occupied to give minute heed to the claims of this railway, let a dozen merchants of London, Liverpool, or Montreal be allowed to build it, with the single advantage of the grant of alternate blocks of land, as on the United States Pacific railways, and the line will be a reality and a success in a few years' time.

The reasons that demand its construction and ensure its success are not all indicated yet. The proposed Dominion Pacific Railroad is on the most direct line possible to China. No map gives a just idea of the shortest lines over the earth's surface. The convexity of the earth cannot be shown on the flat surface of the map. But take a globe; place one end of a string on Canton; draw it by the 'airline' straight to Liverpool, with only those deflections which the configuration of the continent render absolutely necessary. The cord will pass through British territory solely. Crossing the Pacific, the line will enter Vancouver's Island, follow the Saskatchewan, traverse the Red River country touching at Fort Garry, pass north of Lake Superior, cut the St. Lawrence, and reach the Atlantic at Cape Breton. Standing before a globe it is at once intelligible that the proposed Dominion line should be, as estimated, over twelve hundred miles shorter than the existing United States line by San Francisco and New York.

Commerce as certainly finds the nearest and readiest route of communication, as waters do the lowest level.

The true North-West Passage has been found. The commerce of Asia in the ancient world built up a long line of cities whose fame survives their decay—Nineveh, Babylon, Palmyra, Bagdad, Alexandria. This great commerce, now beginning to flow eastwards round the world, may help to raise a new line of cities, from Victoria to St. John, fair with a newer and purer civilisation, to rival the glories of the past.

CHAPTER XV.

THE MARITIME PROVINCES.

THE Canadian Dominion is destined to be, apparently, one of the great maritime powers of the world. Upon the adhesion of Nova Scotia and New Brunswick in the Confederation, the returns of the commercial navy exceeded 800,000 tons. If we allow for even a moderate increase of prosperity since that date, and take into account the marine of the two provinces of Newfoundland and Prince Edward's Island, which are surely gravitating to the New Dominion, the gross tonnage would to-day exceed probably a million tons, a more imposing commercial marine than that of any of the continental powers of the Old World, with the doubtful exception of France.

'The Maritime Provinces, in confederating with Canada, have augmented her importance and power in a degree immensely exceeding the mere proportion of their population or extent of their territory. They have given her an ample seaboard thickly studded with excellent harbours, coalfields nearly as extensive as those of Great Britain, and many thousands of hardy, skilful seafaring men, who, to use the language of Governor Andrews in his report to Congress on the British Provinces, from their superior intelligence and bodily vigour, and their experience in the navigation of cold and stormy coasts, are the best of seamen, and well qualified to maintain the honour of their flag on every sea. The Dominion, though but in the beginning of her power, owns already about 800,000 tons of shipping; bearing a proportion of about 20 per cent. to her population, while that of Great Britain, the greatest maritime power in the world, without her colonies, is only about 18 per cent. per head.' *

The importance of the offensive and defensive powers of a navy of this magnitude can scarcely be overestimated in the event of war, while during peace the fisheries constitute one of the principal sources of national prosperity. This industry tends also to conserve the old national characteristics and the vigour of the race.

Nova Scotia, the ancient Acadia, with Cape Breton, a part of the same peninsula, contains an area of 28,800 square miles, or twenty millions of acres, a territory about twice the size of Denmark. It is a beautiful country of hill and valley, with innumerable streams and lakes. As many as a hundred sheets of bright water are sometimes grouped

* From an admirable pamphlet on the North-West, by A. J. Russell, Esq., of Ottawa.

within a space of twenty square miles. A considerable proportion of the soil is excellently fitted for agriculture. An improved system of farming is being adopted throughout the province.

Coalfields of immense extent occur on the very seaboard, to aid the natural advantages of position possessed by the province for securing the direct trade between the Old World and the New. Mines of tin and copper have also been recently discovered. But this great rocky peninsula, thrust boldly out into the ocean, seems expressly designed for a vast fishing trade, and for a nursery of sailors. The coast is a continuous fretwork of excellent harbours. From Cape Canso to Halifax alone, a comparatively short strip of about a hundred miles, there are no less than a dozen ports capacious enough for ships of the line. In the harbour of Halifax, one of the strongest military positions on the new continent, the assembled navies of the world might ride at ease.

New Brunswick shares the characteristic advantages of the sister province. She possesses a somewhat larger area than Nova Scotia, or about twice that of Switzerland. The country is eminently picturesque, abounding in wooded lakes and rivers, with fair reaches of fertile valley, and great ranges of hills, broken with abrupt masses of rock, and rising often to precipitous elevations, 'which give them an almost Alpine aspect; all the more striking in contrast with the peaceful plains and vales they protect from the tempests of the sea.'

It is estimated that a million acres of her valleys are under cultivation. Her magnificent breadth of forest is a source of great wealth. Her coal fields are of enormous value. But the fisheries of New Brunswick are again of the chief importance to the province. A large proportion of the population is employed in this industry. ' In the harbour of St. John's alone there have been at one time 200 boats with 500 men taking salmon, shad, and other fish. Nearly 600 fishermen have been seen at one period at the Island of Grand Manan; while at the West Isles about 700 men have been thus employed at one moment; and so on at many of the other countless fishing grounds and stations of the New Brunswick and the Nova Scotia coasts.'

By far the most valuable fisheries on the whole coast of the Atlantic are those of Newfoundland, the Gulf of St. Lawrence, and the Bay of Fundy. The mackerel is now rarely caught on the shores of the United States, while cod, herring, and other valuable fish never go south of the cold waters surrounding the coasts of Dominion provinces.

The economic importance of these fisheries is very great. In the Year Book of Canada, a useful publication, compiled with extreme care, there is contained in the volume for 1868 a statement of the value of the annual yield of fish. From the figures collected for the year 1866, the most recent date for which the requisite statistics could be obtained, it appears that the total value to the provinces of the produce of the fisheries, for export and local consumption together, reached the large amount of $10,837,000 (or 2,167,000*l.*); while a nearly equal value was taken from the same waters by the fishermen of the United States. The total gross value, therefore, exceeds four millions of pounds sterling.

The regulation of the fisheries has been deemed of too important and too critical a nature to be left to the control of the provincial governments. A special minister of the Dominion has been entrusted with the charge of this department. The interests involved affect the honour and prosperity of the Dominion very closely, and are not without a bearing on the Imperial policy also.

From the first discovery of these fisheries they have been the occasion of national jealousy, and sometimes of armed strife. French, English, and Americans have fought strenuously for the possession of these rich waters. At the present moment they are likely to give rise to new complications between the Imperial and United States governments.

The cause of disagreement is of easy apprehension.

From 1854 to 1864, during the continuance of the Reciprocity Treaty, under which the markets of the United States and of Canada were open freely to each power, the fishermen of the States were allowed an open entry to all the fishing-grounds of our Atlantic colonies. By the action, however, of the Washington Government, in terminating this Treaty in 1864, they forfeited the privilege of this free entry into Canadian waters. Their fishing rights became once more limited within the close terms of an earlier convention—that of 1818—between Great Britain and the United States. The present misunderstanding arises upon a difference of construction of the terms of this convention.

It must, however, be stated that in 1865 the Canadian Government, hoping for a speedy renewal of the friendly Reciprocity Treaty, adopted a particularly liberal and conciliatory policy towards the United States on this subject of the fisheries, with the express understanding, however, that the concessions granted to the American fishers were provisional in their character, and should not be taken as prejudicing the legal rights of the Canadian provinces. The United States vessels were allowed temporarily all the privileges they had enjoyed under the Reciprocity Treaty upon the payment of a nominal license-fee of fifty cents per ton.

The Dominion Government has now, however, decided upon resuming the privileges thus accorded, and of falling back upon the strict provisions of the 1818 Convention, the only treaty of legal force in this matter.

The reasons for the adoption of this course are simple. In the first place, the payment of the nominal license-fee was systematically evaded by the American vessels, with the possibility, as the Dominion Government feared, that this unrestricted use of our waters would be set up at some future time by the States as a claim established by usage. And further, the express object for which these fishing privileges were provisionally accorded—that of inducing a renewal of the commercial Reciprocity Treaty—appeared to be still a remote probability. Debarred from trade privileges by the United States, Canada has naturally determined to resume the uncompensated privilege which she had accorded.

In a note at the end of this volume will be found the text in full of the Convention of 1818, limiting the fishing-rights of the United States. The terms are briefly these:—

American fishermen have liberty to fish on certain coasts of Newfoundland, of Labrador, and some islands expressly defined; but are debarred 'for ever any liberty heretofore enjoined or claimed to take, dry, or cure fish *on or within three marine miles* of any of the coasts, bays, creeks, or harbours' of the British dominions in America not included in the specified limits.

The present disagreement between the two Governments, in this matter, is limited to a single point. 'Great Britain contends'—I quote the report of 1870 of the Canadian Minister of Marine—'that the prescribed limits of three marine miles, as the line of exclusion, should be measured from headland to headland. The United States Government contends that it should be measured from the interior of the bays and sinuosities of the coast.'

A technical difficulty of this minute character can be readily adjusted, it may be presumed, between the two governments, upon a reference to the usage of nations in similar circumstances. But out of the eminently unsatisfactory condition in which this whole subject of the fisheries rests at present a number of practical inconveniences are certain to arise, calculated to excite still more a feeling of mutual distrust and alienation between the peoples of the United States and of the Dominion, and to provide matter for distasteful discussion between the government of the United States and those of Great Britain and the Dominion.

In pursuance of its newly-adopted policy of protecting the exclusive fishery-rights of the British vessels, reserved in the 1818 Convention, the Dominion Government has equipped a marine police of six sailing vessels and two steamers, to prevent, on pain of seizure, the vessels of the United States from fishing within the prescribed three-mile limits. Several seizures have been made; an occurrence peculiarly aggravating to the body of American fishermen and to the temper of the American people.

This new and most unfortunate grievance naturally finds a prominent place in the last message of the American President.

'The course pursued by the Canadian authorities towards the fishermen of the United States during the past season,' President Grant complains, 'has not been marked by a friendly feeling. . . . Vessels have been seized without notice or warning, *in violation of the customs previously prevailing*, and have been taken into the Colonial ports, their voyages broken up, and the vessels condemned.'

'Anticipating that an attempt may be made by the Canadian authorities in the coming season to repeat their unneighbourly act,' the President proceeds to recommend Congress to confer upon the Executive the power to suspend the operation of the existing laws 'authorising the transit of goods, wares, and merchandise, in bond, across the territory of the United States to Canada.'

The policy here proposed by President Grant, of limiting still more the already closely-restricted commercial relations between the United States and the Canadian people, is scarcely a wise one. The abrogation of the Reciprocity Treaty, instead of increasing the chances of the annexation of Canada, intensified in the northern nation a dread of the tyranny of the Republic, and incited it to a strenuous development of its own resources. The suspension of the privilege of bonding goods will be a political mistake of the same kind, and will produce, in larger measure, the same results. The Dominion of Canada might by possibility be attracted to enter the Union; she will never suffer herself to be compelled.

On their side the Canadian authorities are entirely resolved to disallow to the United States so important a privilege as that of the freedom of the fisheries without receiving some compensating advantage, as, for example, that of the entry of the United States ports for the sale of fish at moderate rates of duty. The demands, apparently reasonable, of the population of the maritime provinces, enforce this policy on the Dominion Government, even if there were not principles at stake of national importance to be established as well.

I will make one further extract from the recent Report of the Minister of Marine and Fisheries :—

'Immense as is the intrinsic value of the exhaustless fisheries which form so large a portion of our material resources, their rightful control and exclusive use possess a peculiar value and significance intimately connected with the new condition and prospects of this country. The actual situation and future development of these inshore fisheries acquire, if possible, additional importance from the selection of a sea-board line of railway connecting the hitherto separated provinces of the British North American Confederation.

'If these provinces must in future depend more fully on their own resources, and open new markets for their native products, our attention cannot now be too soon turned to the development of our vast and valuable fisheries. They should form the staple of an extensive and lucrative trade with foreign countries and with the other British colonies. They provide an important nursery for our seamen, and they afford an inexhaustible field for the skill and energy of our sea-board populations. They possess peculiar value to Canada. Their exclusive use, therefore, affords these united provinces such advantages as a young country cannot too highly estimate, and should on no account neglect or abandon.'

CHAPTER XVI.

INTER-CONTINENTAL COMMUNICATION.

THE inter-colonial railway, now being rapidly constructed across New Brunswick and Nova Scotia, will prove of great value in binding together the provinces of the Confederation, and in opening up the eastern country for immigration and for the development of its buried resources. It will be, also, a military line of the greatest importance; and, once more, it will aid materially in an object of national and imperial consequence—the shortening the time of communication between Great Britain and all parts of the Dominion.

Each year the relations between the Old World and the New become more intimate and more important. The exchanges of a vast variety of products and manufactures grow unceasingly in magnitude and in value. The mail service alone has grown to enormous dimensions; and passengers cross and recross the Atlantic in numbers to be counted by hundreds of thousands.

The great bulk of products and of manufactures

will naturally follow the cheapest and easiest routes of transit, such as require the fewest trans-shipments and avoid unnecessary delays. As inevitably the passenger and mail service will persistently seek out the shortest and speediest line of communication possible.

Already, on the European side, the mails are forwarded by rail and packet to Ireland, and are put on board the Atlantic steamer at Queenstown with a saving of many hours. It is probable that, on the American side, similarly, the mails will before long be forwarded to the last practicable point of departure for the steamer. The inter-colonial railway will provide the necessary means when the lines of travel are established between the port of Halifax and New York and Boston to the south, Montreal and Quebec to the west.

The track of the ocean steamships lies along the Nova Scotia coast. Letters from New Orleans, St. Louis, New York, Toronto, Montreal, could be put on board at Halifax, or some port more eastern still, of several days' later date than by the existing system of mailing from New York City.

The imperious interests of commerce will probably compel before long the adoption of the shortest practicable mail line between England and America. It might not, however, be unworthy the care of Imperial and Canadian statesmanship to aid the establishment of this line, and secure its control, linking so closely together, as it would, the mother country with her greatest colony.

It is conceivable also that the occasion might arise when the possession or control of the fleet of swift steamships needed for this service might prove to be a matter of grave importance to the empire.

CHAPTER XVII.

IMMIGRATION.

THE stream of emigration from Great Britain is beginning to set in to her North American possessions in increasing volume. By slow degrees the especial advantages which Canada presents as a home new to the Englishman are becoming known. Farmers, manufacturers, traders, and enterprising men of all kinds in the pursuit of fortune, with large capital or with small, are finding in this true New England a peculiarly promising sphere for the attainment of independent position and wealth. Various associations in England, and many private individuals of influence, induced by patriotic or charitable considerations, are engaged in assisting suitable families of poor means to cross to the new Dominion. Still, when the overcrowded condition of all professions and occupations in the old country is considered, and when it is remembered that free space and the ready means for the immediate improvement in position of tens and hundreds of thousands of settlers are afforded in the older and newer provinces of the Dominion, it is apparent that only a beginning, though a good one, in this transfer of our people has been made.

The immigration statistics for 1868, given in the Government Report for 1870, are as follows:—

	Cabin.	Steerage.	Total.
Passengers arriving at Quebec	1717	32,583	34,300
Passengers arriving at Hamilton, *via* the Suspension Bridge	.	.	32,004
At Portland, Montreal, and Toronto, by steamers, etc.	.	.	2,294
Total	.	.	68,598

Of these numbers probably one-third, or rather less, remained in Canada. It is impossible at present to obtain accurate information on this head, but from the following figures an approximate estimate may be made:—

Of 14,098 emigrants conveyed by the Grand Trunk line westward from Quebec, 4,513 remained in Canada, against 9,585 taken through to the States, according to returns furnished by the Company.

Again, from the returns made by the different emigration agents in Ontario and Quebec, it appears that in the year 1868 emigrants had settled in various parts of the Dominion in the following proportions:—

In the Hamilton district, about	4,646
„ Toronto „ „	5,197
„ Kingston „ „	1,817
„ Ottawa „ „	1,284
„ Montreal „ „	1,321
„ Quebec „ „	300
	14,565

These figures are necessarily very incomplete. They serve, however, to show that there is already the commencement of a considerable emigration to the Canadian provinces. The excellent Minister of Agriculture and Immigration for the Province of Ontario, the Hon. John Carling, informed me that from data in his possession it appeared likely that the immigration to Canada within the past two years 1869–1870 would approach or possibly exceed 50,000 persons.

There is no need for either surprise or regret in the circumstance that some 40,000 immigrants annually pass to the western States of the Union through British territory. A singular instance of the misuse of statistics is found in the statement, repeated on all hands without consideration, that the population of Canada migrates into the States almost as rapidly as it can be recruited by fresh immigration. The simple fact of the case is that, in regard to the whole mass of these immigrants, their destination is already fixed for some point in the West. In a large proportion of cases they actually bring through tickets from Ireland, Sweden, Bavaria, to the new States and Territories of America. The proper deduction from the existence of this large through traffic is, that the Dominion possesses in the St. Lawrence the natural highway to the west of the continent, and that Canadian enterprise has availed itself of this advantage for securing a large and profitable branch of business.

While there is abundant scope in Canada for every kind of ability, there are some particular kinds of immigration that may be recommended with especial confidence. There is a very large and increasing demand, for instance, for agricultural labourers, for useful artisans, such as carpenters, tailors, masons, smiths, &c., and for female servants.

During the past season Mr. Carling procured returns from the reeves and mayors of a number of Ontario municipalities, stating the kinds of occupation for which immigrants were needed, and the number for whom immediate employment could be found. 'These returns,' the Government Report says, 'show a demand for upwards of 24,000 farm labourers, mechanics, and female servants.'

'Indigent immigrants,' the Report continues, 'on their arrival were each furnished a good wholesome meal, and forwarded as soon thereafter as possible, by free railroad or steamboat passes, to their several places of destination, by the respective immigration agents, at the expense of the local government. By this prompt method of distribution, dependent on the returns from the municipalities, the congregating of large numbers of immigrants at any of the points of debarkation, and much consequent suffering, were avoided. The rate of wages current in the Dominion is, of course, an important consideration for the intending emigrant. I will quote a pamphlet on Emigration issued under the sanction of the Government of Ontario :—

'Farm indoor servants, who are generally treated as members of the family, receive from $10 to $14 a month, by the year. Farm servants with wives can obtain employment with board, in the house, at from $12 to $18 a month, provided the wife is willing to assist in the general female work of the farm. Sometimes farmers give to married servants a cottage and garden, with fuel, and grass for a cow, on the premises. In such cases, the usual wages are from 50*l.* to 60*l.* a-year.

'Female servants receive from $4 to $6 a month, by the year. In country places wages are somewhat lower. The demand is constant for both of these classes throughout the province, and superior servants will sometimes get higher wages than the largest amounts above stated.

'Labourers receive from 75 cents to $1·25 a day, with board. During harvest, wages have often risen to $1·50 to $2 a day, with board. Boys of twelve years of age and upwards readily get employment at proportionate wages.

'Carpenters in towns get from $1·50 to $2·25 per day. Bricklayers, plasterers, and stone-masons from $1·75 to $3; painters and plumbers, $1·50 to $2·25; tinsmiths, $1·25 to $1·50; blacksmiths, $1·25 to $2; wheelwrights, $1 to $1·75. Tailors can earn from $1·50 to $2, and shoemakers nearly the same.'

These amounts coincide with the answers made to my own inquiries in all parts of the Dominion. A large employer of labour in Ottawa gave me the

following items as the wages paid by his firm :—
Carpenters, $1½ or 6s. a day; masons, $2¼ or 9s.;
labourers, $1¼ or 5s. At these rates he could offer
employment to a hundred additional hands at the
time of my visit.

At the Great Western Rolling Mills at Hamilton,
employing at present 175 men, but where, it was
expected, a large addition would shortly be required,
the following figures were given me as the ordinary
wages :—Labourers, $1; engineers, $1¾ to $2½;
puddlers paid by the piece, but making on an average, per day, $3¼; heaters, $4¼ (piece); their helpers,
$1½; rollers (piece-workers), $5. The Canadian
dollar may be reckoned with sufficient accuracy at
four shillings sterling.

A farmer in 'the Garden of Canada' gave me the
wages paid by him as follows :—To single men, 50*l.*
a year, paid monthly; to married men, 40*l.* a year,
with a good cottage rent free, and a liberal supply
of milk, vegetables, and fuel. To harvesters, $1 to
$2 per day.

From Mr. Conolly, whom I met in Canada on his
return tour as a delegate from an English Trades'
Union, inquiring expressly into the condition of the
working-men of this continent, I received the following comparative statement :—

	UNITED STATES. Dollars (paper currency).	CANADA. Dollars (coin, or in currency at par).	LAND. Shillings (sterling).
Carpenters, per day	2 (country)	1½	6
,, ,,	2½ (New York)		
Masons, ,,	3 (country)	2½	6
,, ,,	4½ (New York)		
Bricklayers ,,	3 (country)	2½	6
,, ,,	4 (New York)		
Engineers ,,	2¼	1½ to 2	5 to 7

It was Mr. Conolly's opinion that, taking into account the depreciated value of the American currency and the increased cost of living in the States, the wages received in Canada were fully equal in buying power to those paid in the States.

In regard to the important consideration of living expenses, I will again quote the Ontario Government pamphlet (count the cent as a halfpenny; the 12½ cents is the so-called New York shilling, equivalent to our sixpence) :—

'The cost of living in Ontario for ordinary mechanics and agricultural labourers, when quantity and quality of food are considered, is cheaper than it is for the same classes in the old country.

'Rents—Cottages and small houses in cities and towns, suitable for single families, from $4 to $8 a month, including taxes.

'Flour per barrel (200 lbs.), $5 to $6. Butchers' meat from $5 to $8 per 100 lbs.; cheese, 12 to 16 cents per lb.; butter, 15 to 25 cents; tea, 60 cents to $1; coffee 25 to 40 cents; sugar, 8 to 13 cents. Poultry are generally plentiful and cheap; geese,

30 to 50 cents; turkeys, 50 to 70 cents. Potatoes and ordinary vegetables are usually procured at moderate prices. Working people living in the country commonly raise sufficient of the before-mentioned articles to supply their own domestic wants.

'Clothing, strong and well-suited to the climate, made from cloth manufactured in the province, can be obtained at reasonable rates. A man's winter suit, including the making, from $14 to $20. Summer clothing lower. Calico and the finer descriptions of woollen goods, being generally imported, are consequently dearer than in England.'

From a similar tractate, 'published by order of the Government of Quebec,' I extract a few items, serving to show the cost of living in the French province:—

'Bread, 6 lb. loaf, 12 cents to 15 cents; flour, per barrel of 200 lbs., $5 to $6; meat, per lb., 6 cents to 8 cents; salt butter, 15 cents to 20 cents; cheese, 12 cents to 16 cents; potatoes, per bushel, 40 cents to 50 cents.'

The above sets of figures are substantially accurate. At one of the many market-places I visited, the busy, crowded, morning market at the thriving little city of Hamilton, I asked the prices of a great variety of articles:—

Beef or mutton, best cuts, $12\frac{1}{2}$ cents per lb.; seconds, 10 cents and 8 cents; the brisket, $6\frac{1}{2}$ cents (i.e. the best 6d., the cheapest $3\frac{1}{4}d$.); bacon, 17 cents; hams, per lb., 15 cents; pork, 12½ cents; sugar, 10 cents moist, 12½ cents loaf; tea, 50 cents, 75 cents, and $1 per lb. Coffee, ground, 25 cents to 35 cents per lb.; soap, 6 cents per lb.; salt, 1 cent per lb.; butter, 23 cents per lb.; fowls, 25 cents a pair (when full grown 40 cents to 50 cents a pair); potatoes, 40 cents a bushel; tomatoes (a delicious summer vegetable in common use), 40 cents a bushel; onions, 50 cents a peck; carrots and beets, 12½ cents a peck; heads of cabbage, 6 cents each; of cauliflower, 15 cents; splendid melons, 15 cents each; great pumpkins, 8 cents; pears, 50 cents a peck; grapes, 10 cents a quart; cooking apples, 10 cents a peck; Indian corn, 12½ cents the dozen cobs; capsicums, or 'hotpeppers,' as they were called, 8 cents a dozen; crab apples, for jelly, 20 cents a peck.

As to house rent, four rooms, I was told, could be had at four dollars a month.

The immigrant of small means should not expect to find his 'bread ready toasted, and buttered on both sides,' as the wife of a newly arrived London artisan naively expressed their hopes to me. He will have to work hard, and perhaps to suffer both inconveniences and privations. But in this, at least, the lot of the artisan and labourer will have undergone no change. The advantages presented to the immigrant are mainly these: first, the easy possibility of improving his position, by obtaining a house of his own and a plot of ground or a farm, by purchase at low rates or by free grants. The artisan, if a man of industry and intelligence, may expect to become a master; the labourer a farmer. Second, the assurance of securing an excellent practical education for his children, and giving them a fairer start in life, under more favourable conditions for their success, than he enjoyed himself. Even if he fail himself, the immigrant may expect his children to attain to positions of wealth and consideration. Third, the influence of the climate, and tendency of the general conditions of life, for benefiting his own health, and for raising a hardy and vigorous family. Fourth, the certainty of securing abundant employment at fair rates of payment. The skilled or unskilled labourer must work hard, and may suffer hardship; this will not be new. But the pleasant novelty is that in a few years he may be independent, and in a few more he may see his children foremost in the country in wealth and influence.

But the class to which Canada presents at present the greatest advantages are farmers with small capital. A farm of good land, with fair improvements upon it of dwelling-house and out-buildings, situated in the best parts of Ontario, with easy access to good markets, can be purchased freehold for less money than is paid in England for the year's rent of inferior land. I should be inclined to name $30, or 6*l*. per acre, as the present average price of farm-lands in the oldest settled districts of Canada, this amount being inclusive of the buildings and fences on the farm. An average, however, is very hard to determine; the value varying greatly according to the quality of the land, and still more from its situation.

Farms may be obtained in Ontario for $10 or even $5 an acre (1*l.* or 2*l.* only); while for farm-lands near the great towns $50 or $100 would be a small price. In the uncleared districts, the land can be bought for one or two dollars an acre, or had for nothing in the free-grant districts.

As a rule understood to have many exceptions, the immigrant farmer should wait a season before investing his capital. He will do well to visit the farming districts of the Maritime Provinces and of Quebec and Ontario, and also some of the uncleared regions along the line of the Inter-colonial railway, or up the Ottawa river, for examples, before he makes his choice of a new home for himself and his sons. If he can spare sufficient time, the farmer is not likely to regret the extension of his tour to the Red River country. All this time the English or Scotch farmer will be finding abundant occasion for 'unlearning' much of the system pursued at home. He will see that, with the wide tracts of land to be cultivated, with a summer of novel shortness, and with a great scarcity of labour at his command, the farmer must make rapidity of operation his chief aim, and leave neatness of fence, regularity of furrow, and cleanness of harvesting to the era of steam-ploughs and of the fuller settlement of the country.

In many districts the old stumps, disfiguring the soil and obstructing the plough, will grieve the eyes of the old-country farmer. He will tolerate more readily the unsightly 'snake-fence,' a zig-zag line of tree trunks laid end to end and five or six feet high, which almost universally takes the place of the picturesque hedges of our own country. Happily, however, the stumps rot ; and the snake-fences too.

The farmer will see the necessity of accommodating his practice to the exigencies of a new country. He will not, however, forget the ideal of high farming he saw aimed at in the old. His experience will prove of admirable service.

If the new comer has relatives or friends in one of the provinces, he may wish to settle in their neighbourhood. They will, however, in all probability, advise him to defer the purchase of his farm, or at least his personal management of it, until he has had time to learn the peculiar characteristics of Canadian agriculture.

There is abundant room, with the certain prospect of independence, for tens of thousands of our tenant farmers who find it difficult at home to make the rent and living expenses out of their farms. 'Not one half of the land already in private hands is yet cultivated, to say nothing of the many millions of acres of wild lands still undisposed of by Government.'

The farmer need not fear any failure of the markets. The rapidly-growing towns of the Dominion require a constantly increasing supply. The grain market cannot be overstocked. The export trade will absorb all that can be produced.

The immigrant farmer need not incur the trouble and expense of taking agricultural implements with him. He will obtain them at moderate cost in Canada, manufactured expressly to suit the peculiarities of the soil, &c. But he will do well to carry with him favourite seeds and roots; and his wife or daughter should not fail to take a quantity of flower seeds from the old garden and woods. Canada has a lovely flora; but there are never too many flowers in any country; and, besides, the plants of the old home will make the new one more home-like, and will serve to freshen the memories of the past.

The farmer of capital would do well to take over some of his choice stock. Horses, horned cattle, sheep of good breed, could be sold to advantage if it proved inconvenient to keep them until the choice of a farm was made.

Stock-breeding is rapidly becoming one of the most important and lucrative branches of business in the Dominion.

When the especial advantages of Canada for English emigrants become known, appropriate means of passage and facilities for settlements will be provided to answer the demand. I shall therefore be content to make but one or two slight suggestions, in addition to a strong recommendation to the proposing settler to consult some government emigration agent in the United Kingdom before starting, or in the Dominion upon landing there.

I visited recently a new-born American settlement, Greely, on the Denver Pacific Railway. On April 25, 1870, not a house stood there, and not a clod of the earth was turned up. On November 21, I found a thriving township of about 300 plank-houses, hotels, stores, carpenters' and masons' shops, and neat dwellings. Forty miles of ditches, at an expense of $30,000, had been cut. Business and prosperity had already set in.

A tract of 200,000 acres, all needing irrigation, had been purchased at cheap rates by a Mutual Aid Society. To secure the settlement on this spot, the railway companies had agreed to take the Greely passengers and freight at half rates. The settlement was laid out as follows : First, into city lots ; second, into 5-acre plots round 'the city ;' third, into 40-acre allotments outside; and then into 80-acre and 160-acre farms on the outskirts. Each member of the association was allowed the choice of a city lot and of one of the outlying allotments, the increasing size compensating for the greater distance. The company consisted of 800 members, with paid up shares of $150 (30*l.*) a share.

Similar projects of settlement have been tried in Canada, and in other English colonies, with varying success. The plan seems peculiarly adapted for the choice lands of Red River and the Saskatchewan.

Among the various plans for assisting the emigration of individuals and families from England, the one lately proposed by the Rev. A. Styleman Herring seems to merit especial notice for its easy simplicity and practicability, and for its consequent proved success. This gentleman has commenced several Working Men's Emigration Clubs in his own large parish of 8,000 souls in the east of London. The rules of these clubs are delightfully practical. Each member pays in what he likes weekly. He is at liberty to collect subscriptions for the club, 'but with the distinct understanding that it is for his own benefit if he emigrates; if not, for the general fund.' If the member changes his mind, he can draw out the amount of his weekly subscriptions, forfeiting only the shilling entrance-fee. From funds raised for the relief of London distress, and to aid the emigration of the poor, an equivalent amount is added to the members' subscriptions. Reduced fares are obtained from steamship and railway companies. 'The selection of the emigrants is by payments, lot, election, or by the President.' It is no matter of surprise that over 500 souls have already been assisted to Canada by Mr. Herring. I had the pleasant opportunity of witnessing the delight with which these emigrants met their kind friend in the country of their new home, and of hearing the satisfaction with which they all spoke of the change in their condition.

Mr. Herring has also succeeded in establishing a number of similar Immigration Clubs in Canada, for the assistance of relatives and friends who may wish to join the settlers.

An altogether admirable plan is the one adopted by Miss Rye this year, in removing from the English poor-houses a number of healthy orphan girls to find them homes in families properly guaranteed in Canada. On calling at the spacious and pretty home—a transformed prison—which this lady has purchased and prepared for her good work, I was too late to see more than two, or three of the 120 children brought out this season. In three weeks all had been provided for. Miss Rye kindly allowed me to see some quaintly-written letters from these girls, expressing their regret at the separation from their kind friends, mingled with delight at the novelty and comfort of their new condition. They all wanted Miss Rye to go and live with them, or at least pay them a visit. I was also shown a huge packet of letters from farmers' wives and townspeople, making application for these English children.

It appears to me that Canada presents several advantages of the greatest importance to the inhabitant of the old country wishing to change his home.

First, I should be disposed to reckon its nearness of situation. Quebec is but a week from Liverpool. The Scotchman or Englishman need not feel himself hopelessly expatriated. Upon his establishment in a good position in the new country, he can 'run over' to see his friends in the old land. From the older provinces the journey is now only a short pleasure trip; that is, if the traveller escapes sea sickness.

I shall be bold enough to reckon the climate as a second great advantage.

The opinion popular in England and in the United States, that Canada has a 'thirteen months' winter,' is scarcely an accurate one. The Canadians do, however, count four months of snow and frost, but without any disposition to accept our commiseration. My repeated questions about the severity of the season were answered with amusement, and sometimes with a pretty resentment.

To the two principal industries of the Dominion, farming and lumbering, the winter presents especial advantages. It makes all the country traversable. Snow roads are formed across rivers and swamps, through vast forests, and over broken tracts of rock, for the easy transport of all kinds of freight. By the gliding sleigh, and by 'runners' of various ingenious construction, agricultural implements, heavy grain, cumbersome timber, and produce and goods of all kinds, can be transported with less cost, and in less time, than over the best macadamised roads in summer.

'Our vast lumbering operations could not be carried on without our long winter,' an Ottawa merchant said to me.

'Our winter in the woods is the best part of the year to us,' a lumberman told me in one of the upper shanties. 'We can work so easily, and we never feel the cold. We generally pull off our jackets. Of course we keep a roaring fire in the shanty, and our evenings there are the jolliest I have ever spent.'

Farmers talked to me with a similar inability to perceive that the long Canadian winter was a disadvantage.

The professional men, merchants, and traders of the cities and towns find leisure in the winter for snow-shoeing excursions into the country, and for skating and sleighing at home.

To the ladies of Canada the long winter is the gayest and brightest season of the year. Balls, 'hops,' and concerts innumerable, make brilliant the nights. The days are enlivened with delightful 'to-boggonning' excursions. Hill-side slopes and river-banks are made gay with this pretty exercise throughout the Dominion. The 'to-boggon' is a curved slip of birch bark, extremely light, and daintily ornamented, on which the fair Canadian girl takes her seat on the top of the slope; once started it glides down with a delicious rapidity, and, skilfully guided, carries its charming occupant far along the level ground at the base. The cavalier, who has shot down in his clumsier snow-canoe, draws the two to-boggons up the slope again without effort by the side of his companion.

I had to make many promises of returning to Canada to enjoy its winter myself, in order to become disabused of my last prejudices against the season.

In all seriousness, I am persuaded that, despite

its severity, the climate of Canada is one of the healthiest in the world. It is expressly fitted to develope a hardy race. For the bringing up of a young family it is to be preferred very decidedly to the climate of almost all the States of the Union south of the chain of Canadian lakes. The fact of the generally healthy condition of the people, the splendid development of the men, the preservation of the English type of beauty of the women, may be taken in proof of the excellence of the climate, and may well be allowed to influence the choice of an Englishman who seeks a new home for his family.

I venture to think that to many Englishmen considerations of patriotic duty would be of weight in determining their choice of a new home. Third among the reasons for selecting Canada, I shall name the usual influence which each new settler may exert in strengthening the bonds that unite our chief colony with the mother country, and in securing the adoption of a policy which shall preserve intact the integrity of the British Empire.

CHAPTER XVIII.

THE POLITICAL QUESTION.

THE next great question likely to disturb the public mind of Canada relates to the future of the country—whether the Dominion shall remain attached to England, or be annexed to the United States, or become a sovereign and independent power. Advantages of no mean character are presented by each of these courses. Wise statesmanship might easily control the result; it seems only too likely, however, that a policy of 'letting things drift' will be followed both by the Imperial and Dominion Governments, and the future of this great northern empire be left to the play of circumstance, or the hasty decision of some popular excitement.

Let us endeavour to estimate without undue partiality the advantages of the several courses of policy indicated, and the chances of their adoption. Beyond all question the people of the United States expect to annex the Canadian provinces. They would be prepared at any time to make large sacrifices to this end, were it not for a profound conviction that the result is certain, even without any pains taken to secure it. 'When the Canadian apple is ripe it will fall,' they always say. East and west, from the Atlantic to the Pacific, the eventual annexation of the English colonies is the dream of the whole American people; and even the dreams of a great people have an odd way of finding fulfilment. The incorporation of the vast range of our northern possessions would add to the wealth and numbers, and above all to the dignity, of the American Union. The removal of the British flag from the continent would be a piece of flattery to the national pride to which every American would prove susceptible. The annexation of the north would be a happier achievement than the subjugation of the south. The Americans are not accustomed to consider very carefully the amount of advantage which Canada would gain by this change. The honour of belonging to the great Republic would immeasurably exceed, as they suppose, any pride of connexion with an Old World monarchy. A new era of progress and of rapid improvement, they say, would follow the change. Canada would cease to be conservative and old-fashioned. Real estate would increase in value fifty per cent., they promise, on the day of union with the Republic. Labour would be better paid, new railways would be opened, the mines would be worked, a great immigration would be attracted, and generally the whole country would be changed by 'Yankee' enterprise. The long double line of custom-houses would be abolished.

The evil of smuggling would be done away. A ready and vast market would be opened for all Canadian produce. The northern provinces would immediately have their full share in all the prosperity of the Union. An equitable arrangement would be made in regard to the burdens of the war debt. If the new provinces strongly objected to bear their proportion, a complete immunity might be indulgently granted them.

Of these advantages the only one, it is safe to say, that at present would be greatly appreciated in Canada is the opening of the American markets to her produce. To obtain this from the States, the Dominion government would willingly arrange a renewal of the Reciprocity Treaty, with or without modification, or agree to the institution of some kind of customs' union.

It is probable that a great increase in material prosperity would be attained by union with the States; at least it is thought so generally, though by no means universally, in Canada. But at present the presumed disadvantages of the course outweigh in the popular mind any such possible increase in the national wealth. There has grown up in the Dominion an extreme repugnance to the mobocratic elements of the great neighbouring republic. It is certainly a fact that the Canadians prefer, very decidedly, their own ordered and free mode of government to the more democratic institutions of the States. An American can scarcely be expected to realise this; an Englishman may. The Canadians are disinclined to permit within the Dominion the disruption of affairs which takes place with each Presidential election; they hesitate to change their parliamentary system for one in which the President's veto might stop legislation; and they fear the adoption of democratic changes which might lead to the election of the judges by the populace, the periodical removal of the business officials of the nation, and similar measures. There appears to be in Canada a greater fear and dislike of 'Americanising' their institutions than we feel at home. It is easy to account for this. The States are their next-door neighbours. The Canadians are compelled to overhear the party strifes within the Republic, and to listen to the threats of a certain order of politicians to 'Americanise' and annex the northern provinces with or against their will. This, together with the overt course of action pursued by the United States Government, has induced a feeling of alienation from the republic, the force of which we are not prepared to estimate rightly at home.

The Reciprocity Treaty was repealed by the action of the United States in 1864, avowedly for the purpose of chastising Canada for the misdirection of her sentiments during the rebellion, and with a view to forcing her into the Union for the salvation of her commerce. The decisive alienation of Canadian feeling dates from the adoption of this policy. Canada has been compelled to discover that she can exist in complete commercial independence of the States. The period which was to have witnessed her financial and industrial ruin has been the most prosperous in her history. Thrown back expressly on her own resources, Canada has found them practically inexhaustible. There are not, indeed, wanting some sanguine spirits in the Dominion who dream of a future time when the British North American Empire shall become a worthy rival of the States in all the elements of national prosperity and greatness.

This feeling of Canadian distrust of the States has, unfortunately, not lacked further provocation. The canals and navigable waters of the Dominion have always been open to United States vessels on precisely the same terms with the native shipping. The American barge or boat passes anywhere without hindrance on payment of the ordinary dues. This courtesy has not been reciprocated. The transport vessels of Canadian owners lie under certain disabilities. They are not permitted, for instance, to trade from one American port to another. The interests of American protectionists have here coincided with the settled policy of the government.

So, similarly, in regard to the passage of material of war. During the rebellion in the States stores and troops were allowed to pass freely across Canadian territory from Detroit to Niagara along the Great Western Railway. But a vessel of ours containing stores for the Red River expedition was not permitted to pass the four miles of canal at Sault Ste. Marie belonging to the States. Only after much trouble, and the unloading of the stores, was the vessel allowed a passage. A persistent policy of this kind has not proved efficacious in increasing a desire for union with the States. It was surely little calculated to have that effect upon a high-spirited people.

But, further, it is urged in Canada that the promised rapid development of the country upon its annexation might well be bought at too dear a cost. The prosperity of a country is not shown solely, or mainly, by the numbers of its population, and the returns of its imports and exports. England, in the Elizabethan era, was not a rich country, and did not count the number of souls that Canada possesses to-day. There is a feverishness of haste, a painful crudity and excitability, in the character of the progress of the modern American cities and States, which presents an unfavourable contrast with the slower growth of Canadian prosperity, at least in the estimation of our colonists themselves. They believe their progress to be as much more sound and wholesome as it is less spasmodic and startling.

A sentiment of nationality also is slowly arising throughout the Dominion. The people want to be themselves, and not part of another nation, even though a greater one. They desire to work out their own course of civilisation, to fulfil their own destiny, and not to become merged in another people.

They no longer ask for any help; the only favour they wish is to be let alone; and they have no fear about the future. There are not lacking some spirits among them who dare believe that no amount of interference can prevent this.

In considering the probability of annexation to the United States an important element of the case is often overlooked. It is this, that the American and Canadian peoples are fast becoming sundered by the development of distinct types of national character. Two races are here forming side by side. The Canadians are still sturdily Anglo-Saxon. The climate of the north involves a slighter change for the race than that of the middle and southern portions of the new continent. In so far as the climate is changed at all, it is by a return to the severity of the northern regions from which the Scandinavian peoples came. The old race bids fair to attain a new vigour in being transplanted to a bleak clime once more. The Canadians, as a rule, are hardy, well-developed, fresh-coloured; they love the country and the life of a farmer; they are fond of field sports and of vigorous exercise; they are all born soldiers, and learn to handle the rifle well. They are like the English of past generations.

To a certain extent this description applies also to the French Canadians. The English, as a race, however, are but little affected by their presence among them; intermarriages not being frequent. For the sake of distinctness, I speak expressly of the English-speaking people.

The American people, though distinctly Teutonic, is ceasing to be Anglo-Saxon or English. It will soon become, if indeed it is not already, a nationality of more mingled elements than ever the world has known before. American thinkers perceive the fact, and argue from it a great future for the nation. The English nation was made up of many elements— Celtic, Roman, German, Norman—and proved a good one. The American nation will be more mingled still, and should unite the best qualities of the foremost peoples of the age. Already the new race claims to possess the solidity and practical good sense of the English, the vivacity of the French, the wit of the Irish, and the breadth and thoroughness of the German. It is certainly impossible to travel east and west through the States without perceiving that changes from the old English type have taken place. In further support of this position some well-known facts may be advanced.

First, an enormous immigration of Irish, Germans, South Germans, and Swedes has been attracted from the Old World, and for a series of years has been overflowing the American continent. The English immigrants are lost in the multitudes of other races. Second, the new-comers rear large families, of eight, twelve, sixteen children; the native American, the descendant of the English race, chooses to have but one child or two. In the West, if he is a farmer, he has more; but, as a rule, the American prefers a trade or profession; and in all the cities,

West as well as East, the small family is the recognised rule. An increasing proportion is thus secured for the foreign elements, and used up in the fusion of the new race. The amount of negro or Chinese blood likely to be mingled in the American people is too slight to require consideration. The race is, and will remain, Teutonic.

Thirdly, in estimating the growing divergence of type of the American and Canadian peoples, account should be taken of the difference of climate of the two countries. This influence, acting persistently as it does, and upon every individual of the masses, must exercise a great though insensible power in modifying the physique and the character. And, singularly enough, the operation of this cause appears to be directly in the line of those already indicated. Climatic influences tend to intensify the differences created by divergence of race. The long and severe Canadian winter produces vigour and hardihood in the people. The summer heat, though more intense than in the mother country, has not the extreme dryness of the middle and southern portions of the new continent. The hot breezes coming from the south are tempered by the great chain of lakes that stretches along the Dominion border. The climate of the New England and central States is one of extremes; the winter is severe, the summer heat excessive. All the year round the air is keen, dry, exhilarating. No one has any real need of stimulants. Not a little of the restless, eager excitability of the typical American is probably due to this subtle influence.

To summarise the arguments. The Canadians prefer their own representative institutions to the democratic republicanism of the States. They are proud of their social order, their general well-being, their system of education, the tone of thought in society, the sound basis on which their increasing prosperity rests. A sentiment of nationality, too, is slowly arising. The Canadians are growing proud of the extent of their Dominion, and of their inexhaustible resources. They would not now willingly submit to be 'swamped' in the superior greatness of another people. And they are eminently English, cherishing fondly many dear old insular prejudices. They speak the language as we do, with no noticeable change of accent. They are jealous to a fault of the English honour, and proud of the English fame and power. In race they are wholly one with us. The immigrants they receive are from the old country. Climate has fostered, not changed, the national characteristics. They are conservative of the old traditions of English liberty, and honour, and national greatness. They are the English of the English.

It is certain that only the humiliation of being cast off by the old country, and the discovery that Canada could not stand alone as an independent power, would at present induce her to enter the American Union.

Whether the annexation of Canada would prove an advantage to the States themselves, and to the world at large, are questions difficult indeed to answer.

The immediate effect would be the Americanising both of the people and of the institutions of the country. The formation of a purely Anglo-Saxon nation on the new continent would be stopped. Promiscuous immigration would overflow and obliterate the boundary line. The nuisance of the army of custom-house officials would be swept away. The North American Union, more complete than ever in its variety of climes and productions, would probably adopt an indefinite extension of the system of commercial protection. The idea does not lack grandeur of the whole of this vast continent being filled with a new, freshly mingled, Teutonic race, to be counted presently by hundreds of millions, and forming one single gigantic republic. A citizen of the States must naturally cherish the glorious vision.

But it would be hard indeed to determine whether human progress and the development of the race would be advanced or retarded by the realisation of this dream. The big world, however, could well afford to let the experiment be tried.

One element in the case the American politician should not overlook. The presence of Canada in the Union would add materially to the chances of a future disruption of the Republic. In some grave national crisis, or on the breaking out of a new war, if Canada seceded from the Union, she would probably carry with her the Western States that find in the St. Lawrence the natural outlet for their productions, together with all the States that border upon the great river on its way to the sea.

The way is now prepared for considering more briefly the probability of the English connexion ceasing, and of Canada becoming an independent power.

In the Dominion it is suspected that this is the set purpose of the home government. It is regarded as a weak and blundering policy, and is looked upon with much regret and some contempt.

The Dominion is not powerful enough yet to stand alone. Its men are too few; its resources are too little developed; its means of inter-communication too incomplete; its power of defence too weak. The consolidation of the government is scarcely effected. The confederation of the various provinces is too recent; in fact, is still imperfect. The sentiment of a common nationality is too partial. The population does not count five millions, while the Dominion Territory equals two-thirds of Europe.

It is generally held in Canada that independence now would lead quickly to annexation. The country would be overrun by political agitators, who would address themselves skilfully to the prejudices of the French and Irish among the population, and to the sectional interests of some classes of the people—the manufacturers and holders of property in the cities, for example. Lavish promises would be made on the one side to attract the Canadians; on the other high tariffs would be threatened or imposed to compel them into the Union. Grievances against the Dominion government would be discovered with extraordinary frequency, and would fill the newspapers. A *plébiscite* would quickly be demanded, and the era of independence would close. It is in this way, at least, that Canadians forecast the future.

The few public men in the Dominion who advocate the policy of independence are particularly careful to disavow this ulterior project of uniting the Canadas to the States; but the popular mind retains its suspicions. The independence party at present is insignificant both in numbers and influence.

The time has not yet come when the Dominion may stand alone. The time need never come when the connexion with England should terminate. It is an incomplete statement of the fact to say that Canada has no desire for the separation. On the contrary, speaking generally of the people, they are proud of the English name, and are ambitious of adding to the wealth and power of the empire. The Canadians have their dreams, too, of an Anglo-Saxon confederation belting the world, with England at its head and London as its metropolis. The sons of England in these colonies fret at the thought of English decadence, the signs of which they think are apparent in the indifference she manifests towards her colonial possessions. A wise policy, they believe, might consolidate an English Empire which the world would be compelled in continuance to respect; our present policy, they fear, will reduce England to a third-rate power.

The imperial policy, favouring Canadian independence, is regarded, I have said, with some contempt as well as with sorrow. It is supposed to indicate a weak fear of rival power—a feeling which no great nation can consciously entertain without a fatal loss of self-respect. Such a fear, if it exist, Canadians say proudly, is wholly unreasonable. The United States would not fight for Canada; nor could they obtain Canada by fighting. The States, the Canadians say, dare not provoke a new conflict. They do not hold securely all their present territory. The South is still impacified. By the time the States are prepared to undertake a war of conquest— could such a course, so alien to the spirit of the people, be dreamt of—the Canadians will be ready to oppose an effectual resistance. Or, should the country be overrun, an indemnity would have to be made at the close of the war for the damage inflicted. Again, at the very worst, should Canada be conquered, the loss and the suffering would be hers, and not England's, and at least this task would not be effected without diverting from other employment a large proportion of the American forces. 'If,' say the Canadians, 'we choose to expose ourselves to this possible risk, for the sake of our connexion with England, why should you object? We have no fear for ourselves; please do not allow yourselves to suffer so much fear for us.'

In reply, however, it may be fairly urged that our retention of Canada exposes us to increased risks of misunderstanding with the States, and of the defeat of our arms in the event of war.

England has never yet, however, been accustomed to attach very much consequence to considerations of this nature. We have never yet doubted our ability to defend our rights and succour our allies. In the day when England adopts for her policy the careful removal of possible causes of dissatisfaction to other nations, the period of her decline will have set in. No people can possess the consideration of the world that has ceased to respect itself.

The destiny of the Dominion appears to rest mainly with England.

Canada would prefer a continuation of the connexion with us, with a prospect of a share befitting her position in the consideration of questions of imperial consequence.

In determining her future we shall probably decide our own.

CHAPTER XIX.

CANADIAN DEFENCE.

THE feasibility of the defence of Canada still remains a subject of legitimate concern. If a just perception of the facts of the case prevailed generally in England, it is likely that we should cease to view our great colony as a source of national weakness, and the probable occasion of a grievous humiliation.

Our ordinary conceptions at home, I suspect, are these: that Canada is not worth fighting for; that the Canadians themselves would not fight; that, if they did, they would be crushed immediately by the overwhelming might of the United States, the sole power likely, in any event, to make this war; that Canada lies exposed to America along two or three thousand miles of indefensible frontier; that, finally, not all the military power of England, could it be employed, would suffice for this task of Canadian defence. A more complete mass of popular misapprehensions cannot probably be produced on any subject of human concern.

The facts are directly opposite. It is likely that these pages have at least raised a presumption that

Canada, whether independent or joined to the States or to England, is sure to become one of the great countries of the world. The Canadians themselves are a peculiarly warlike people, both in their training and temper; presenting, in this characteristic, inherited from England, a distinct contrast to the growing disposition of the people of the United States. Certainly the Canadians, upon sufficient provocation, would fight for their country, even if they had to fight unaided; and they would be very hard to beat. 'It was difficult to conquer the South,' they say, with quiet assurance; 'but to subdue the North would be impossible.' They are hardy, stubborn, valorous; a nation of soldiers more truly than any people of this age, with the doubtful exception of Prussia. The difficult character of the country and the severity of their winter would give them extreme advantages. Nature would fight for them. Considering that it is a continental boundary, Canada possesses a frontier singularly suited for defence. The magnificent St. Lawrence and the great system of lakes make Canada a vast intrenched and moated camp. Guarded by gun-boats, by far the greater proportion of the country would be inaccessible. The landing of a large invading force, except at some few points, would be to court disaster. The weak places in the natural line of defence are well-known; they have been fought over before, and defended, by the fathers of the present generation. These points could again be protected by earthworks and resolute armies. That Canada can be taken at one gulp, 'like an oyster to tickle the appetite,' as an American lately said to me, is a statement only to be smiled at. A gourmand would enjoy better the swallowing of the oyster shell.

It is a significant fact, not commonly known, that all men in the Dominion between the ages of eighteen and sixty are liable by law to military service. The proportion of the adult population that has received some amount of training is very considerable. The period of service in the militia is three years, with sixteen days' drill each year, during which the men receive a pay of half a dollar a day. The returns in the Government report, made to December 31, 1869, show an active force of 43,541 men, with a militia reserve of 612,467; total, 656,008 men.

Nor are these pen-and-ink forces. On the occasion of the Fenian raid in 1862 20,000 men turned out in four and twenty hours. This year, 1870, when 40,000 were called for, 43,000 responded within the specified time. With what efficiency they did the work then needed of them is within the popular recollection. They executed forced marches, and chose and used advantageous positions, to the satisfaction of military critics. These slight affairs were but playing at war, but they served to show the military capacity of the people.

Respecting the present condition of the militia force, I will quote briefly the report of Colonel P.

Robertson-Ross, made to the Dominion Government, March, 1870:—

'There are few of these battalions [of infantry] without some officers or men who have previously served in the regular army, and many of them, at some time, actively in the field. The presence of these men in the ranks is of the utmost importance, and tends to impart a feeling of military strength and steadiness throughout the whole; for there is a very large number of men who have previously served as soldiers settled in the Dominion. The rural battalions are almost entirely composed of the agricultural population—the bone and sinew of the land, who have a stake in the country, and in very many instances are the proprietors and sons of proprietors of the land; *and it is impossible to see a hardier race, or finer material for soldiers.* In many instances their physique is most remarkable, and they all appear imbued with a spirit of the greatest loyalty to their Queen and country, and the same spirit and aptitude for military service are exhibited by the city battalions, who are composed mainly of intelligent and educated artisans and mechanics. Considering, moreover, the short period of time allowed for the annual drill, the degree of advancement at which they have arrived is most creditable, and they are all now quite ready to go into brigade.'

The arm chiefly used is the Snider-Enfield rifle. It is proposed, however, to supply by degrees to all the Dominion forces the last improvement in breech-loading arms. The use of the rifle seems natural to the Canadian; every man in the country is accustomed to arms. Rifle matches are everywhere popular. As many as 181 took place during the year 1869,—an increase on the preceding year; and rifle-practice is becoming still more common.

I attended a volunteer corps shooting-match at Ottawa. The practice made during my stay was twenty-three, twenty-four, and twenty-five points (twenty-eight the highest possible) with the Snider. I remarked particularly the splendid physique of the men. For employment in a region of country like that of Canada, where the personal qualities of the individual soldier would still necessarily count for much in determining the practicability and success of military manœuvres, the stalwart farmers, backwoodsmen, and lumberers of the country would produce the finest army conceivable. 'Great heavens!' exclaimed an English officer to me, at the sight of these tall, broad-shouldered, resolute-looking men, 'what superb fellows I would make of these, if I might only lick them into shape.'

A significant example of the military proclivities of the race, and a proof that Canada is resolved to make herself respected, may be found in the fact of the large attendance at the schools for the practical training of officers. These institutions were commenced in 1864, on the occurrence of the Trent affair. Four of them—those of Quebec, Montreal, Kingston, and Toronto—have continued in constant operation. 'The number of cadets who have been granted certificates by the several commandants (officers of the regular army) who have had charge of these schools now exceeds 5,000, of whom 24 per cent. have taken first-class certificates. The whole of these cadets are distributed throughout the two provinces of Ontario and Quebec, and so continuous have been the applications from the provinces, that the number of cadets in Quebec only exceeds that of those from Ontario by eighty-eight.'

Since the adhesion of New Brunswick and Nova Scotia to the Dominion, schools of military instruction have likewise been established at St. John and Halifax.

The necessity, however, of a higher grade of military instruction than is contemplated in these schools of practical training, is now becoming felt somewhat generally. An academy of military science, like that of West Point in the States, should be established without unnecessary delay. The Dominion might then expect to find ready, within the ranks of her own population, her Lees, or Grants, or Shermans, in the unhappy event of the defence of the country requiring them, or possibly to aid the mother country in some future struggle for empire or existence.

Canada has already prepared for self-defence, without a great dependence upon military aid from England. She believes that the moment chosen to attack her, should it ever come, would be when

England was engaged in some European or Asiatic war, straining all her resources in disciplined soldiers. Novel as the statement may seem to English ears, it is nevertheless a fact that the Dominion calmly expects to be able to hold its own, even under such circumstances, against any force likely to be brought against her. I will quote again the Report of Colonel Robertson-Ross, already cited :—

'In the event of war, sufficient numbers of men could always be obtained from the large Militia Reserve to swell the ranks of the active force to any strength likely to be required, for it is a fact that the population of the Dominion comprehends nearly as many men within the fighting ages as the Southern States in the neighbouring Republic ever brought into the field, and the men of Canada, both morally and physically, are not only equal to any that the world can produce, but in point of hardihood, manliness of spirit, and fitness for military service, are not to be surpassed.'

It is not pretended, however, that the Dominion, with a population of less than five million souls, would be able to oppose a successful resistance for an indefinite time to a power numbering forty millions. The Dominion must needs expect the action of the English fleet in drawing off large American armies for the defence of the long line of populous coast cities open to attack. Canada would thus be left, she believes, to encounter no more than the considerable odds for which she considers herself prepared; she would be fighting on the defensive, with the many advantages which a people always find over an invading foe.

But the Dominion population will not long rest at four and a half millions. At the present rate of increase—and the proportion is likely to increase rather than lessen—the numbers will exceed six millions in 1880, and will reach twelve millions by the close of the century. With each year Canada increases in strength, in confidence, and in the pride of nationality; and in the same proportion the chances of her absorption into the great Republic diminish. If no war of annexation takes place before the Dominion possesses ten millions of souls, it is safe to predict that it never will. From the time when this northern empire shall count its tens and scores of millions of population, it appears more reasonable to expect rather the breaking up of the Dominion itself into an Atlantic and a Pacific power, unless the dream of a great Anglo-Saxon Confederation be earlier realised.

In discussing the possibility of the defence of Canada, it should scarcely be forgotten that she has already once successfully withstood the power of the United States in a three years' war of invasion. It is half a century ago, and the Republic has in that time increased vastly in wealth and in numbers. But Canada has advanced also in at least a proportionate degree. The relative increase in strength, indeed, is in favour of Canada, since in this interval the confederation of the North American Colonies has been effected. It can scarcely, therefore, be unreasonable to expect a similar issue of the struggle in the unhappy event of its renewal.

The news of the declaration of war on the part of the United States did not reach the English government until after the commencement of hostilities. There happened to be but some 4,000 regular troops in Canada at the time. The resources of Great Britain were taxed to the utmost in the great European war then raging, and no troops could be spared for our remote dependency. The moment for an invasion of Canada appeared well chosen; the Americans anticipated an easy conquest. But the war of 1812–14, memorable for the victory of Queenstown Heights and for the battle of Chateauquay, by which the safety of Montreal was assured, terminated distinctly in favour of Canada. The invasion wholly failed. Canada defended all her frontier. In the third year, 1814, when a few regiments of Wellington's veterans were added to the Canadian militia forces, offensive operations on a large scale were undertaken. By this time, also, the American coast was blockaded by an English fleet, and the commerce of the Republic almost destroyed. In complete disgust the Americans closed the war.

It is worthy of remark that in this war no portion of our colonists proved more loyal than the French, no troops fought better than they. It was anticipated beforehand in the States that the French, remembering bitterly their conquest in old days by the English, would be willing to change their rule, and enter the Union as an independent State. But England had consistently respected her treaty engagements with the French, and had won their entire good-will. Since then broader liberties than ever have been accorded the French, in common with all our American colonies. The province of Quebec exercises the fullest control over its own affairs, and fails to see any likelihood of advantage in any change of her political condition. The French of Canada are as favourably disposed towards the English rule as ever, and would prove this decisively if the necessity arose. They believe that their interests are bound with ours. In defending the Dominion they would fight for their own honour, the integrity of their institutions, the continuance of their social and material well-being. The Quebecois, too, are Canadians. They have begun to feel the influence of the new national sentiment.

There is no disaffected class within the Dominion.

The numerous Irish Canadians form no exception to this statement. They have never shown any sympathy with the Fenianism common in Ireland and in the States. The fact is singular, but not unaccountable. They are not tampered with by political agitators. They find themselves fairly treated and moderately prosperous under English rule, and without a single grievance. And, to name perhaps the principal reason, they are more completely under the influence of their religion in Canada than in Ireland or America. The Catholic Church in Canada is emphatically loyal. By treaty-right she holds many special advantages which would be put in immediate jeopardy upon a union of the French province with the States. It need not be doubted that the Irish Canadians, equally with their French co-religionists, would strenuously support the Dominion Government in a war of national defence.

Hitherto, in considering the possibility of the defence of Canada, I have been mainly concerned with various objections. The Dominion, however, possesses a number of unusual advantages for the conduct of a war, which must be briefly mentioned.

She has already a splendid marine, the third in amount of tonnage in the world. Her seafaring population, accustomed to hazardous fishing ventures, is especially hardy, able, and daring. From her secure ocean recesses on the Gulf of St. Lawrence and Bay of Fundy armed flotillas could swoop down on the exposed commercial sea-board of the States from Boston to New Orleans, and make terrible reprisals. She could thus inflict ten times, or a hundred times, the injury which she could be made to suffer. Even without the aid of English men-of-war, the rock-bound coasts of New Brunswick and St. Lawrence, full of armed vessels, with the first-class military station of Halifax, would render the eastern portion of the Dominion practically unassailable.

Her fishermen and sailors would supply the best possible material for the gun-boats with which she would line the 2,000 miles of inland sea and river which form the natural protection of her southern boundary. From Lake Superior to the mouth of the St. Lawrence no large invading force could land on Canadian soil, exposed to the attack of fleets of gun-boats, without extreme peril. On the other hand, the rich and populous cities of Rochester, Buffalo, Cleveland, Detroit, Chicago, and Milwaukee lie on the shores of the great lakes, peculiarly exposed to sudden attack or the horrors of bombardment.

Nature herself, with barren wilderness and impassable regions of perpetual ice, provides effectually for the defence of the Canadian north. The Dominion will never be taken 'in reverse.'

The seasons, too, in their courses would favour Canada. The shortness of summer would allow but little time for an offensive campaign. The rigours of winter would dishearten, or even destroy, any alien army that could succeed in encamping on the soil. 'General Frost,' the Canadians say, is one of their first commanders. Storms of snow and hail would be no mean auxiliaries to mitraille and grape in driving back invaders.

The farmers and lumbermen of Canada are a splendid material for an army. They are accustomed to the use of arms and the care of horses. They are peculiarly adapted for artillery service, and for a light cavalry as mounted riflemen.

The country is peculiarly suited for defence, from its broken and irregular character, and especially from its water-boundary. It stands like a great citadel built against the frozen north, and boldly facing the south. Quebec, with its recently-formed lines of earthworks; Montreal, with its similar outer-lines; Kingston, with its strong system of fortified works, are three mighty bastions in the grand line of defence. Similar strong points, at Toronto, at London perhaps, and at some spot commanding the Georgian Bay, ought to be prepared by earthworks to complete the chain of posts. Then what a moat has this citadel! Lakes fifty miles across, and a river that is the glory of the northern continent, wind along the whole course, to give protection and stop an invader.

'The reason we were so long taking the South was this, that the Almighty jest made that damned country on purpose to be defended,' an American once said to me, unconscious of the extraordinary claim he was making for his nation. I fancy that this inquirer into final causes might be still more disposed to believe that Canada was designed for defence from the creation.

Of course this does not apply to the Red River country, where an imaginary line on the flat prairie is the sole boundary. That country, doubtless, might be invaded with ease. The piece of Canadian territory also south of the St. Lawrence might possibly be occupied by an enemy. In either case, possession would be restored, with compensation for all damage inflicted, if the Dominion were successful in the struggle to retain her independence.

To sum up our considerations of Canadian defence: the population is a warlike one; it is already to a large extent trained to arms; it is willing to bear the chief strain of a struggle on this continent should the United States ever declare war against England. The country, from its position and climate, is eminently fitted for a long defence. Its well-manned fleets could make destructive reprisals. Its growing wealth and power will soon put the question of its conquest beyond ordinary discussion. England may well be reassured in regard to the possibility of maintaining her prestige and influence in the New World. The mother country need not think of abandoning her chief colony from a weak fear that her power is insufficient to protect it.

But further, in the event of a war between Great Britain and the United States—a possibility to be prepared for as diligently as it should be shunned—the fleets and armies of the Dominion would probably turn the scales of fortune. Driven to the States by the inconsiderateness of English policy, or cajoled into union with the Republic by large promises, Canada would assure to the American people a naval, military, and commercial precedence over the pent-up race of the English. United permanently with Great Britain, and growing always stronger from an overflow of the English population to her boundless territories, the Dominion may materially assist in prolonging the period of Anglo-Saxon ascendency.

It may possibly have appeared ungracious that throughout this discussion so constant a reference has been made to the United States. This has arisen from necessity, and from no feeling of inclination. No other power has ever expressed the least wish to attempt the taking of Canada. But the public men and the press of the American Union constantly engage the popular mind with projects of this order. The absorption of the Dominion appears to have become one of the fixed ideas of the people of the great Republic.

Still, they will pause long before undertaking a war. They feel heavily the burden of their debt. If a war of invasion against Canada proved unsuccessful, America would be called on to pay a bill of many figures for the injury she inflicted, after the example set in recent instances. This consideration will have weight in the States. Besides, the still disaffected condition of the South excites apprehension in the minds of thoughtful American politicians. Such men would prefer the consolidation of the existing republic to any further extension of its boundaries. It is by no means impossible that some of the States in the Union would withhold their forces from joining in an unprovoked war upon Canada, following in this the example of Maryland, Massachusetts, Connecticut, and Rhode Island in the war of 1812–14. It is not even beyond possibility that some of the States would take part with the Dominion.

The American Government will not hastily adopt a policy of annexation at the risk of a disruption of the Union.

CHAPTER XX.

THE FUTURE OF GREAT BRITAIN AND HER COLONIES.

For a long period Great Britain has occupied a foremost place in the eye of the world. Her achievements in all departments of human enterprise and ambition have won for her a lasting fame. Her arms have compelled victory the world round. Her colonies are growing into great states in each quarter of the globe. Her civilisation and liberty have influenced all modern nations. The story of her slow growth to power, and of the sweep and vigour of her ascendency, is one continuous romance. It is possible that, in coming ages, the student will rank after Greece and Rome the name of England next in time and next in fame.

But, without question, the ascendency of England is now threatened. There are at least three rival powers that aspire to stand before her in the rank of nations; and Prussia, Russia, and the United States can each advance very imposing claims to greatness. Each is an eminently progressive people; each possesses a vast and growing population; each indulges in an inordinate ambition.

These rivalries will have to be settled eventually as all rivalries of race have been hitherto. The great wars of the world have still to be fought. England will have to take her part, or drop in the rank of nations.

The mere mass of an empire and bulk of its population are becoming rapidly material elements in determining its place and power. War-power has now to be estimated by the million of men. Valour and science are essential as ever, but mainly to wield vast masses whose chief merit must be a perfection in military discipline.

To hold her front place England must be prepared to meet her rivals on these new terms. Her insular policy must be abandoned. Cooped up in a narrow island, she will sink to insignificance, for simple lack of men, if she pursues her recent course of alienating her colonies.

Her rivals are vast confederations. Russia contains eighty millions of people, of various races, held firmly under one central power. The American Union is composed of forty-five States and Territories, each as large as an old European kingdom. The population is forty millions; it will reach a hundred millions, possibly, by the end of the century. Germany has become an empire. Prussia is but the controlling member of a mass of States held in union in the North German Confederation. The South German States gravitate towards this powerful Union. By virtue of its weight and density, and inspired by intelligence and patriotism, Germany may take the first position in Europe, and the next great place in history.

England possesses, however, advantages beyond either of her rivals for the formation of a powerful empire. Her colonies and dependencies embrace about one-third of the surface of the globe and a quarter of its population. The colonies of her own blood and language afford abundant opportunity for the preservation of the hardihood of her sons, and room for their increase to hundreds of millions. England should adopt as her national policy the strengthening of her colonies, and the attachment of them to her permanently in a great Anglo-Saxon Confederation.

Failing some course of this kind, England must sink to the position of a second or third-rate power. Upon the realising of this policy, the English race would be assured of a new era of prosperity and ascendency.

The difficulties to be encountered are slight compared with those we have had to meet already. Our scattered colonies are nearer together in travelling time than our counties used to be; and they are within talking distance by telegraph. The pretence will scarcely be made that we have not statesmanship enough to arrange fairly for the representation of each colony in a Confederation Convention, and for a wise determination of the limits of its powers. If we followed our practical national instincts, we should probably commence our scheme for colonial representation in a tentative and informal way. A Deliberative Assembly might first be convened to discuss certain specified subjects, and present reports and recommendations to the English, the Canadian, and the Australian parliaments. This assembly might become periodical or permanent, as the subjects arising for its consideration might require, and according to the measure of respect which its method of treating them might secure. Subsequently, a power of legislation would possibly be granted to the assembly on certain intercolonial subjects carefully defined. Finally, the convention might acquire a control over affairs of imperial policy similar to that which the English Parliament has obtained over the whole range of subjects affecting the interests of our people. In such a consultative or legislative assembly England would naturally exercise a leading influence similar to that which Prussia has in the North German Parliament. More she could not wish.

But the discussion of any particular method by which an Anglo-Saxon Confederation might be organised, though of some consequence as showing the practicability of the scheme, is of infinitely less importance at present than the conviction in the public mind of the necessity of some kind of close and permanent union of Great Britain and her colonies. This is absolutely essential, to prevent the breaking up of the empire and the degradation of the English fame.

Following upon a national conviction of the importance of strengthening the bonds that unite the English race, some measures of the greatest practical moment might be carried into effect.

Great Britain has a redundant population. Our colonies need the overplus. Transport is now easy and inexpensive. An imperial scheme of emigration might be adopted with the greatest advantage to the mother country and to our dependencies. In view of the future, it would be only a measure of national protection to direct the ceaseless outflow of our people to the countries likely to remain united or allied with us, rather than to those which are alien in their feeling towards us. This proposal, at least, is neither utopian nor sentimental.

The adoption and consistent development of a national policy of strengthening our colonies, and at the same time of strengthening the bonds of interest and sympathy that unite them with us, would render the task always more easy of consolidating a great Anglo-Saxon empire.

After all, the fame of England is but young. The vigour of the race is unimpaired. It is too early in our history yet to suspect that England will forfeit willingly her first place among the nations of the world. A destiny of influence and of honour beyond that of the past is open before her. England will be true to her old fame, and to her generous and unquenched ambition.

APPENDIX.

SHORT NOTES.

1. *English Ignorance of Canada.*

An amusing instance of the ignorance of Canada, too prevalent in England, was told me privately, but not confidentially, in Toronto. My informant was a personal acquaintance of the heroine of the story. A cultivated English lady, who came on a lengthened visit to the Dominion in the present year, actually brought over with her a barrel of butter and six dozen of eggs, to assist her in existing on the barbarous fare of the country. These stores were disposed of as quickly as possible upon the lady's arrival at Quebec.

2. *Government Information.*

In former days the gun-boats sent for service on the lakes of Canada were provided with an apparatus for condensing salt water. It was presumed apparently that, being so large, these inland waters could not be fresh.

The story is told in Quebec of an old wooden guard-house arriving there once from a military station in southern Australia. The thing was of more value as firewood in Melbourne, where wood is scarce, than it was as a guard-house in Canada, where lumber is the great article of export.

The story is scarcely incredible. On the quay at Montreal, at the time of my visit, were a number of heavy sentry-boxes brought down from a distant post, waiting for transport to England, where they would not be worth a tenth of the cost of their removal.

3. *The Meaning of 'Canada.'*

'Le nom de Canada, donné ici par les indigènes eux-mêmes à une partie du pays à la totalité duquel il s'étend maintenant, ne laisse aucun doute sur l'origine de ce mot, qui signifie, en dialecte indien, *amas de cabanes*, village.'—*F. X. Garneau*, '*Histoire.*'

'Laissant ensuite la baie de Gaspé, Cartier découvrit la grande rivière de Canada, ou *Kanata*, qui signifiait, dans la langue algouquine, un assemblage de cabanes, et qui les Français prirent pour le nom du pays.'—*L'Abbé Bourbourg*, '*Histoire.*'

4. *Steamer Travelling.*

It is an extreme advantage to the traveller in Canada that he can traverse all parts of the Dominion by the easy and luxurious mode provided by river steamers. He has the use of a private berth; meals are served at the *table d'hôte*; there is a commodious deck for smoking, walking, talking, and seeing the scenery. At night some fellow-travellers will usually join in whist, or possibly in dancing. There is frequently a piano in the saloon. No time need be lost; it is as easy to read, write, talk, as in a house on shore. At night one sleeps, after a little experience, without waking up at the stopping stations.

5. *The Climate.*

The climate of Canada, so decried by outsiders, excites the enthusiasm of actual residents. It is a theme which can exalt the sober style of a government pamphlet to poetic fervour.

'Nowhere on earth do the seasons of the year move on in a lovelier, grander procession. In spring we have a quick awakening of vegetable life, and Nature puts on her best attire, promptly as a bride on her wedding morn. Our summer is short, but gorgeous with splendour, and bedecked with flowers that can hardly be surpassed; we have oppressive heat at times, and occasionally drought, but how do our summer showers refresh the face of all things; how welcome is the rain, and how green and beautiful are the fields, and the gardens, and the woods when it falls. In autumn we have the waving fields of tasselled corn; our orchards display apples of gold in baskets of silvery verdure, and we can reckon even the grape among our fruits ; our forests present a richly-tinted and many-coloured foliage. We have mid-October days in which the weather is superb ; our Indian summer is a splendid valedictory to the season of growth and harvest ; a bright and beautiful hectic flush sits upon the face of universal nature as death draws on and we glide imperceptibly into winter. This, though confessedly severe, is exhilarating, hardening animal as well as vegetable fibre, while it has its ameliorations and joys in the fireside warmth that tempers into geniality the clear, frosty air ; we have also the merry jingle and fleet gliding of the sleigh, and the skater's healthful sport, together with almost entire exemption from damp and mud, two most disagreeable accompaniments of winter in milder climes.'—*The Province of Ontario: issued by order of the Government.*

6. *The Autumn Foliage.*

All the world knows the glory of the Indian Summer of the North American Continent. I think, however, that the spectacle of most startling beauty to a traveller accustomed only to the sober tints of the foliage of the Old World is afforded by a Canadian forest after the first slight early frost. Here and there only, in infrequent masses, a single branch of the maple tree hangs in the midst of the deep verdure a flaming mass of scarlet, orange, rosy-hued opal, or purple dripping with gold. Aglow in the sunlight, these patches of magnificent colour seem like sprays of resplendent gems. Later in the year the whole forest blazes with colour, and the force of the contrast is lost.

7. *The Climate Ameliorating.*

In Harper's 'Statistical Gazetteer' the statement is made that the climate has lost as much as 8° of its former severity in the neighbourhood of Quebec, and that the river St. Lawrence remains open for navigation nearly one month later than when the country was first settled.

8. *The Province of Ontario.*

'I am delighted to have seen this part of the country; I mean the great district, nearly as large as Ireland, placed between the three lakes Erie, Ontario, and Huron. You can conceive nothing finer. The most magnificent soil in the world, four feet of vegetable mould—a climate certainly the best in North America—the greater part of it admirably watered. In a word, there is land enough and capabilities enough for some millions of people, and in one of the finest provinces of the world.'—*Lord Sydenham's Memoirs.*

9. *Population to the Square Mile.*

England	. 250	Upper Canada	. $9\frac{1}{2}$
France	. 179	Lower ,,	. $5\frac{6}{10}$
Germany	. 182	British Columbia	. $\frac{1}{3}$
Belgium	. 436	North-West Territories	$\frac{1}{10}$
Italy	. 219	United States	. $7\frac{1}{15}$

(Estimate made in 1860.)

10. *Free Grant Lands.*

'No grant is to be made to a person under 18 or for more than 200 acres. The patent shall not issue for five years after location, nor until the locatee has cleared and cultivated fifteen acres, and built a house thereon fit for habitation, has resided continuously on the lot, clearing at least two acres per annum; absence of six months during each year is, however, allowed. Failure to perform settlement duties forfeits the location. The mines and minerals on such lots are reserved to the Crown. The settler may not cut any pine timber on it, except for fencing, building, or other farm purposes, and in clearing, until the issue of the patent; or, if it be cut, the settler must pay timber dues to the Crown. On the death of the locatee, the land vests in his widow during her widowhood, unless she prefers to accept her dower on it. The land cannot be alienated or mortgaged until the patent issues, nor within twenty years of the location, without consent of the wife, if living. Nor will it at any time be liable to be sold under execution for any debt contracted before or during the twenty years after the patent issues, except for a mortgage or pledge given during that time. It may be sold for taxes.'—*Summary of the Amended Free Grant and Homestead Act of Ontario.*

11. *Burden of Public Debt.*

The public debt of Canada is $23·50 per head of the population; that of the United States is $80·18.

12. *The Laws.*

Though mainly the same as those of England, the laws are simpler and less expensive. Some differences are worth noting.

'The law of primogeniture has been abolished, lands descending to all children, male and female, in equal shares. Married women hold their own property free from debts and control of the husband. Trial by jury in civil cases is optional, being dispensed with unless either party desire it.'—*Government Pamphlet.*

13. *Montreal.*

The name of the commercial capital of the Dominion is a corruption of the old name of the fine hill rising behind the present city, Mont Royal.

The place has been thrice named. At the time of the first visit of Jacques Cartier the site of the present city was occupied by an Indian village, Hochelaga. The French dedicated the city they founded here to the Holy Virgin, and called it Ville Marie. In 1760, the date of the English possession, the present name usurped the place of the old. In 1800, the population was but 9,000. It is now probably over 150,000.

The situation of the city, at the junction of the picturesque Ottawa with the magnificent St. Lawrence, commanding naturally a great number of lines of communication with the interior of the country, and in the best position for securing the import and export trade with Europe, is one of the most important on the whole of the American continent. It will yet probably become a worthy rival in commerce with New York. It is already, I think, the most substantially built city of the New World. Its appearance, too, is already an imposing one. 'Montreal,' an American book of description says, 'with its beautiful villas, its glittering roofs and domes (the latter covered with tin), its tall spires and lofty towers, and its majestic mountain in the background, bursting on the eye of the tourist, forms, together with the noble river, a vast and picturesque panorama that is perhaps unequalled in the whole of the American continent.

'Its quays are unsurpassed by those of any city in America; built of solid limestone, and uniting with the locks and cut stone wharves of the Lachine Canal, they present for several miles a display of continuous masonry which has few parallels. Unlike the levees of the Ohio and the Mississippi, no unsightly warehouses disfigure the river side.'

The city boasts one of the engineering marvels of the world, the great Tubular Bridge. The church of Nôtre Dame, popularly but incorrectly called the cathedral, will seat 10,000 persons. The streets are adorned with fine churches and public buildings. The private residences of the merchants clustered round the mountain form one of the finest city suburbs in America.

14. *The Queen City.*

The capital of the province of Ontario is one of the most busy and prosperous cities on the American continent. Standing in one of its handsome and crowded thoroughfares, I was assured by a merchant of the city that within his recollection the forest woods crept down over the spot to the margin of Lake Ontario. A deep gulley then occupied the present site of the Town-hall. An acre on King Street sold for 250*l.* a few years ago. This property now fetches one hundred guineas a foot frontage, with a depth of a hundred feet. In 1833, the town happily changed its name from York, and entered upon its career of prosperity. It now contains about 10,000 public and private buildings, with a population of some 70,000. The assessed value of the property is about ten million dollars.

It possesses many fine piles of building, churches, halls, libraries, distilleries, blocks of stores, as little interesting as all the other big masses of buildings are on the new continent. But, to its honour, the city can boast of one piece of architecture imposing in simple grandeur, and exquisite in its appropriate internal decoration. The University of Toronto is, perhaps, the only piece of collegiate architecture on the American continent worthy of standing room in the streets of Oxford. It is a Norman pile. In the interior, massive wooden columns, joists, and rafters are freely exposed to view, giving a suggestion of the style of decoration naturally suitable to a country of great forests. Every Canadian should visit this building before instructing his architect on the style of a new house he wishes built.

15. *Golden-haired Women.*

The type of beauty in Canada is peculiarly English. The women are well-proportioned, well-developed, often very fair, and sometimes stately and tall. There is a greater admixture of Scotch blood than is found in most parts of England proper.

In the city of Toronto especially, I was struck with the large number of beautiful women with golden hair. I believe that this is due to the purely Saxon origin of many of the families settled there.

A lady of the city, herself of Scotch extraction, and boasting a glorious mass of golden hair, assured me that, among all her acquaintances with flaxen, or auburn, or golden locks, there was not one lady who used dyes. I believed her implicitly.

16. *Hamilton the Ambitious.*

The rapid progress in material prosperity throughout the Dominion has occasioned a great increase in the number and in the importance of the centres of commercial activity. The growth of Hamilton may be taken as an example of a large class of towns of the secondary rank.

In 1847, the population was about 7,000; it is now over 25,000. The assessed value of property is some ten million dollars. In 1869, 1,105 immigrants settled in the city. Up to September 1870, 906 had already chosen this bustling town for their new home. In 1868, small houses could be rented at $3 per month; the rates are now nearly double in consequence of the increasing demand. Hamilton manufactures in large quantities boots, hats, furs, glass, brushes, brooms, sand-paper, agricultural implements, steam-engines. It exports sewing-machines to the United States and to Europe. 'More than $100,000 worth of manufacturing machinery has been put up in the different establishments of the city during the present year.'

The grain trade for 1869 of this one city amounted

to about 1,575,000 bushels. The receipts of coal at one wharf have reached 50,000 tons during the current year. 'The freight passing inwards,' a local paper says, 'in 1860 amounted to 11,036 tons, while in 1869 it had reached 24,879.' It has projected and commenced several lines of railway to develope the interior country, and expects from these a great addition to its prosperity.

17. *London the Little.*

London, Ontario, is one of the most enterprising and prosperous of the cities of Canada of the second rank. It is not by these characteristics, however, that it is peculiarly distinguished. London, Ontario, can boast an increasing population, increasing wealth, large manufactories, a central position, converging lines of railways, and an energetic body of townspeople resolved to rival the other growing towns of the province. But for nothing of all this will the city be remembered by the ordinary traveller.

The little city has chosen to affect a resemblance, or comparison, or rivalry with the metropolis of England. London, Ontario, is built on a little stream, called the Thames. Her bridges across are named Blackfriars and Westminster. Her principal church is St. Paul's. Her streets are Piccadilly, Oxford Street, Regent Street, and Pall Mall.

From what singular mental condition of the inhabitants such a naming of their town can have arisen, it would be a difficult task to determine. The mystery is too high for me; I cannot attain to it.

There seems a touching simplicity, a delightful innocence, about the matter. These names were chosen, perhaps, as a father might christen his baby Cæsar, Shakespeare, Bacon, or Napoleon, in the hope that the name might work as a subtle spell in developing a rival hero. In this delicate way, or in some other no less profound, there was presumably an intention of paying a compliment to that London of which the world has already heard.

The motives were probably, however, mingled that led to this piece of public display. Possibly the little town felt the swelling emotions of an ambition that threatened to burst it on the spot, without some relief of its sense of its magnificent future. Or again, distrustful of the strength of its resolve to be great, possibly the young city chose this means of pledging itself publicly to continuous effort, on pain of meriting some such contemptuous epithet as 'petty London' if it failed to become big. Or have the borrowed names been given out of pure affection to old London by emigrated cockneys? But imagination tires in the attempt to discover an adequate cause for this extraordinary phenomenon.

Is it yet, however, quite too late for this busy, prosperous little city to resolve to be herself, and make a new name famous? However patriotic, or complimentary, or ambitious the intentions of the community were in choosing these old names, the unhappy result has been to make the city ridiculous.

18. *Newspapers.*

The following is a recent estimate of the dimensions of the newspaper and periodical press in the Dominion :—Ontario, 239 publications; Quebec, 88; Nova Scotia, 45; New Brunswick, 34; total, 406.

19. *Art in Canada.*

One of the few paintings of any artistic merit to be found on the new continent is a Crucifixion, attributed to Vandyke, in the Catholic Cathedral at Quebec. In this fine composition four weeping cherubs fill from the wounds on the cross large sacramental cups. The darkness of the scene is scientifically accounted for; an eclipse of the sun is taking place with great distinctness.

20. *Religious Recusants.*

In the province of Quebec the Catholic Church has the power of assessing the property of its members for the erection of church buildings, &c. I was told of an instance of $50,000 being assessed on a certain town, whereupon twenty-four families, liable to one-third of this amount, incontinently turned Protestant. This kind of conversion is a reproach to human nature rather than to the consistency of any particular religion. In Salt Lake City the chief recent defection from the Mormon Church occurred upon the decision of the Executive to limit the dangerous growth in wealth of some of the merchants by enforcing the co-operative system on the whole trading community.

21. *The Clergy Reserves.*

In 1823 an Act was passed in Upper Canada authorising a reservation of land, for the support of the Protestant clergy, equal in value to one-seventh of all lands disposed of to settlers. No authority existed, however, for a long time, for the sale of the Clergy Reserves; a Clergy Corporation simply granted leases. The system answered badly; freeholds were commonly preferred throughout Canada, and the Corporation found difficulty in obtaining adequate rents. The Legislative Council constantly rejected the Bills for dealing with these reserves sent up by the House of Assembly. This disagreement was one of the main grounds for the agitation for responsible Government, and was one of the chief causes of the rebellion of 1837.

In 1827, 1829, 1830, 1831, and 1832, Bills were passed by the Lower House to appropriate these reserves to purposes of education. In 1832, 1833, and 1834, Bills were passed to vest the reserves in the Crown. In 1835 and 1836 still other Bills were voted in the House of Assembly of similar purport.

In 1840 the Imperial Clergy Reserve Act passed

both Houses and became law, admitting the Church of Scotland to share the exceptional advantages of the Church of England. This measure, though a partial one, was accepted provisionally by the people for the sake of peace.

In 1853, under the Duke of Newcastle's administration, this Act of 1840 was repealed. The next year, under the Hincks-Morin Ministry, the question of the Reserves was finally settled. The life interests of the clergy were capitalised, and the lands reverted to the State.

22. *Endowed Rectories.*

In 1836 Lord Seaton, while Governor of Upper Canada, determined to establish a number of rectories, with an average of 400 acres of land each for their maintenance. By the mere accident of the omission of his signature to a number of these grants before his supercession by Sir Francis Head, only forty-four out of fifty-seven rectories which he had purposed to establish were legally entitled to the endowment. The question was afterwards brought before the English law courts, whether the endowment of the rectories was beyond Lord Seaton's authority. The validity of the grants was finally affirmed.

23. *Religion in the Backwoods.*

I attended Divine service one Sunday at the Methodist chapel of the picturesque village of

Portage du Fort, sixty-five miles above the City of Ottawa, on the lovely river of that name.

The minister became eloquent once in his prayer, when he entreated for 'the land darkened with God's judgments, and desolate with conflicting flames.' The sermon was suggested by the text, 'They have Moses and the prophets; let them hear them.' One application of the subject was a quaint one, considering the rustic character of the audience, and the small probability of the preacher's well-meant remonstrance having any influence on the dignitary of the English Church whom he named.

'I think,' said the good man earnestly, 'that if Bishop Colenso had only meditated humbly on these words, in which the Saviour acknowledges the sufficiency of the teaching of Moses for the salvation of precious souls, then, whatever his mathematical calculations might have been, he would have exclaimed with renewed faith—

> Whate'er the forms that men devise,
> To assault my soul with treacherous art,
> I'll call them vanities and lies,
> And bind the Gospel to my heart!

24. *Races.*

The Canadians have certainly not lost the love of the turf that seems natural to the English blood.

Waiting for my train at the small station of Guelph, on the Great Western, I took down the headings of a number of flaming placards on the walls, of autumn races about to take place in this part of Ontario :—

Brantford Races, premiums $1,000
Guelph Turf Club, premiums $2,400.
Ingersoll Fall Races.
Autumn Races, Napanee.
Mineral Springs Fall Races.
Aurora Turf Club Autumn Meeting.

25. *Ogdensburgh and Prescott.*

Half a hundred times I was told in the States that an easy means of judging of the relative property of the Union and the Dominion was afforded by the contrast between the go-ahead city of Ogdensburgh on the south shore of the St. Lawrence and the quiet town of Prescott on the opposite bank. I was duly mindful of the fact when I finally reached the place. The explanation of the difference of size and business of the two towns was a simple one: Ogdensburgh is the junction of several railways, while no reason exists at present for the rapid growth of Prescott. As far as an example could go in proof of a general assertion, the question was settled.

But at the next stopping-place of the steamer this relation of things was reversed, with even a greater advantage to the Canadian shore. Brockville in Ontario is a busy, thriving, substantial-looking town;

Morristown on the American shore is an insignificant cluster of frame houses.

I think it would prove inconvenient to form and change and reform one's ideas on a large subject upon recurring examples that perpetually differ. It is easier to take an example, and stick to the conclusion from that alone.

There is no doubt that each succeeding traveller through the States will be favoured his half-hundred times with the characteristic example which was urged on my notice.

26. *Accent.*

Among the minor reasons which might influence an Englishman in preferring Canada to the United States for his new home may be mentioned the freedom of the Canadian, generally speaking, from the peculiar accent, or rather intonation of sentence, peculiar to the Americans, and especially characteristic of the true-born Yankee. This accent is often quaint and amusing, and gives peculiar pungency to the delicious Yankee yarn; and on the lips of a Boston lady it is extremely fascinating. I think, however, that most Englishmen would prefer that their children spoke without it.

27. *The Far West.*

'The region from Lake Superior to Lake Winnipeg is of the primitive or crystalline formation. In its general aspect it is a hilly and broken country, intersected by rapid rivers and wide-spread lakes. . . . Dense forests cover the whole of the region, and the most valuable kinds of woods are seen in various places and in considerable quantities.'

The Red River and the West—'an undeviating flat spreads out everywhere, vast prairies open up where the eye seeks in vain for some prominent point to rest upon, and the rivers, richly bordered with trees, flow with a sluggish course through the great alluvial plain.'—*Report of Mr. S. J. Dawson*, 1859.

28. *The Fertile Belt.*

What sort of crops grow?—Oats, barley, and wheat, chiefly, but all sorts of vegetables.

Did the wheat ripen?—In ninety days from the sowing.

It ripened very perfectly?—It was the finest wheat I ever saw.

Was the soil fertile?—Along the immediate banks of the rivers, and extending for perhaps the breadth of two miles, no finer soil could be seen, with a limestone formation.

Is it geologically limestone?—All.

And wherever lime is, there is fertile land, is not there?—I think that is the consequence.

Do you know how far the limestone extends, looking at that map?—I have ascertained from servants of the Hudson's Bay Company that it extends as a base of the whole prairie land to the Rocky Mountains.

So that, in fact, that part of the territory is fit for agriculture?—Quite so.

And would make a good colony?—It might maintain millions.—*Col. Crofton's Evidence before a Committee of the House of Commons appointed to investigate the claims of the Hudson's Bay Company.*

29. *Native Skill of the Half-Breeds.*

The half-breeds of the Red River country have obtained a high reputation for their faculties of observation. Bishop Taché, for instance, in his work on the North-West, says: 'A glance suffices to enable them afterwards to recognise all the horses of a large herd which do not belong to them, and after a considerable lapse of time they can tell the difference between one horse of the herd and another which they may or may not have seen at the same time.'

An instance was given me in Red River of one of these half-breeds, a herdsman, who, the morning after a herd of 200 cattle had been brought, informed his master that he missed two animals, which he particularly described. Upon counting the cattle it proved that two were gone. The herdsman received authority to pay a trifling sum to any person who should succeed in finding the animals. By a singular coincidence they were brought in next day by a cousin of the half-breed who had described them so carefully.

30. *Indian Names.*

The Indians are forced to live indolently, if it were only in order to find sufficient time to repeat each other's names. Here are the ordinary titles of some chiefs in the north of Lakes Huron and Superior:

Pameguonaishueng, by the river Maganatiwang; Ketchiposkissigun, near Lake Nessinassung; Shawanakeshick, at Wanabitesebe; Nebenaigoching, near Wanabekinegunning.

Of course all these words are expressive. Here is an example from the Sioux language of the way in which these long words are constructed: A saw-mill is thus called Chan-bassen-dassen-dassen-bassen-da-madah-tepee; i.e. a log cutting-up, cutting-down, cutting-down, cutting-up, plank, out-there house. I give this example, on the authority of an Indian scout, I confess, with some dubiousness.

31. *The Fisheries.*

The Canadian Fisheries are protected along 900 miles of coast.

The hump-backed whale is harpooned in large numbers in the Gulf of St. Lawrence. It frequently measures from fifty to sixty feet long, and yields from 300 to 2,000 gallons of oil. In 1861 the produce of this fishery was 33,600 gallons of oil, value $17,680.

Seals were captured in the Gulf of St. Lawrence alone to the number of 26,591, in the year 1862; and yielded 208,439 gallons of oil, value $120,463.

Cod weigh from five to 100 lbs. They are voracious, and take any bait. The female spawns several million eggs. Vast as are the quantities of fish taken from the Newfoundland Banks, the supply is likely to answer the demand in perpetuity.

The total yearly produce of the cod fishery is estimated at one and a half millions of tons of fresh fish. Half is thrown away as refuse, but would yield 150,000 tons of manure as good as guano.

'The Bankers' range from thirty to 100 tons, with crews of from eight to thirty men. 300 to 400 lbs. of fish is a good day's average for each man. The cod are usually taken with a hempen line strung with hooks thirty fathoms long, let down into the submerged banks. Sometimes, however, the 'seine' is used, and as many as 5,000 may be taken at a single haul.

The summer fishing is from April to August. Fish then caught are exposed to the air and sun. These are the 'dried cod' of commerce.

The autumn fishing, during September and October, yields better fish. These are salted and barrelled as the 'pickled cod.'

In 1862 the oil from this fishery was estimated at 100,000 gallons. The cod are sometimes so abundant in Moisie Bay that a dry Government Report is betrayed into the statement that one 'could walk upon them over the waters of the bay on snow shoes.'

Herring in 1861 was taken to the amount of 48,000 barrels, at $1.50 = $72,000, in the spring fishery; with the addition of 5,000 barrels, at $3 = $15,000, as the yield of the autumn fishery.

The exports of mackerel for the year 1865 are said to have amounted to a million dollars.

Salmon are caught annually to the value of $30,000. Nova Scotia boasts that she possesses finer salmon streams than any country in the world, with the one exception of Scotland.

The yield of the fisheries of the north and south shores of the St. Lawrence, from Quebec to the Baie des Chaleurs, amounted in 1867 to $1,070,622.

The yield of the lakes and rivers of Ontario came to $187,865 in the same year (in 1868 the figures increased to $198,082).

New Brunswick exports in products of the sea $300,000 a year.

Nova Scotia, $3,000,000 a year.

These figures amount to four and a half millions of dollars, or a million sterling, a year, and do not include all the North American fisheries.

32. New Brunswick.

'A few years ago the country round the Bay of Chaleurs was considered unfit for raising wheat; experience has proved this unfounded, and it now produces all the kinds of grain raised in Eastern Canada. The climate does not appear colder than in the district of Quebec. Fogs are little known. Showers of snow fall about the end of October; winter generally sets in in the month of November, but fine weather often continues to the end of the month. The average height of the snow is four to five feet when deepest; it disappears about the beginning of May, and the ground is fit for sowing a few days afterwards.

' Owing to the direction of the Baie des Chaleurs and River Restigouche, the winds are either westerly or from the east; strong gales are of rare occurrence.

' The well-cultivated grounds in the neighbourhood of Dalhousie yield, of wheat, thirty to thirty-two bushels per acre; peas, about the same; oats, forty to forty-eight; barley, forty-five to sixty; potatoes, three to four hundred; carrots, two hundred and seventy to three hundred bushels per acre; hay, two to four tons per acre. The weight of grain exhibited at the agricultural shows in the district has been as follows: spring wheat, per Winchester bushel, sixty-four to sixty-seven pounds; fall ditto, sixty-six; Siberian wheat, sixty-four to sixty-five; oats, forty-two to forty-eight and a half; barley, fifty-four to fifty-six; field peas, sixty-six to sixty-seven pounds.

'On new land, not cleared of stumps, the yield of wheat has been thirty to one; fifteen to twenty to one is not unusual.'—*Report to the Hon. the Commissioner of Crown Lands, by A. W. Sims, Nov. 1848, inserted in Blue Book on the Intercolonial Railway,* 1870.

33. *Average Crops.*

	Average produce per Imperial Acre.	
	State of New York.	New Brunswick.
Wheat	14 bushels	20 bushels
Barley	16 ,,	29 ,,
Oats	26 ,,	34 ,,
Rye	9½ ,,	20½ ,,
Buckwheat	14 ,,	33¾ ,,
Indian Corn	25 ,,	41¾ ,,
Potatoes	90 ,,	226 ,,
Turnips	88 ,,	460 ,,
Hay	— ,,	1¾ tons.

'The superior productiveness of the soils of New Brunswick, as is represented in the second of the above columns, is very striking. The irresistible conclusion to be drawn from it appears to be, that looking only to what the soils under existing circumstances and methods of culture are said to produce, the Province of New Brunswick is greatly superior as a farming country to the State of New York.'—*Government Report on New Brunswick,* 1870.

34. *The Remaining Provinces.*

The terms are already arranged, subject to formal authorisation, for the admittance of British Columbia and Vancouver's Island into the Confederation. It is expected that Newfoundland and Prince Edward Island will follow.

35. *Prince Edward Island.*

This Island is admirably situated for fishing, and possesses excellent harbourage. 'Its coasts are so much indented by bays that no part of the Island is more than ten miles from salt water.' It has an excellent soil, and a climate more moderate than that of Quebec. It is some 140 miles long, with an irregular breadth reaching to thirty-four miles at the widest part. The area is 2,100 square miles; the population perhaps 100,000.

A considerable proportion of the people are of French origin, the descendants of the men who were expelled from lovely Acadie, now Nova Scotia, on September 10, 1755. The anniversary of the sorrowful day is still kept by them.

36. *Newfoundland.*

Its area is estimated at 42,000 square miles; the population at 150,000 souls. In the year 1867 its exports, consisting principally of the products of the cod and seal fisheries, amounted to five million dollars. Its imports, of breadstuffs and animal food chiefly, came to five and a half million dollars.

37. *Labrador.*

This coast was discovered A.D. 986 by Northmen, who called it 'Helluland it Makla,' the Great Slate Land, from its stratified rocks. It was re-discovered in 1501 by Corte Real, and misnamed by him 'Terra Labrador,' the Labourer's Land, or land capable of cultivation, from the growth of trees which he saw. It consists of a high table-land, with mountains rising to 3,000 and 4,000 feet. It possesses dense forests of spruce, fir, and beech. Its fisheries are of great value. It is estimated that a million seals are killed annually by Esquimaux and other fishers.

38. *British Columbia.*

British Columbia contains 280,000 square miles, a territory greater than the whole of the States of the North German Confederation, with the South German States counted in.

Its harbours on the Pacific are destined probably to receive a large proportion of the Japan and China transit trade with Europe, on the construction of the Canada Pacific railway.

At present the imports are but some five million dollars; the exports about the same, principally of gold. The population is estimated at 25,000 whites and Chinese and 35,000 Indians.

The country possesses minerals of all kinds. It has great and valuable forests. Its fisheries are of importance. It is well adapted for stock-raising.

39. *Vancouver's Island.*

'The serenity of the climate, the innumerable pleasing landscapes, and the abundant fertility that unassisted nature puts forth, require only to be enriched by the industry of man, with villages, cottages, mansions, and other buildings, to render it the most lovely country that can be imagined; whilst the labours of the inhabitants would be amply rewarded in the bounties which nature seems ready to bestow on cultivation.'—*Capt. Vancouver.*

40. *The Direct China Route.*

'Victoria is but 6,053 miles from Hong-Kong, or about twenty-one days' sailing; and if a roadway were constructed from Halifax to some point in British Columbia, the whole distance from Southampton would be accomplished in thirty-six days—from fifteen to twenty days less than by the overland route *via* Suez. . . .

'Millions of money and hundreds of lives have been lost in the search for a North-West passage by sea. Discovered at last, it has proved worthless. The North-West passage by land is the real highway to the Pacific.'—*Milton and Cheadle.*

41. *Lines of Traffic.*

'An air line from St. Louis to Liverpool passes northward of the city of Ottawa. An air line from New Orleans to Liverpool passes through the Straits of Belle Isle. . . .

'A railway from Montreal to the Pacific might not exceed about 2,500 miles, and Fort Garry is about midway on the route. . . .

'The lands granted to railway companies in the United States amount to 232,000 square miles or 154,000,000 acres (written June, 1869). . . .

'We have by a long way the best engineering route for a railway across the continent, the shortest line for through traffic, and the greatest amount of arable land for local traffic. The through traffic would be from the Pacific coast, China, and Japan. The foreign commerce of China is worth $500,000,000 annually (100,000,000*l.* sterling), and is in British hands.'—*From Letters by Thomas C. Keefer, Esq., Engineer, Ottawa.*

42. *Railway Enterprise.*

In the year 1869 I find that nearly 3,000 miles of railroad were open; and railway enterprise has not stopped since then. With a view to the more rapid opening up and development of a new country, wooden railways are being laid down in the province of Quebec; and in the province of Ontario railroads of a three-feet-six-inches gauge, at a cost of but 5,000*l.* a mile, similar to lines laid in Norway and Queensland.

43. *Commercial Inter-Communication.*

'Toronto is as near Liverpool, viâ St. Lawrence and the Straits of Belle Isle, as New York is by the ordinary sea-route. If large and commodious steamers could come down through our improved canals with western produce, carrying equal to 7,000 barrels of flour, and these meet ocean-vessels at Montreal or Quebec, it may fairly be expected that both freight and passengers would be attracted to a route which, by means of but a single trans-shipment, would convey them from any foreign port to the cities of the west. . . .

'Freights by the St. Lawrence can be despatched as early and as late in the season, by the route of the St. Lawrence, as can be done by the water communication of the United States.

'Montreal is nearer Liverpool by about 200 miles by a direct navigable line than New York is by the sea-route.'—*Letters by the Hon. John Young, M.P.P. Montreal.*

44. *The Port for England.*

Halifax is 550 miles nearer Liverpool than is New York, 357 miles nearer than Boston, 373 nearer than Quebec, and 316 nearer than Portland.—*Blue Book on Inter-Colonial Railway.*

45. *Canadian Ocean-Steamers.*

The Allan line started in 1856 with 4 vessels, 6,536 tons. By 1868 the number of vessels had increased to 23, and the tonnage to 96,887. Quebec and Montreal are the summer ports; Portland the winter one.

No more safe, speedy, and commodious vessels cross the Atlantic.

46. *Le Canada.*

The French muse has not been dumb in the old Quebec province. Here are two stanzas written in 1859 by one of the many French Canadian poets, M. Cremazie, interesting for its expression of the sentiment of nationality slowly growing up among the people :

> Salut, ô ciel de ma patrie !
> Salut, ô noble St.-Laurent !
> Ton nom dans mon âme attendrie
> Répand un parfum enivrant.
>
> Ah ! puisse cette union sainte,
> Qui fit nos ancêtres si grands,
> Ne recevoir jamais d'attente
> Par les crimes de tes enfants.

> Et si jamais pour te défendre
> Suivait le grand jour du combat,
> Comme autrefois qu'ils sachent prendre
> Le glaive vainqueur du soldat.

47. *Consolation.*

When Canada was lost to France it was said in Paris, 'Après tout, que nous font quelques arpents de neige en Amérique?'

Do we undervalue Canada in England from an impression that we cannot retain the connexion, and that it is philosophic to make light of a prospective loss?

48. *Removal of our Troops.*

' The feeling in Canada respecting the removal of the national troops may be easily misunderstood. It is not that the people expect or desire that England should bear the burden of the defence of the colony. But they prize highly the moral support which the presence of our troops affords. It is the pledge of protection of a great empire. The departure of our regiments one by one seems to threaten the final withdrawal of English power and influence from this continent. For a long time yet England ought to retain some of her troops here, unless indeed we have resolved to shirk the responsibility imposed upon us by our fame and our history, and abandon our old national policy. "There are many things which England can make better than we can, better than the rest of the world," a Canadian officer lately said to me. "Soldiers, for one example. We cannot make troops with the British discipline, and order, and esprit de corps. You must try to teach us the secret of this manufacture. Your troops ought to remain here as a pattern to ours. And especially we should need the example of their steadiness and order in actual war. The regulars would give confidence to the volunteers, and show us how fighting ought to be done.'"—*From an Article in Fraser's Magazine for November* 1870 *by the Author.*

49. *Counter-Alabama Claims.*

Canada considers that she suffered a very large direct loss, and an enormous indirect loss, through the two Fenian raids made on her territory by citizens of the United States. She considers that a claim for compensation can be preferred against the Government of the Republic with at least an equal show of justice with the more celebrated Alabama claims made against England.

50. *Bill of Rights.*

Drawn up by the Red River Convention during the Rebel Interregnum.

1. That the people have the right to elect their own Legislature.

2. That the Legislature have the power to pass

all laws local to the Territory over the veto of the Excutive by a two-thirds vote.

3. That no act of the Dominion Parliament (local to the Territory) be binding on the people until sanctioned by the Legislature of the Territory.

4. That all Sheriffs, Magistrates, Constables, School Commissioners, &c., be elected by the people.

5. A free homestead and pre-emption land-law.

6. That a portion of the public lands be appropriated to the benefit of schools, the building of bridges, roads, and public buildings.

7. That it be guaranteed to connect Winnipeg by rail with the nearest line of railroad, within a term of five years; the land grant to be subject to the Local Legislature.

8. That, for the term of four years, all military, civil, and municipal expenses be paid out of the Dominion funds.

9. That the military be composed of the inhabitants now existing in the Territory.

10. That the English and French languages be common in the Legislature and Courts, and that all public documents and acts of the Legislature be published in both languages.

11. That the Judge of the Supreme Court speak the English and French languages.

12. That treaties be concluded and ratified between the Dominion Government and the several

tribes of Indians in the Territory, to insure peace on the frontier.

13. That we have a fair and full representation in the Canadian Parliament.

14. That all privileges, customs, and usages existing at the time of the transfer be respected.

51. *The Fishery Treaty.*

Article 1 of Convention between His Britannic Majesty and the United States of America, signed at London, October 20, 1818:

Whereas, differences have arisen respecting the liberty claimed by the United States, for the inhabitants thereof to take, dry, and cure fish on certain coasts, bays, harbours, and creeks of His Britannic Majesty's dominions in America, it is agreed between the High Contracting Parties that the inhabitants of the said United States shall have, for ever, in common with the subjects of His Britannic Majesty, the liberty to take fish of every kind on that part of the southern coast of Newfoundland which extends from Cape Ray to the Rameau Islands, on the western and northern coast of Newfoundland from the said Cape Ray to the Quirpon Islands, on the shores of the Magdalen Islands, and also on the coasts, bays, harbours, and creeks from Mount Joly, on the southern coast of Labrador, to and through the Straits of Belle Isle, and thence northwardly indefinitely along the coast, without prejudice, however, to any of the exclusive rights of the Hudson's Bay Company. And that the American fishermen shall also have liberty, for ever, to dry and cure fish in any of the unsettled bays, harbours, and creeks of the southern part of the coast of Newfoundland here above described, and of the coast of Labrador; but so soon as the same, or any portion thereof, shall be settled, it shall not be lawful for the said fishermen to dry or cure fish at such portion so settled without previous agreement for such purpose with the inhabitants, proprietors, or possessors of the ground. And the United States hereby renounce, for ever, any liberty heretofore enjoyed or claimed by the inhabitants thereof, to take, dry, or cure fish on or within three marine miles of any of the coasts, bays, creeks, or harbours of His Britannic Majesty's dominions in America not included within the above-mentioned limits; provided, however, that the American fishermen shall be admitted to enter such bays or harbours for the purpose of shelter and of repairing damages therein, of purchasing wood, and of obtaining water, and for no other purpose whatever. But they shall be under such restrictions as may be necessary to prevent their taking, drying, or curing fish therein, or in any other manner whatever abusing the privileges hereby reserved to them.

INDEX

INDEX.

ABE

ABERCROMBIE, Fort, 127. Farmsteads round, 128, 132. Inspection of, 133
Abraham, plains of, 16. Battles of, 16, 17
Acadie (now Nova Scotia), expulsion of the French from, 301
Accent of the Canadians, 293. Compared with the intonation peculiar to the Americans, 293
Africa, Little, Negro settlement so called, 99, 101
Agriculture, importance of, to Canada, 70. Necessity for the best agricultural implements, 73, 77, 232. *See* Farming interest; Settlers
Agricultural exhibitions, 74–78
Ague, prevalence of, in some parts of the North-west territory, 186, 188
Alabama claims, losses of Canada by the Fenian raids as a counter-claim to the, 308
Alexandra Villa, log-houses of, 127
Algonquin Indians, their league with the French under Champlain, 2
Allan line of steamers, increase in the tonnage of the, 306. Their safety and rapidity, 306
Andrews, Governor, his Report to Congress on the British Provinces, 207

BEE

Animals of Canada, domestic, 57, 77. Wild, 57. Birds and small game, 57. An Indian's natural love for, 109
Ann, St., church of, 27. Miraculous cures performed at the, 28. Visit to, 30. Crutches suspended in the, 30
Ann, St., river, 30
Annexation of Canada to the United States, chances of, 239, 240
Apples of Canada, 5, 76
Archibald, Hon. Mr., appointed Lieutenant-Governor of Manitobah, 172
Assiniboine river, confluence of the, with the Red River, 143, 180. English settlers on the, 148. Its course, 180
Athabasca, Lake, its height above the sea, 177, 193. Its beauty, 193
Athabasca river, woodland and fertile prairie land of the valley of the, 193. Its junction with the Peace River, 193
Axe, a Canadian, 61. Mode of using it, 61

BASS, 58
Bays and inlets of Canada, 9
'Bee,' the, in the backwoods, 62

316   INDEX.

BEL

Belle Ewart, town of, 49
Bellevue, Chateau, visit to, 26
Bill of rights drawn up by the Red River Convention, 308
Birds, wild, 57
Bitumen in the valley of the Peace River, 193
Bracebridge, town of, 55. Visit to, 55. Its romantic situation, 55. Stores and buildings at, 56
Brantford, Ontario, agricultural settlement of the Six Nation Indians at, 109
Breton, Cape, area of, including Nova Scotia, 207
Brick-making, opening for, at Red River, 150
Brixton, Negroes of the town of, 100
Brockville, Ontarian town of, compared with that of the American town of Morristown, 292, 293
Bruce, John, first president of the Red River Provisional Government, his proclamation to Governor McDougall, 152. Supplanted, and at work as a journeyman carpenter, 163
Brunet, the Abbé, visit to, 21
Brunswick, New, incorporated with the Dominion, 10. Advantages of, 208. Area of, 208. Beauty and fertility of the country, 208. Extent of land under cultivation, 209. Importance of the fisheries of, 209. Railway across, 217. Annual exports of, in produce of the sea, 298. Wheat grown round the Bay of Chaleurs, 299. Yield of crops in the neighbourhood of Dalhousie, 299. Weight of grain per bushel, 299. Average crops compared with those of the state of New York, 300
Buffalo, herds of wild, on the prairie lands of the North-west, 185

CAN

By, Colonel; his military canal, 45
Bytown, now Ottawa, 45

CACOUNA, fashion and gaiety of, 34
Canada, name of, 1, 276. Settlement of by Europeans, 1. The English occupation, 1. Discovery and settlement of by the French, 3. End of the French rule, 3. Loyalty of the people of, 3, 4. Fertility of the country, 5. Its produce, 5. Development of the Canadian race of people, 5. Increase in their material prosperity, 6. Quantity of land under cultivation, 6. Increase of the population, 7. Its future prosperity, and importance of its resources, 7. Advantages of the route across Canada between Europe and Asia, 8. Importance of the Dominion to the mother country, 9. Its active militia force and trained reserve, 9. Its seamen, fisheries, and marine, 9. Extent of the country, 10. Its future greatness, 11. Advantages of the union of Upper and Lower Canada, 22. Lumber and lumber-trade of, 37. The free-grant lands, 49. The steps of progress of the settler in Canada, 66. The farming interest, 70. Canada as an agricultural country compared with the United States, 80, 81. Increase of the population, 81. Fertility of the Canadian soil, 84. The Falls of Niagara, 85. Oil and salt springs, 93. Little Africa and the Negroes in Canada, 99–104. The Indians, 105. The Prairies, 123. The Red River revolt, 145. The great North-west, 174. Line of the

CAN

Dominion Pacific Railroad, 197. The air-line to China, 199. Growth of another and larger England, 199. Canada destined to be one of the great maritime provinces of the world, 206. Its fisheries, 209, 296. Effect of the abrogation of the Reciprocity Treaty, 214. Intercontinental communication, 217. Statistics of immigration, 220. And of food and clothing, 224–228. Advantages of the climate, 236, 237. The political question, 239. The various courses of policy indicated, and the chances of their adoption, 239–250. Distinct types of national character in Canada and the United States, 245. The only present inducement to Canada to enter the United States, 248. The wisest policy of England as to its future, 252, 253. Its defences, 254. Its increase in strength, confidence, and pride of nationality, 261. Complete failure of the American invasion of Canada in 1812-14, 262. Unusual advantages of Canada in the conduct of a war, 264. Suitability of the country for defence, 266. Its value to England in the event of war with the States, 267. Ignorance of Canada in England, 275. Its climate, 277–279. Its population to the square mile compared with that of other countries, 280. Law respecting free grant lands, 280. Public debt of Canada, 281. The Queen city of the Dominion, Toronto, 283. The newspaper press of the Dominion, 288. Art in Canada, 288. The Clergy Reserve Act in Upper Canada, 289. One of the chief causes of the rebellion

CHA

in 1837, 289. Towns of Canada compared with those of the United States, 292. The fertility of the Far West and Red River, 293, 294. Admittance of the remaining provinces into the Dominion, 301. The through traffic to China, 302. Railway enterprise, 304. Commercial inter-communication of England and the Dominion, 305. Remark in Paris on the loss of Canada, 307. The feeling in Canada respecting the removal of British troops, 307. The Fishery Treaty of 1818 quoted, 310

Canada Pacific Railway, Indian country through which it will pass, 119, 199, 304

Carling, Hon. John, Commissioner of Agriculture for Ontario, his account of the progress of Canada, 81. His statistics of immigration, 222, 223

Carling, Port, school at, 67

Cart, a springless, 27

Cartier, Jacques, his discovery of Canada, 3

Catholics, Roman, loyalty of their Church in Canada, 264

Cattle of the settlers, 57

Caughnawauga, settlement of Iroquois Indians at, 108

Cereals of Canada, 75. Yield of grain in various places, 79

Champlain, Samuel de, his exploration of Canada, 2. His league with the Hurons and Algonquins, when he puts an army to flight, 2. Establishes the first French colonies, 3

Charles, St., river, beauty of the, 12. Settlement of Huron Indians on the, 108

Chateauquay, battle of, 262

Chateau Richet, visit to the French

CHA

village of, 24. Church and school of, 25. Falls of La Puce at, 25

Chatham, town of, agricultural exhibition at, 78. Negro settlement at, 100, 101

Chaudière, Falls of the, 17

Chauveau, Hon. Mr., minister of instruction for the province of Quebec, 18. His Indian name, 19

Chicago, city of, 121. Houses and public buildings of, 121. Go-a-headiveness of the people of, 122. Sights of the city, 122. Population of, 122. Meaning of the name of, 123

China, the through traffic from England to, 199, 304. Annual value of the foreign commerce of, 304

Clergy reserves, Act of 1823 relating to, 289. Acts of 1827-36 respecting them, 289. Act of 1840, 289, 290. Final settlement of the question, 290. Endowed rectories of Lord Seaton, 290

Climate, melioration of the, 4, 279. Of North-western British America, 177. Of the Dominion generally and its advantages, 236–238. Its effect on the national character of the Canadians, 245, 247. And on the character of the Americans, 247. Its advantages in the defence of Canada, 255, 265. Realities of the Canadian climate, 277

Clothing, cost of, in Canada, 227

Cloud, St., station, on the St. Paul and Pacific Railway, 124

Coal, vast beds of, on the banks of the Saskatchewan river, 179. In the valley of the Saskatchewan, 191. And at Peace River, 193. The coal-beds on the proposed line and at the termini of the Dominion

DEF

Pacific Railroad, 200. The lignite coal of the eastern base of the Rocky Mountains, 200. The coal-fields of the maritime provinces of Canada, 206. Of immense extent in Nova Scotia, 208. Of New Brunswick, 209

Cod fishery of the Dominion, 209. On the banks of Newfoundland, 297. Total yearly produce, 297. The 'Bankers' and their takes, 297. Periods for fishing, 297. The dried and pickled cod, 297. Cod oil, 298. Abundance of the supply, 298

Colonial possessions, apprehensions as to the result of the present English policy respecting, 252

Columbia, British, admittance of, into the Dominion, 301. Its area, 302. Its harbours, 302. Its probable future trade, 302. Its imports and exports, and population, 302, 303. Its forests and fisheries, 303. Its capabilities for stock-raising, 303

Confederation, a great Anglo-Saxon, proposed, 272, 273

Copper, mines of, discovered in Nova Scotia, 208

Couchiching, Lake, beauties of, 50. Meaning of the name, 50

Cows, the settler's, 65

Cremazie, M., his French poem on Canada, 306

'Cribs' of lumber, 41

DALHOUSIE, yield of crops in the neighbourhood of, 299

Defences of Canada, concern respecting the, 254. Conceptions and misapprehensions in England regarding the facts, 254. The Canadians a warlike people, 255.

DEN

The militia and numbers of the militia reserve, 256. Forces turned out in 1862 and in 1870, 256. Report of Colonel P. Robertson-Ross respecting the present condition of the militia, quoted, 257. Schools for military instruction of officers, 258, 259. Preparations for self-defence, 259, 260. Failure of the invasion of 1812-14, 262. Advantages of Canada in the conduct of a war, 264. Suitability of the country for defence, 266. Summing up of our considerations of Canadian defence, 267. Advantages of the country in the event of a war between England and the United States, 267

Dennis, Colonel, receives a commission authorising him to commence civil war in the Red River territory, 160. Issues proclamations, and disappears from the country, 162

Dresden, Negroes of the town of, 100

Droughts, occasional, of the North-west territory, 186

Ducks, wild, 57

EDUCATION in the backwoods, its difficulties, 67

Elk, 57

Emigrants. *See* Immigration

Encampment, an, on the prairie, 134-136

England, her policy respecting the future of Canada, 252, 253. The future of, and her colonies, considered, 270. Position occupied by her, 270, 271. Her ascendancy threatened, 270. Claims of Prussia, Russia, and the United States to power, 270. Future settlement

FAR

of these rivalries, 271. Advantages of England over all her rivals, 272. Proposal for a great Anglo-Saxon Confederation, 272, 273. And for an imperial scheme of emigration, 274. Ignorance in England respecting Canada, 275

Exports of Canada in 1851, 1861, and 1869, 6

FARMING interest in Canada, 70. Increase in the produce in ten years, 70, 71. And in the quantity of land brought under cultivation, 71. Extent of the farms generally, 72. Scientific farming little in use, 72. Importance of labour-saving machines, 73. Improved methods of draining, 74. Agricultural fairs, 74, 75. The farmers attending them, 75. Produce exhibited at them, 75, 76. Live stock shown, 77. Stock farms, 79, 185, 232. Peculiarities of the farmers of Red River, 49. Advantages of the wild prairie lands of the North-west over all the countries in the world, 184, 185. Wages paid to farm servants and labourers, 224. Advantages of the Dominion to farmers with small capital, 229. Value of land, 229, 230. Advice to the immigrant farmer, 230-232. Stumps of trees, 230. Snake-fences, 231. Agricultural implements, 232. Advantages of the winter to the farmer, 236. The farmers considered as material for an army, 265. Period in which grain ripens in the fertile belt, 294. Yield of the crops in the neighbourhood of Dalhousie, 299, 300. Crops of New York

FEN

State compared with those of New Brunswick, 300

Fenian party, aim of the, in the Red River revolt, 156. No sympathy shown by the Irish in Canada for Fenianism, 263. Losses suffered by Canada in the Fenian raids as a counter-claim to the Alabama claims, 308

Fever, prevalence of, in some districts of Red River, 186, 188

Fires, prairie, 131, 132

Fish of the lakes and streams, 58

Fisheries of Behring's Straits, 206. Of the maritime provinces of the Dominion, 207. Of New Brunswick, 209. Of Newfoundland, the Gulf of St. Lawrence, and Bay of Fundy, 209. Statistics of the fisheries, 209. Minister for the regulation of the fisheries of the Dominion, 210. Jealousies and disagreements to which the fisheries have given rise, 210. Action of the Washington Government, and termination of the treaty in 1864, 211. Liberal and conciliatory policy of the Dominion, 211. Resumption of the rights of the Dominion government, 211. Reasons for this resumption, 211. Terms of the Convention of 1818, limiting the fishing rights of the United States, 212, 213. Seizures of vessels of the United States, 213. Report of the Minister of Marine of the Dominion respecting the fisheries, 215. Extent of coast along which the fisheries are protected, 296. Whales and seals, 296, 297. Cod, 297. Herring and salmon, 298. Value of the yield in the lakes, rivers, and at sea, 298. Fisheries of Labrador, 302. And of British

GAR

Columbia, 303. The Fishery Treaty of 1818, quoted, 310

Flowers and foliage plants of Canada, 77

Food, cost of, in the Dominion, 226–228

Forests, magnificent colours of the, in the sunlight, 278, 279

Free-grant district, tour of inspection in the, 49. Land disposed of in two months at the, 56. Proportion of land capable of cultivation in the district, 57. Progress of the settlers, 60–65. Regulations of the government grant, 68. Extent of the free-grant lands, 68, 69

French in Canada, settlement of the, 1, 3. Ally themselves with the Hurons and Algonquins against their foes, 2. Their number in the country, 3. Their discoveries, 3. End of the period of French rule, 3. Loyalty of the people to England, 3, 4. Cost of living in the French province, 227. Character and distinctness of type of the people, 245. Their loyalty in the war of 1812–14, 262. And of those of the present day, 263. Sentiment of nationality growing among them, 306

Frog Point, 137

Fruits of Canada, 5, 76

Fundy, Bay of, importance of the fisheries of the, 209

GAME, small, 57

Garry, Fort, distant view of, 143. The principal station of the Hudson Bay Company, 147. Seized by the Red River rebel half-breeds, 155. End of the revolt, 320

Gaspé, Jacques Cartier's cross at, 3
Georgian Bay, settlers at, 60
Georgetown, the United States Northern Pacific Railroad at, 137
Gibraltar, in Canada, precautions against Fenians at, 52. Mr. Cuthbert and his shanty at, 53
Goderich, oil and brine springs of the town of, 97
Goose River, junction of the, with Red River, 137
Gold dust in the Peace River, 194. In the country between Lake Superior and Red River, 196
Gophir, mole-hill mountains of the, in the prairies, 186
Grain, crops of, in North-western British America, 177, 182, 183. Average weight of the yield, 184. The grain trade of Hamilton city, 285. Period in which it ripens in the fertile belt, 294. *See* Farming interest; Wheat
Grapes of Canada for dessert, 76. For wine, 77
Great Northern Railway, farmsteads and villages on both sides of the, 49. Future of the line, 50
Greely, visit to the township of, 233
Grand Forks, the river at, 137
Grasshoppers, or locusts, periodical plague of, in the North-west territory, 186, 187. Their probable extinction, 187
Gravenhurst, the door of the free-grant district, 50, 51

'HABITANS,' or French Canadians, 30. Houses of the, 30, 31. Their industry and frugality, 32. Their large families, 33. Sir George Cartier's description of a French Canadian, 36. Their style of farming, 73
Ha-ha Bay, 35
Half-breeds, native skill of the, 295, 296
Halifax, in Nova Scotia, harbour of, 208. School for military instruction at, 259. The nearest port to England in North America, 306
Hamilton city, cost of living in, 227. And of house rent in, 228. Its rapid increase in prosperity and population, 285. Immigration into in 1869-70, 285. Its manufactures, 285. Its grain trade, 285. Railways projected and in progress at, 286. The freight passing inwards, 286
Harbours of Nova Scotia, 208
Hennepin, Father, his impression respecting the Falls of Niagara, 88, 90
Herring of Canada, 58. Herring fishery of the Dominion, 209, 298
Herring, Rev. A. Styleman, his plan for assisting emigration, 233, 234
Hochelaga, a former name of Montreal, 282
House-rent in the Dominion, 226, 228
Hudson Bay Company, territory of the, ceded to the Dominion, 10. The seat of government of the, 147. Battle of Red River, and death of its governor, 147. Amalgamation of the Company with the Northwest Company, 147. Contempt into which its government had fallen at the time of the Red River revolt, 154. Its neglect to secure Fort Garry against the insurgents, 161. Its policy respecting the North-west territory, 174
Huron Indians, league of, with the French under Champlain, 2. Settlement of, at La Jeune Lorette, 18,

IMM

107. Professor Wilson's remarks respecting them, 108. Their long names, 296

IMMIGRATION into Canada, increase of, 69, 220. Statistics for 1868, 221-223. The particular kinds of emigrants most in demand, 223. Method of distribution of immigrants, 223. Rate of wages in the Dominion, 224, 225. Advantages to the immigrants, 228, 229. Suggestions to intending settlers, 232. Mr. A. Styleman Herring's plan for assisting emigration, 233, 234. Miss Rye's plan, 235. Advantages to emigrants, 235. Proposal for an imperial scheme of emigration from Great Britain to the colonies, 274

Indian summer of Canada, 278

Indians, origin of the name, as applied to the Red Men, 2. How treated by the first European settlers, 2. Improvement in their condition, 2. The native tribes not fated to immediate extinction, 105, 115. Results of British policy of conciliation and protection, 106, 117. Gradual civilisation of the tribes, 107. Their village of La Jeune Lorette, 107. Caughnawauga Indians, 108. Indian dexterity, 109. An agricultural settlement at Brantford, 109. Employment best suited for them, 110. Influence of the various religious missions on the native tribes, 110. Ojibways at Sarnia, 111. Indian love for colours and personal ornament, 111, 112. Their mixture with the white races, 112. Methodist and Episcopal chapels, 112. An Ojib-

LAB

way church, 113. Condition of the red men of Canada, 114. Total Indian population of Canada in 1868, 115, 116. Their employments, 116. End of the wars of the whites with them, 117. Proofs of their attachment to British rule, 118, 119. Their long names, 296.

Inns in the backwoods, 45

Inundations, occasional, of rivers in the North-west territory, 186, 188

Iron ore in the valley of the Saskatchewan, 191. And in the north, 193. In the valley of the Peace River, 193

JOHN'S, ST., fisheries of the harbour of, 209. School for military instruction at,

Joseph, St., Lake, beauty of, 56

Jury, trial by, optional in civil cases in Canada, 281

KAMINISTIQUIA River, part of the old canoe route to Red River, 195

Kanata, the Indian name of Canada, meaning of the name, 1

Kashaboiwe, Lake, part of the old canoe route to Red River, 195

Kildonan army, the, in the Red River insurrection, 165. Their demonstration and dispersion, 165

Kingston, town of, 51. Defences of, 266

LABRADOR, discovery of, 302. Name of, given by the discoverers, 302. Re-discovery of, by Corte Real, 302. Meaning of the

LAC

name of Labrador, 302. Its forests and fisheries, 302. Its seal fishery, 302

'La Crosse,' the Canadian game of, 108. Dexterity of the Indians at, 108, 109

Lakes, ignorance in England respecting the, of Canada, 275

Land, extent of, under cultivation in 1851, 1861, and at the present time, 7, 71. Scientific methods of treating it, 73, 74. In Canada as compared with that of the United States, 81. Fertility of that of the valley of the Saskatchewan, 191

Laval University, at Quebec, 13. Origin of the name, 13. Visit to, 21

Laverdière, Rev. Mr., librarian of Laval University, 22. His yacht, 23

Lawrence, St., river, its width at Quebec and lower down, 12. A sail on the, 23. Disposition of the farms along the, 30. Climate of the banks of the, 33. Junction of the Saguenay with the, at Tadousac, 34

Lépine, Hon. Mr., his part in the Red River revolt, 163, 164

Lévis, De, his victory at the Plains of Abraham, 17

Léry, St., river, 17. Gold obtained near the source of the, 18

Lévy, Point St., masses of lumber at, 14

Little Lake, encampment on, 141

Locusts in the North-west territory. *See* Grasshoppers

London the Little, agricultural fair at, 74-78. Mineral oil at, 96. Preparation of it for the market, 96. Other manufactures of, 97. Characteristics of the city, 286. Its increasing wealth and population,

MAC

286. Its resemblance to or rivalry with the metropolis of England, 286, 287

Lorette, La Jeune, village of Huron Indians at, 108. Visit to it, 18. The cascades at, 19

Lumber, masses of, on the St. Lawrence, 14. The lumber trade of Canada, 37. Winter work, 37. Operations in felling a tree, 38. Floating rafts, 41. The saw-mills, 42. Principal seat of the lumber-trade, 43. Statistics of the trade, 47. Advantages of the winter to the lumberers, 236

Lumber-man, the, of Canada, 37. His shanty, 38. His food, 39. His way of life, 40. Lumber-men considered as material for an army, 265

Luna Island, lunar rainbows at, 89

Lawrence, Gulf of St., importance of the fisheries of, 209. The whale fishery of, 296. Quantity and value of whale oil, 297. Seals captured in, 297

McDONALD, Hon. Sandfield, at Gibraltar, 53

McDougall, Mr., notice served on, by the Red River Provisional Committee, 141, 153. The document, 154. Riel's proclamations, 154. Mr. McDougall's proclamation, 159, 160. His commission to Col. Dennis, 160

McKenzie River, formation of the, 193. Its great advantages, 194. Its future importance, 194

Mackerel rarely caught on the shores of the United States, 209. The mackerel fishery of the Dominion, 298. Exports of, 298

MAC

McTavish, Mr., Governor of the Hudson Bay Company, his indignities, 162. Leaves the country and dies, 162

Mail service, importance of the, between Europe and America, 217. Future improvements in the, 218

Maize, produce of, in Ontario, 79

Manan, island of Grand, fisheries of, 209

Manitobah, Lake, 181. Meaning of its name, 181

Manitobah, new province of, 141

Manure, how disposed of, by the farmers of Red River, 149

Marine, importance of the, of Canada, 9, 206, 264

Maritime provinces, hardihood, daring, and ability of the seafaring population of the, in case of a war with the United States, 264, 265

Market, want of a, in the North-west territory, 186

Métis, or half-breed, story of a, and a Sioux, 129

Militia and trained reserve of Canada, 9. The militia and militia reserve, 256. Number turned out in 1862 and 1870, 256

Mille Lacs, Lac des, part of the old canoe route to Red River, 193

Milton, Viscount, on the Pacific Dominion Railway quoted, 201, 202

Mineral riches of the valley of the Saskatchewan, 191. Of the northern parts of British North America, 193. And of the belt of country between Ontario and Red River, 195, 196. Wealth of the country north of Lake Superior, 198, 203. And of Nova Scotia, 208

Mole-hill mountains of the little gophir in the North-west prairies, 186

NEW

Montcalm, Marquis of, tablet to, at Quebec, 15

Montmorenci, Falls of, 20

Montreal, defences of, 266. Origin of the name of, 281. Its former names, 282. Population of, in 1800 and at present, 282. Its important situation, 282. Its buildings and public works, 282, 283. The Tubular Bridge and church of Nôtre Dame, 283

Moose, 57

Mosquitoes, plague of, in the North-west territory, 186, 187

Mules, zebra-marked, their patience and strength, 134

Murray Bay, old settlement of Scotchmen at, 34

Muskoka, Lake, meaning of the name, 52. Beauty of, 55

Muskoka River, 56

NAMES of towns, 50, 51. Indian long names, 296

Nationality, growth of a feeling of, in Canada, 244. Distinct types of national character in Canada and the United States, 245

Navy, commercial, of the Dominion, 206. Its tonnage, 206, 207. Its importance, offensive and defensive, 207

Negroes, settlement of, in Canada, 99-101. Their schools and scholars, 101. Men of superior intelligence among them, 103. Their farms, 103

New York, agricultural statistics of, compared with those of Canada, 84

Newfoundland, importance of the fisheries of, 209. The cod fishing on the Banks of, 297. Admittance of, into the Dominion, 301. Its area and population, 301. Its exports and imports, 301, 302

Newspaper press of the Dominion, 288

Niagara, Falls of, 85. View of, by moonlight, 86, 87. Calculations of the masses of water passing constantly, 88. Luna Island, 89. Stories of the dangers of, 89. Recession of the Falls, 91

Nipigon, Lake, its extent and beauty, 198. Its fitness for settlement, 198

North-west passage, the true, found, 205. The passage by sea, its discovery and worthlessness, 303, 304. But value of that by land, 304

North-west Company opposes the Hudson Bay Company, but finally amalgamates with it, 147, 148. The British American territory little known until recently, 174. Policy of the Hudson Bay Company respecting it, 174. Its value and importance, 175. The three great sections of the country, 176. Its width and extent, 176. Its climate and soil, 176, 177. Probable causes of the mildness of winter and of the heat of summer, 177. Water communication, 178-180. Advantages of the prairie lands for steam-farming, stock-breeding, and railway making, 184, 185. Disadvantages of, and objections to, the country, 186. Its future prosperity after the construction of the Pacific Dominion railway, 198

Nova Scotia incorporated with the Dominion, 10. The ancient Acadie, 207. Its area, including Cape Breton, 207. Its beauty and fertility, 207, 208. Its coal-fields, 208. Its abundance of harbours,

208. Railway across, 217. The fine salmon streams of, 298. Value of the fisheries of, 298. Expulsion of the French from Acadie, 301

O'DONOGHUE, Hon. W. B., represents the Fenian party in the Red River insurrection, 163. At the battle of Winnipeg, 165

Ogdensburgh, American city of, its progress compared with that of the Canadian town of Prescott, 292

Ojibways, settlement of, at the town of Sarnia, 111. An Ojibway church and divine service, 112

Oil, whale, in the Gulf of St. Lawrence, 297. Seal, 297. Cod, 298. The mineral oils of Canada, 93. Value and produce of the crude mineral oil, 96. Refining it, 96

Ontario, Lake, 283

Ontario, province of, its wheat, and excellence of the, 5. Increase of its produce in ten years, 70. Stock farms of, 79. Indian corn grown in, 79. Agricultural statistics of, compared with those of New York, 82, 83. Lord Sydenham's account of the province of, 279. Its busy and prosperous condition, 283. Price of building land in, 283. Its public and private buildings, 283. Its population, 284. The University Buildings, 284. The golden-haired women of, and their beauty, 284. Three-feet-six-inches gauge of railways in, 305. Cost of these lines, 305

Orchards of Canada, 5

Orillia, town of, 50

Orleans, Isle of, 12. Woods of the, 14

Ottawa, capital city of, 45. The

former Bytown, 45. Streets and buildings of, 46
Ottawa, river-valley of the, the principal seat of the lumber-trade, 43. The river, 43. Settlements on its banks, 43, 44. Its picturesqueness, 44

PACIFIC RAILROAD, United States Northern, course of the, 137, 197-205. *See* Railways
Palliser, Captain, his Report on the valley of the Saskatchewan quoted, 191
Parliament House at Quebec, 13. At Ottawa, 283
Parry's Sound, settlers at, 60
Partridges, 57
Paul, the Saulteaux Indian, 134, 135
Paul, M., chief of the Hurons, settled at Lorette, 18
Paul's, St., town of, 123. The St. Paul and Pacific railway, 124
Peace River, fertility of the valley of the, 193. Plaster quarries in the, 193. Gold in the, 194
Pears of Canada, 76
Peau River, fertility of the valley of the, 193
Pembina, Fort, 141. Mr. McDougall at, 141
People of Canada, 5, 6
Peterborough, North, townships of, open for settlement, 69
Petrolea, town of, 93. Mode of working the oil wells at, 93
Petroleum springs in the north, 193. In the valley of the Peace River, 193
Pigs, the settler's, 65. The breed of, in Canada, 77
Pithole, the petrolea district of, 93

Plumbago in the valley of the Peace River, 193
Pomme-de-Terre, city of, 127. The last sign of settlement at, 128
Population of Canada, 5, 6. In 1841, 1852, 1861, and in 1870, 7. Of the city of Quebec, 16. Of Toronto, 284. Of Hamilton, 285. Of London the Little, 286. Of Prince Edward Island, 301. Of Newfoundland, 301. Of British Columbia, 303
Potatoes of Canada, 75
Poultry, the settler's, 65
Prairies, the, journey over, 123-144. Swedish settlers on, 124. Shanty inns on the roadside, 125. A supper at one, 126, 135. Prairie fires, 131, 132. Sunset in, 132, 140. An encampment in, 134. A camp fire in, 135. A night in, 136. Sunrise in, 137. Thieves in, 138. A prairie adventure, 139. Weather in, 140. A celestial spectacle in, 141, 142. The prairies west of the Rocky Mountains, 146. Advantages of the wild prairie lands beyond all other countries in the world, 184, 185. Herds of wild buffalo on, 185. Pastures of, 185
Prescott, Canadian town of, its progress compared with that of the American city of Ogdensburgh, 292
Primogeniture, law of, abolished in Canada, 281
Prince Edward Island, admittance of, into the Dominion, 301. Its fisheries and harbours, 301. Its soil and climate, 301. Its area and population, 301. People of, 301
Puce, La, Falls of, 25

QUE

QUEBEC, city of, 12. River flowing at her feet, 12. Origin of the name, 12. Lines of the citadel, 13. Streets and public buildings, 13. Defences, 15, 266. Convent of the Ursulines, 15. Tablet to Montcalm, 15. Population, 16. Trade, 16. Nearness of the city to Liverpool, 16. Means of constructing docks, 16. Beauty of the environs, 16. The Falls of Montmorenci, 20. Local legislature of, 22. Picture attributed to Vandyke in the cathedral of, 288

Quebec, province of, townships of, open for settlement, 69. Stock farms of, 79. Broad liberties accorded to the French in common with our American colonies, 263. Loyalty of our French subjects, 263. Causes of defection from the Roman Catholic church in, 288. Wooden railways in, 305

Queenstown Heights, victory of, 262

RACES and the turf, love of the Canadians for, 291. Meetings in Ontario, 292

Railways, ease with which they can be laid down on the prairies of the North-west, 185. Future development of branch lines, 185. A practicable railway route to the Pacific, 197. The air-line to China, 199. Its importance to the English empire, 199. Favourable conditions of the Atlantic and Pacific termini and of the course of the line, 201. Value of the country traversed by it, 203. Imperial policy concerned in it, 203. Proposals for its execution without delay, 204. Reasons which de-

RED

mand its construction and ensure its success, 204. Importance of the inter-continental communication, 217. Air-line from Liverpool to St. Louis and to New Orleans, 304. Length of line from Montreal to the Pacific, 304. Lands granted to railway companies in the United States, 304. Railway enterprise in Canada, 304, 305. Wooden railways in Quebec, 305. The three-feet-six guage in Ontario, 305

Rainy Lake, communication through the, 180. Part of the old canoe route to Red River, 195

Rainy River, fertility and beauty of the banks of the, 180, 195, 196

Rebellion of 1837, one of the chief causes of the, 289

Reciprocity Treaty, object of the repeal of the, on the part of the United States, 242. Alienation of friendly feeling for the States from this time, 242. Further causes of distrust in Canada, 243

Red River, Battle of, 147

Red River, settlement at, 128. The stream, 133. Junction of the Goose River with it, 137. Confluence of the Assiniboine with it, 143, 180. Account of the Red River revolt, 145, 153. Exceptional state of the country, 145. Peculiarities of the farmers of, 149. Dwelling-houses of the old settlers, 149. Scarcity of timber in the settlement, 149, 150. Abundance of limestone at, 150. Brick-clay but no brick-kiln at, 150. Character of the settlers, 150. Their exploits, 151. Commencement of the revolt, 153. Ingredients of the quarrel, 155–157. The initial and chief blunder in the

328   INDEX.

REL

affair, 157. Other mistakes, 159. Colonel Dennis authorised to commence civil war, 160. Mistakes of the Canadian or loyal party, 161. The prime movers, 163. Riel recognised as president, 164. Demonstration of the Kildonan army, 165. Murder of Thomas Scott, 167. Riel's proclamation, 170. End of the revolt, 171. Present state of the settlement, 172. Its future importance, 173. Account of the country 1,000 miles to the west of Red River, 176. Climate at Red River, 177, 178. Facts respecting the country, 181. Marvellous fertility of the soil, 183. Objections to the country, 186–188. Length and severity of the winter in, 186, 189, 190. Low temperatures at, 189, 190. Route from Lake Superior to Red River, 195. The Hudson Bay Company's trails, 195. Ease with which the Red River country could be invaded from the United States, 266. Bill of Rights drawn up by the Rebel Convention, 308

Religion in the backwoods of Canada, 290. Divine service at a Methodist Chapel at Portage du Fort, 290, 291. The preacher's remonstrance against the views of Bishop Colenso, 291

Riel, Louis, account of, 163. His title of the 'Little Napoleon,' 163. Recognised as president of the provisional committee, 164. His fatal mistake in Scott's death, 168. His proclamation to the people of the North-west, 170. His disappearance, 171

Rifle shooting natural to every Canadian, 258. Matches in rifle prac-

SAR

tice in 1869, 258. A match at Ottawa, 258

Robertson-Ross, Colonel P., his Report on the present military condition of Canada quoted, 257. And on the preparations for self-defence in the event of war, 260

Rocky Mountains, beds of lignite coal on the eastern slopes of the, 200. The Yellow-head or Leatherhead Pass, and the Dominion Pacific Railway, 201. Lord Milton on the practicability of the railway quoted, 201, 202

Roman Catholic College at Quebec, 13. The Roman Catholic Church at Red River, excitement caused by the influence of the priests of the, 169. Defections from the Church in Quebec, 288

Rousseau, Lake, its picturesqueness, 56. Islands of, 56

Russia, war-power and population of, 271

Rye, Miss, her plan for assisting emigration of healthy orphan girls, 235

SAGUENAY RIVER, junction of the, with the St. Lawrence at Tadousac, 34. Magnificent scenery of the, 35

Salmon fishery of the Dominion, 298. The salmon streams of Nova Scotia, 298

Salt, produce of, at Goderich, 97. The salt springs, 97. Extent of the salt deposit, 98

Salt Lake City, causes of recent defection from the Mormon church in, 288, 289

Sandfield, Port, a spot on Lake St. Joseph christened, 59, 60

Sarnia, settlement of Ojibways outside the town of, 111

SAS

Saskatchewan, valley of the, its fertility and beauty, 146. Rise and fall of the river, 178. Beds of coal on the banks of the, 179. Herds of wild buffalo in the valley of the, 185. The 'Fertile Belt' of various travellers, 190. Captain Palliser's report of the country, 191. Report prepared for the New York Chamber of Commerce quoted, 191. Its extent, 192. Measureless extent of the coal-fields of the valley, 200

Saulteaux Indian, a pure one, 134. The Saulteaux round Red River Settlement, 152

Schultz, Dr., party of loyalists, or the Canadian party, in his house in Winnipeg, 161. Taken prisoner by the rebels, with his men, 162. Escapes from prison, 162

Scotch settlers on Red River, 148

Scott, Thomas, offences charged against him, 166. Tried by court martial and shot, 167

Seal fishery of the Gulf of St. Lawrence, 297. And of Labrador, 302

Seaton, Lord, his establishment of a number of endowed rectories in Upper Canada, 290

Seine River, water communication through the, 180

Selkirk, Lord, his settlement of Scotch families at Red River, 147

Sentry-boxes at Montreal, story of the, 276

Settler, his selection of a piece of land, 60. His mode of proceeding, 61. His first house, 63. His essentials, 64. His progress, 64, 65. His crops, 65. Pleasure and ease of a journey to the Red River, 143. The farmer's best mode of proceeding, 143. Settlements on Red River and on the Assiniboine, 148, 149.

STE

Crops of an old Scotch settler at Red River, 182. Another settler's first crop, 182. Advantages of the wild prairie lands for steam-farming, stock-raising, and railway making, 184, 185. Statistics of settlers in various parts of Canada in 1868, 221. The Hon. Mr. Carling's statistics of immigration, 222, 223. Rate of wages, 224. Mr. Conolly's statement, 225, 226. Cost of living, 226, 227. Advantages to the settler in Canada, 228, 229. Advice to immigrant farmers, 231, 232. Suggestions to intending settlers, 232. Modes of settlement, 233. Laws respecting free-grant lands, 280, 281. *See* Farming interest; Immigration

Sewing-machines manufactured in Hamilton, 285

Shebandowan, Lake, part of the old canoe route to Red River, 195

Sheep, breed of, in Canada, 77

Simcoe, Lake, settlement on, 49. Passage over, 50

Sioux Indians, their long words, 296. Story of a Sioux warrior and a Métis, 129

Sleighing in a hogshead, 66

Smith, Mr. Donald, his efforts to save Thomas Scott, 167

Snake-fences in Canada, 231

Soil of Red River, 181, 182

Spectacle, a celestial, in the prairie, 141, 142

Spragge, Mr. W., his Report on the condition of the Canadian Indians, 114

Steamboat travelling in Canada, advantages of, 277. The ocean lines of steamers between Europe and North America, 306. The summer and winter ports, 306

Stimulants, why not needed in the United States, 247
Stock, live, excellence of the, in Canada, 77. Stock farms, 79
Stock-breeding, advantages of the prairies of the North-west for, 185. As a business in Canada, 232
Sturgeon Lake, fitness of the land near, for cultivation, 198
Sulphur in the valley of the Peace River, 193
Sunset on the prairie, 132
Superior, Lake, route from, to Red River, 195. Country north of the, 197
Swamps, ague-breeding, in the North-west territory, 186

TACHÉ, Dr., Bishop of St. Boniface, his influence among the French of Red River, 169. His services to the cause of order, 169. His description of Lake Athabasca, 193
Tadousac, Champlain's chapel at, 34. Junction of the Saguenay with the St. Lawrence at, 34
Tait, Mr., his wagons, 132–133. A journey to Fort Garry in them, 133
Thunder Bay, Lake Superior, route from, to Red River, 195
Timber, scarcity of, in the North-west territory, 186. Trees suitable for Red River, 188. The timber of the country between Lake Superior and Red River, its value and importance, 196. On the streams flowing towards Rainy Lake, 197. Value and importance of that of New Brunswick, 209
Tin, mines of, discovered in Nova Scotia, 208

To-boggons and to-boggonning in Canada in winter, 237
Tonnage of the Dominion, 206, 207. *See* Maritime provinces; Navy, Commercial.
Toronto, formerly Little York, 51. Meaning of the name Toronto, 51. Its dignity and importance, 51. Nearer to Liverpool than New York, 305
Tourment, Cape, visit to, 25
Travelling to Red River, routes for, 146, 147
Trinity, Cape, scenery at, 35
Trout, 58
Turnips raised in Canada compared with those of New York, 84

UNITED STATES, agricultural statistics of, compared with those of Canada, 81–83. Terms of the fishery convention of 1818, 212. Resumption of the rights of the Dominion, 211, 212. Seizures of American vessels by the Canadian marine police, 213. Grievance in consequence, 213. President Grant's complaint in his Message, 214. Effect in the Dominion of the abrogation of the Reciprocity Treaty, 214. Demands of the Dominion in return for the fishing privileges, 215. Wages in Canada as compared with those of the States, 226. Chances of annexation of Canada to the States, 240–243, 248. Alienation of friendly feeling dating from the abrogation of the Reciprocal Treaty, 242. The people of the States a distinct type from those of Canada, 245. The American people ceasing to become

VAN

Anglo-Saxon or English, 246. Effect of the climate in this direction, 247. Review of the question of annexation, 249. Possible future danger to the Republic by the admission of Canada, 249. Failure of the invasion of Canada in 1812–14, 262. Value of Canada for or against England in case of a war between her and the States, 264, 268. Risks in attempting annexation of Canada, 268, 269. War-power and population of the United States, 271. Its public debt as compared with that of Canada, per head, 281. Lands granted by the States to railway companies, 304

VANCOUVER'S ISLAND, admittance of, into the Dominion, 301. Its climate and fertility, 303. Capt. Vancouver's account of it, 303
Vandyke, picture attributed to, in Quebec cathedral, 288
Vegetables and roots of Canada, 75
Victoria County, townships of, open for settlement, 69
Victuallersville, abandonment of, 51
Ville Marie, a former name of Montreal, 282

WAGES, rate of, in the Dominion, 224, 225. As compared with those of the United States, 226
Waterfall, a splendid, 29. Of the Chaudière, 17. Of Montmorenci, 20.
West Isles, fisheries of the, 207

YOU

Windigoostigan, Lake, part of the old canoe route to Red River, 195
Winepegoos, Lake, 181
Winter, length and severity of the, in the Red River Settlement, 186
Whale-fisheries of Behring's Straits, fished by Americans, 194. Of the Gulf of St. Lawrence, 296
Wheat, increase of the produce of, in Canada during ten years, 70. Its average yield in Canada, 80. Excellence of that grown near Toronto, 80. Crops of, in British Northwestern America, 177. And at Red River Settlement, 182. Period in which it ripens in the Fertile Belt, 294
White fish, 58
Wine, grapes grown for, 77
Winnipeg, Lake, its height above the sea, 177. Fed by the Saskatchewan, 178, 179. Its future value for communication, 179. Its area, 179. Its advantages and disadvantages, 179. Its name, 181
Winnipeg River, its value and importance, 179, 180
Winnipeg, town of, 143, 152. Trails from, to the West, 146. Houses of, 152. Population of, 152. Convention of Representatives at, 164. Battle of, 164–166
Women, married, laws respecting the property of, 281. The type of beauty of those of Canada, 284
Woods, Lake of the, communication through the, 180. Part of the old canoe route to Red River, 195. Its fitness for cultivation, 198

YOUNG, Rev. George, his efforts to save Thomas Scott, 167

www.ingramcontent.com/pod-product-compliance
Lightning Source LLC
Chambersburg PA
CBHW031433230426
43668CB00007B/520